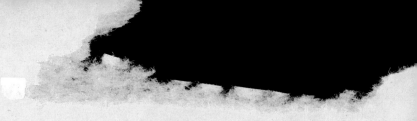

PENGUIN BOOKS

The Hurricane Girls

Jo Wheeler is a writer and radio producer who has written books with Battersea Dogs and Cats Home and worked with a 1950s policewoman to write her memoir, *Bobby on the Beat*. She has also produced numerous historical and arts documentaries for the BBC.

The Hurricane Girls

*The inspirational true story
of the women who dared to fly*

JO WHEELER

PENGUIN BOOKS

PENGUIN BOOKS

UK | USA | Canada | Ireland | Australia
India | New Zealand | South Africa

Penguin Books is part of the Penguin Random House group of companies
whose addresses can be found at global.penguinrandomhouse.com.

First published 2018
001

Copyright © Jo Wheeler, 2018

Picture permissions can be found on page 334.

The moral right of the author has been asserted

Set in 12.5/14.75 pt Garamond MT Std
Typeset by Jouve (UK), Milton Keynes
Printed and bound in Great Britain by Clays Ltd, Elcograf S.p.A.

A CIP catalogue record for this book is available from the British Library

ISBN: 978–0–241–35463–6

www.greenpenguin.co.uk

MIX
Paper from
responsible sources
FSC® C018179

Penguin Random House is committed to a
sustainable future for our business, our readers
and our planet. This book is made from Forest
Stewardship Council® certified paper.

In memory of Dai Evans, 1928–2017,
who always encouraged me.

Contents

CONTENTS

Introduction

Since the birth of powered flight there have been women pilots. In 1903, nineteen-year-old American Aida de Acosta became the first woman to fly solo in a motorised airship. Six months later, the Wright brothers made their own historic flight, in the first heavier-than-air plane, and flung open the doors to the golden age of aviation. Women like the American inventor Lillian Todd designed some of the earliest planes, and Raymonde de Laroche, Blanche Scott, Harriet Quimby and others took to the skies.

Hilda Hewlett was the first woman in Britain to get a pilot's licence, in 1911. She started and ran the country's first flying school and set up a company which produced over 800 military aircraft during the First World War. Other women aviators went on to set records, fly solo in ground-breaking long-distance journeys, and make their names in the flying races and daredevil air circuses of the 1920s and '30s. Despite these achievements, prejudice about what constituted 'women's work' meant that flying was a largely male domain, and only a small percentage of women were ever able to break through into commercial aviation. Flying of any kind was restricted to those who could afford the expensive lessons.

By 1939 war was looming in Europe. To guard against the prospect of being outgunned in the sky, a subsidised flying scheme, the Civil Air Guard, was set up in Britain to train both male and female pilots. Not very happy about the prospect of a lot more women capering about in planes, one magazine editor responded sharply: 'The menace is the woman who thinks that she ought to be flying a high-speed bomber, when she really has not the intelligence to scrub the floor of a hospital properly.'

Two years later Flight Captain Winifred Crossley stepped out of a Hawker Hurricane. She had just experienced the kick and whoosh of the fast fighter which the previous summer had blazed its trails across the sky and helped to win the Battle of Britain. In her flying helmet and goggles, she smiled as she greeted the waiting crowd: 'It's lovely, darlings! A beautiful little aeroplane.' She had just made history as the first woman to fly an operational RAF fighter. Two years after that twenty-eight-year old Lettice Curtis became the first woman to fly a four-engined heavy bomber. She was soon flying the Halifax, Stirling and celebrated Avro Lancaster. Measuring nearly 22 metres in length with a wingspan of 30 metres, the aircraft towered over the pilot. But it was no problem for Lettice, or the other women who flew four-engined planes during the war.

Women were not allowed to join the RAF, but they

were allowed to fly with the Air Transport Auxiliary, a civilian organisation which ferried over a hundred different types of aircraft. In everything from open-cockpit biplanes to nifty fighters, cumbersome seaplanes and heavy bombers, they flew without radio, dodging unpredictable weather, barrage balloons and anti-aircraft fire, with only a map, compass and their eyesight to navigate the treacherous wartime skies. During the Second World War, 168 women, along with over 1,000 male pilots, moved over 300,000 aircraft from factories and maintenance units to air force squadrons across the country, and eventually to the Continent, ensuring the Allies had a steady supply of operational planes.

The 'ATA Girls' were celebrated in the press as glamorous heroines of the air, and the war offered them opportunities that would have been unthinkable outside the urgency of conflict. But it could also be tough, gruelling and dangerous work, and not everyone survived. In the winter of 1941 the celebrated pilot Amy Johnson disappeared into the Thames Estuary with a plane she was flying for the ATA. Others fell foul of aircraft malfunctions and accidents, and at least fifteen airwomen lost their lives during the war.

This book tells just a few of the remarkable stories of the wartime women pilots. Thanks to the efforts of their tenacious leader Pauline Gower, who fought tirelessly for her pilots at every turn, they even achieved equal pay, and the ATA became one of the country's first equal opportunities employers. Being women in what was seen as a man's world had its challenges. But then there was always the prospect of settling into the cockpit of a 350 mph fighter and, just for a moment, leaving the earthly world and all its concerns behind.

1. Learning to Fly

Tensions were high in 1938. Austria was annexed by Nazi Germany and, despite Adolf Hitler's promises to the contrary, an attack on Czechoslovakia was his likely next move. When he made a vitriolic and warmongering speech in Berlin that September many people's fears were confirmed: war in Europe was coming.

Rosemary Rees had flown to Germany in her own plane many times. She had lots of friends on the Continent and had been flying all over Europe for several years. She was a member of a flying club at the exclusive Heston Aerodrome in London and a regular at the rallies and parties organised by European flying clubs. These were glamorous, champagne-quaffing affairs, where the top aviators of the day mingled over tales of aviation daring. They were hosted in each other's towns and cities by mayors and dignitaries. Rosemary was proud of her most treasured possession, a newly developed, sleek, silver monoplane, a Miles Whitney Straight, and she had hand-stitched a massive 'coat' for it to wear in the hangar. It was always the cleanest, shiniest aircraft at every rally.

It wasn't unusual for Rosemary to be in Berlin,

because her cousin's husband worked at the embassy there. On this occasion, he was jittery.

'I think you should take your plane home as quickly as possible. War could be declared very suddenly,' he said. 'It could come at any moment, the way that man's talking, and the first thing they'll do of course is ground all aircraft and not let anyone get any petrol. It'd be awful if you lost the plane. I really think you ought to go home.'

The prospect of losing her beloved Whitney persuaded Rosemary to hop straight back in it and head for England.

Neville Chamberlain was keen to avoid another war. In September, he met Adolf Hitler to discuss the terms of a possible peace agreement. After their talks in Munich the Prime Minister landed at Heston Aerodrome and addressed the crowd:

'This morning I had another talk with the German Chancellor, Herr Hitler, and here is the paper which bears his name upon it as well as mine,' he announced triumphantly, waving the document in the air. 'We regard the agreement signed last night and the Anglo-German Naval Agreement as symbolic of the desire of our two peoples never to go to war with one another again.'

There were cheers and cries of 'hear, hear' from the crowd, but many believed war was still the only option to stop Hitler's advances. Later, outside 10 Downing Street, the Prime Minister said:

'My good friends, for the second time in our history,

a British Prime Minister has returned from Germany bringing peace with honour. I believe it is peace for our time. We thank you from the bottom of our hearts. Go home and get a nice quiet sleep.'

Getting a nice quiet sleep may not have been easy for twenty-four-year-old Irene Arckless. Her fiancé, Tom 'Titch' Lockyer, was a pilot in the RAF. If war did break out, he would very likely be called on to risk his life.

Irene was a high-spirited young woman from Carlisle, who sang in the chorus of the local operatic society and was a keen artist. Her father was an organ builder, but she had been mad about flying since she was a schoolgirl. She completed her first solo flight at the Border Flying Club in Carlisle when she was twenty-one, and she became the first woman at the club to complete her 'A' Licence, the first step on the flying ladder. Tom, whose father was a retired army officer, had joined the RAF in 1935. She and Tom had been childhood sweethearts and they shared their passion for aviation.

Flying wasn't cheap and the high costs put aviation as a hobby out of the reach of most working people. On an average salary it was difficult enough to afford the number of hours it took to keep up a licence, let alone buy a private plane. Irene found work as a secretary which may have helped her pay for lessons, but it was only when she qualified that she eventually told her parents she had been learning to fly. Her grandfather had been heard on the wireless tuning the organ in Westminster Abbey at

3

the King's coronation, but the Arckless family had none of the social privilege afforded to many aviators of the age. Irene achieved her ambitions through pluck, energy and determination.

As the daughter of a prominent Conservative MP and baronet, Rosemary Rees did have the financial means and the social connections it took to pursue a flying hobby. She was a natural fit at the glamorous flying rallies. But aviation was by no means the standard pursuit for a young woman of the time, even for someone in Rosemary's position. It took guts and hard work in the face of prejudice. Women of her class were generally expected to look decorative and marry the right man. When she was in her twenties, Rosemary had already bucked the trend by pursuing a career as a dancer. She was a tall, witty and athletic young woman, but was expected to act demure and be 'presented' at court as a debutante. She found it all thoroughly tedious.

'You should learn to fly,' a family friend told her one day. He had been at university with Rosemary's brother and was the son of the department store owner Gordon Selfridge.

'Fly? What for?' she asked. 'Whoever would want to learn to fly?'

Young Selfridge was persuasive and Rosemary agreed to have a trial lesson. The moment she was up in the air, she was hooked.

The instructor was a man called Valentine Baker, who

had been a First World War pilot and had a bullet still lodged near his spine. He formed a civilian flying club at Heston and taught many notable people, including the Princes of Wales and Kent. He enjoyed the challenge of teaching and took all sorts – nervous people, old and young, girls and boys. Rosemary learnt to fly in an Avro Cadet, a biplane with an open cockpit. Against the din of the noisy engine, with the rushing of the wind against their faces, Baker gently guided her through the basics of flying via the trumpet microphone. She swooped and glided, juddered, came into land with bumps and jolts and eventually got a handle on the little aircraft.

Rosemary's father had died by the time she learnt to fly, but her mother thought it was all rather amusing to have a flying daughter and helped her buy her first aircraft, a Miles Hawk, for the princely sum of £800. It was a bit flashier than the Cadet, a modern two-seater monoplane with elegant wings. Rosemary was proud to go about in her flying suit. She even carried a murderous-looking knife in her boots for a while, in case she had to cut herself free from the plywood aircraft – until she realised the metal blade was altering the dial on the compass. With the knife safely stowed away in the back, Rosemary flew all over Europe, to Poland, Germany and the Balkans. It was the golden age of the private flyer, with no wireless distractions, nobody shouting from air traffic control telling pilots not to land, just the freedom of the skies, away from the troubles of the earth, and the whole of Europe just a few hours away. But everything was about to change.

On 1 October 1938, Nazi troops took control of the Sudetenland, a predominantly German-speaking part of Czechoslovakia, where Hitler had whipped up German nationalism. Britain and France agreed not to respond, on the proviso that Germany would not invade the rest of the country. Nazi aggression continued.

In November, in a night of terror and violence against Jewish people in Germany, Austria and Czechoslovakia, shops and synagogues were destroyed, dozens were killed and 30,000 Jewish men were arrested. This was Kristallnacht, the 'Night of Broken Glass'.

Despite Chamberlain's faith in a peace agreement, preparations were already underway in Britain for the ultimate national emergency. Gas masks were issued to the general public in July, in case of a poison gas attack from the air. Wary of Hitler's ambitions and the Nazis' air capabilities, the British Government got behind a new organisation called the Civil Air Guard, the purpose of which was to create a reserve of new pilots. The ambition was to train men and women between the ages of eighteen and fifty at civilian flying clubs across the country. The clubs were given a subsidy for every pilot they trained, which meant those who would not otherwise be able to afford it were now able to access cheap flying lessons.

Women pilots were not a new phenomenon in the

1930s, but since the early days of flight their numbers had been very few compared to their male counterparts. In 1911 just two women were given aviator's certificates, compared to 168 men. Only eight women had certificates before 1927, out of a total of 8,205 certificates issued. There was something of a boom, if you can call it that, in the 1930s. In 1931 fifty certificates were issued to women (588 to men), and it was reported that a whopping forty British women had their own aeroplanes.

The most famous British female pilot of the 1930s was Amy Johnson. Born in 1903, Amy was from a family of fish merchants in Hull. After graduating from Sheffield University, she moved to London where she became fascinated by flight and determined to make a career of it. Lessons were £5 an hour at her favourite flying club, Stag Lane, but there was another club on the site which charged 30 shillings. She could just about manage that, but it was still a lot of money, so she got a job as a secretary with a law firm. Amy wanted to learn the engineering side of flying, too, but women weren't allowed in the maintenance hangars. In the end they gave her the nickname Johnnie and she wangled her way in. She proved the sceptics wrong and in March 1930 Amy became a fully qualified ground engineer.

Despite Amy's achievements, women weren't taken seriously in the world of commercial aviation, so she decided to do something to get everyone's attention. She publicised an ambitious plan to fly alone in an open-cockpit biplane from London to Australia. This was a bold idea for a twenty-six-year-old who had only achieved her pilot's licence a year earlier and never flown further than Hull. Before she left she tried to sell her story to the press for £25. No one was interested. She did manage to get some sponsorship for petrol and towards the cost of her plane. She also had the solid support of her father, who helped her buy her first aircraft, a de Havilland Gipsy Moth, which she nicknamed *Jason*, a contraction of the family fish business trademark, Johnson.

Amy pushed herself to her limit on the solo trip, both mentally and physically. She had only a few hours' sleep a night as she followed her route to the other side of the world. The first stop was Vienna, and by day six she had reached Karachi. She crash-landed at Rangoon and damaged *Jason*'s wing, but patched it up with local help and continued, finally reaching Darwin in nineteen and a half days. When she returned to the awaiting and enthralled press, this previously unknown fish merchant's daughter from Hull was met by a 200,000-strong crowd. She received a cheque from the *Daily Mail* for £10,000 and became a darling of the aviation world and an immediate public sensation.

Buoyed by her success, Amy went on to make record-breaking trips to Moscow and Tokyo in her second plane, *Jason II*, a Puss Moth. In 1932 she married Jim Mollison, a dashing pilot who was already making his own name as a record-breaking aviator. Amy continued her own daring deeds and travelled to Cape Town solo, beating existing records. Amy and Jim became a celebrity couple and attracted huge crowds before they went on flying journeys together. They broke records to India and America, although they crash-landed after running out of fuel. When they had recovered, they were honoured with a ticker tape parade in New York and treated like film stars.

Behind the celebrity photo shoots and the glamour of flying portrayed by the press, it was gruelling and dangerous, and took a great deal of endurance and resilience. Amy and Jim's marriage came under strain. He was a heavy drinker and, it transpired, something of a playboy. There was also a darkness behind Amy's shy smile and sparkling eyes. In 1929 her sister Irene, who was in an unhappy marriage, had taken her own life by gassing herself in the kitchen oven. The family's grief was exacerbated by the taboo surrounding suicide, and the subsequent reports in the press did nothing to help them deal with their loss. The death of her sister gave Amy a gritty determination, perhaps even a kind of recklessness, which pushed her to pursue her dream in aviation to its limits. Flying became the outlet through which she channelled her grief and her emotion.

Veronica Innes was another woman with a taste for excitement and speed. She was a keen horse rider and developed a love of motor cars. In 1938, she was the proud owner of a new Aston Martin with an open roof, which she drove in all weathers, merrily arriving at parties covered in motor oil, her hair unkempt from the wind. She was also bitten by the flying bug after being taken by a friend to Brooklands Flying Club in Northamptonshire. It was a balmy summer day and the sheer exhilaration of rising up to 3,000 feet beat the Aston Martin any day. The plane looped and turned and came in for a perfect landing. Veronica found the whole thing thrilling and was adamant she wanted to learn to fly herself right away, but winced when she heard the price of lessons.

The creation of the Civil Air Guard provided a more affordable alternative for people like Veronica who were eager to learn to fly. As soon as the announcement was made, enquiries from thousands of aviation hopefuls came flooding in, 'minute by minute', according to the Air Ministry. They had some 16,000 responses in the first few days. The catchy promise to 'learn to fly for 5 bob an hour' attracted many people for whom flying had been largely out of reach. But this wasn't about having a lot of fun messing about in planes. Training with the Civil Air Guard was on the strict condition of an 'honourable undertaking' that in times of emergency members would serve their country.

Captain Harold Balfour, First World War flying ace and now Under-Secretary of State for Air, was instrumental in the formation of the Civil Air Guard.

'At the present time, some 4,000 members have been enrolled for immediate flying,' he told the House of Commons in late 1938; '33,886 applications were received up to 15th October.'

'Is it not a fact,' asked another MP, Rear-Admiral Sir Murray Sueter, a former First World War naval officer, 'that the Civil Air Guard scheme is the only way in which young men of the towns can learn to fly at small cost?'

'Yes, sir,' replied Balfour.

Others wondered what it was all for. Particularly when it came to all those women being trained. Sir Walter Robert Perkins, a pre-war aviation enthusiast and former RAF pilot, demanded to know exactly 'What is the object of teaching women of forty-nine to fly?'

Another asked, 'What will be the position of women pilots in time of war?'

Balfour laid out hopeful, if non-committal, plans for the possible role women might play:

'I would say that in a certain number of cases women will undoubtedly be of value in ferry pilot work or instructional work.' But he added cautiously, 'I would not like to lay down any hard and fast rule as to the degree of utility that women pilots might show in time of war.'

The Civil Air Guard was the perfect opportunity for someone like Veronica Innes to pursue her aviation dreams. However, by the time she heard about it places had already filled up and she was met with nothing but waiting lists. Not the kind of girl to give up easily, she managed to get herself to the top of the list at a flying club in Cambridge where a friend's father worked. She stayed with an aunt and uncle who lived nearby, and in February 1939 she joined the CAG. Her father was oblivious to his daughter's new hobby, but she couldn't hide it for long. Some years earlier, she had been cajoled into taking part in a pageant at Runnymede in Windsor, playing the Fair Maid of Kent, Queen of Beauty, and placing a laurel wreath on the head of the victor in a re-enactment of a medieval jousting tournament. She had found it all rather amusing at the time. Now, years later, she opened the daily paper and read the glaring head-line 'Beauty Queen Joins Civil Air Guard'.

Veronica's instructor was a kind, calm man called Wallis who took her up in a Gypsy Moth. In spite of the winter cold, the weather was clear with good visibility. After just six days Wallis climbed out of the instructor's seat after their lesson.

'Right, now do one on your own,' he said.

Veronica felt a churning in her stomach. This was it: solo. She taxied back to the take-off point. She didn't have time to panic. After a cockpit check she turned into the wind and opened up the throttle. The plane lifted gently into the air and she held her face in a position of ultimate concentration. She could not afford to mess up. She did a circuit of the airfield and hardly had enough time in the air for it to sink in that she was alone.

Climb at 65. Wings level. Keep straight, she thought to herself, focusing on everything she had learnt that week. Before she knew what was happening, she was heading back towards the landing spot. The aircraft came in just over a hedge. It was close. 'A bit of engine,' she said quietly. Her stomach heaved again. There it was. She hit the ground smoothly. Her first solo. 'Daisy cutter!' said her instructor, stepping back into the plane. But he was grinning, so she must have done all right.

Veronica didn't have the financial means to be a wealthy aviator of leisure. She needed to earn a living. Her next challenge was how to become a commercial pilot. This took at least 100 hours solo, and that amount of flying time wasn't covered by the Civil Air Guard scheme. She needed to find more money if she was to pursue her dream.

2. Going Solo

Margot Gore wanted to be a doctor. When her father's engineering business shut down during the Great Depression, it was clear that there would be no chance of her going to university and she would have to earn her own living. She took a typing course and got a secretarial job with British Reinforced Concrete. In 1938 a piece in the newspaper caught her eye: 'National Women's Air Reserve ... meet at the Greyhound public house, Piccadilly'.

Inspired by the daring deeds of Amy Johnson, Margot had always been fascinated and enthralled by the idea of learning to fly, but in early 1938 it seemed to her like a distant dream. A few days later she found herself heading down to central London for a meeting which would change her life.

On arrival at the Greyhound she looked around the smoke-filled pub. There was a group of men at the bar chatting and laughing. Others were nursing pints on their own at tables. In the corner was a group of women deep in conversation. You didn't see that many women in pubs in those days. Margot made her way over.

'Come, sit,' said a woman, catching sight of her. 'We

don't bite!' She had a wavy brown bob and piercing eyes. 'Gabrielle Patterson,' she said, holding out her hand and smiling.

Mrs Patterson was in her thirties, a few years older than Margot. She had a strange mix of quiet self-assurance and shyness. But she clearly knew her stuff when it came to flying. She was one of the very few women instructors in the country and was based at a flying club in Romford.

Mrs Patterson thanked everyone for coming and explained she was hoping to form a reserve of all-women pilots, who could make themselves useful in the air in the event of any impending conflict. She was, she continued on, aware of the shortfall of women instructors and she wanted to change that.

'Even I don't have nearly enough hours working as an instructor as I would have hoped by now,' she said and told the assembled group she was worried about whether there would actually be enough women pilots to become instructors. The reason for this, she concluded, was that 'Women pilots hitherto have consisted only of those with large enough bank balances'.

Margot had been inspired enough by her evening with Mrs Patterson to enrol at Romford Flying Club. Lessons were about 15 shillings an hour. They were cheaper than the usual top flying clubs, but not yet the '5 bob' of the Civil Air Guard which would come shortly.

Flying at Romford was a whole new world for Margot: the vast hangars, the smell of motor oil, the chatter of men and women in their flying suits wheeling the planes out by hand. She soon learnt how to handle the aircraft on the ground herself, and it was always a buzz to watch them taking off and landing.

The plane Margot learnt on was called a Cirrus Moth. It was a training biplane which was first produced in the late 1920s by the famous de Havilland manufacturers. The old Moth was becoming something of a relic by that point, but learning on a plane like this one from the Moth family would serve her well later on.

Margot attended lectures about the theory of flight, and Mrs Patterson's husband, who was an aeronautical engineer, taught them about the mechanics of the engine.

'You've got potential,' said Mrs P to Margot one afternoon after their lesson. She had only done eight hours' flying, but she was already getting the hang of it. They had done a take-off, circuit and landing, and Margot was about to go home for the day.

'You can go back up on your own now,' said Mrs Patterson. Margot didn't have time to think before Mrs Patterson got out of the Moth and left Margot to go around again. As she took off for her first solo flight, Margot was in a daze. She didn't feel at all frightened. She did another circuit of the airfield, and it seemed as though no sooner had she taken off than she was back down on solid ground.

'Well done,' said Mrs Patterson as Margot got out of the plane. 'Not so hard now, was it?'

The second and third times going up on her own were more frightening. Now she knew it was coming and had time to worry and think about it, and about what might happen if something went wrong at several thousand feet. It was quite terrifying when she realised again that there was no one else there telling her what to do. But she soon got used to it and gained more confidence with every lesson.

Margot made a good friend at the club. Alison King was another of the 'flying ladies' from London who had been keen to try out something exciting and take advantage of the cheaper lessons. They flew once a week at the weekend on a rota system, and if they were on together, Alison and Margot would catch up after the day's flying on the long summer evenings as they travelled back to London.

'You're really smitten with all this flying lark, aren't you?' Alison asked Margot as they waited for the train.

'I can't think about anything else!' she replied. 'And you'll never believe – Mrs P wants me to consider being an instructor one day! Can you imagine? It feels like only a few seconds ago I was a fledgling waddling out for my first solo.'

'You should go for it,' Alison said. 'Who knows when it might come in handy?'

In order to pay for more lessons during the week,

Margot got a job at Smithfield meat market. She was a secretary and earned the princely sum of 32 shillings and 6 pence a week. Her shift started cruelly early, at 5.30 a.m., but this meant she could finish at midday, giving her enough time to catch a train at Liverpool Street and walk to the aerodrome from the station. Mrs Patterson decided she was ready to take the assistant instructor's course, and she learnt the 'patter' required to teach new pilots through the speaking tube above the din of the engine. She had to speak clearly and confidently and say things like: 'now demonstrate a spin', 'now will you get out of it', and learn how to encourage someone to come in to land safely. There were several types of teachers. Some were snarling and sarcastic. Others were just plain cruel. Margot took the quiet but firm approach and it seemed to work. The Civil Air Guard soon started sending more and more new recruits to the aerodrome, which Margot assumed was a ploy to get young men ready to fight the Luftwaffe. By August 1939 she was instructing those new pilots herself. They were not really in a position to object to a woman instructor, given that they were all new to flying themselves, although there was always the odd one who was difficult or reluctant to be taught by a female. Margot proved her worth, and taught both men and women, putting them at their ease with her calm confidence.

Veronica Innes had finally managed to get a bank loan to pay for her extra flying lessons. She also indulged in a snug, pale blue flying suit and matching helmet and embarked on the next stage of her great adventure. She moved from Cambridge to join an airfield in Woodley. By 1939 she was building up her solo hours in order to get a commercial licence. All summer she got as much cross-country experience as she could with her new instructor, an amiable chap called Tommy Rose. She got a bit of a shock when Tommy said to her one day out of the blue that he thought she was to ready to try a cross-country on her own. Before she left he said, 'Oh, and if you do happen to get lost' – just what Veronica needed to hear – 'just find a field, any field, land in it, and ring us. All right?'

She started off confidently enough, but there was a growing number of obstacles for pilots as preparations for a possible war were underway. She headed over Bedfordshire towards her final destination, Cambridge, and a dark shape appeared which was not on her map. She was flying near RAF Cardington. It wasn't another aircraft. As the dark shape loomed larger she noticed there were suddenly more of them. She realised to her horror that it was a balloon barrage. The site had produced airships during the last war, and they were now trying out the giant silver balloons which were built to deter enemy aircraft from flying low over vulnerable areas. The problem was, balloon barrages couldn't tell an enemy aircraft from a friendly one. They did not discriminate. The RAF had already started training staff to operate and drive the barrages and Veronica was heading straight towards their thick grounding cables. She veered off and narrowly missed them, but her troubles weren't over. It should have been a straight run to Cambridge, but there was a strong easterly wind which was tugging her off course. To top it off, a thick mist descended. Veronica couldn't see Cambridge, or anything else. *I might as well be in the desert*, she thought.

The reality of the situation pressed in on her. She had no radio to communicate with the ground. She remembered what Tommy had said: 'Find a field and land in it.' That was all well and good, but she couldn't see the ground – and imagine the ribbing she would get if she had to tell him she'd got lost! After a while she picked out the shape of a railway line through the mist, then, miracle of miracles, the shape of what could be an aerodrome appeared. She had no choice but to land on it, wherever it was. When she had touched down she asked someone at the tiny airfield where it was and they told her it was called Wyton. This was a mere twelve miles away from Cambridge. She took off again and followed the railway line successfully to her destination. She got back to Woodley later that day without any trouble and decided not to tell anyone about her little mishap. *Must improve map reading and course plotting*, she thought. It had all been a bit too close for comfort.

Rosemary Rees continued to fly in Europe, but she had been avoiding Berlin since the political situation had become very tense. After hearing the news about the invasion of Czechoslovakia, she hatched a plan to fly there at Christmas to give out food and presents at the refugee camps. That December she loaded up her plane with all kinds of goodies, but she was prevented from taking off from Heston by a thick snowfall. It was becoming more difficult to fly around the Continent as a private pilot, and with authorities getting nervous there were more restrictions and visa checks. Rosemary decided instead to take her instructor's licence in Britain. She learnt all the patter and passed the exam, but found she didn't really like teaching much. There was another, more exciting way for civilian pilots to make a bit of money in the lead-up to war. It paid a lot more, too. It certainly wasn't the average job for a woman, flying in the path of a gunner.

'Army Co-operation' involved giving new RAF gunners a flying target so they could practise training their weapons on incoming aircraft, and Rosemary got a job based at the aerodrome at Portsmouth. Because she had her own plane, she and the aircraft could be called on any time together as a unit, and she would get a call at a moment's notice to head down to the South Coast and fly for about two hours a day, morning or afternoon, on a set course. Trainee fighter pilots would try and get Rosemary's plane in the cross of the gun as practice for shooting down real raiders in the event of war. She also flew to and fro along the coastline while the anti-aircraft gunners on the ground tried to train their guns on her, learning to hit enemy aircraft.

For Rosemary, whose only real passion was flying, it was something for her and her beloved aeroplane to do to pass the time and make some money. The pay was about £10 an hour, a lot in those days, and she was satisfied, as she played the role of sitting – or flying – duck, that she was earning 3 shillings and 6 pence a minute. This was just as well, because although most of the gunners weren't really firing at her, every now and again she was asked to tow a 'drogue', a target, from the back of the plane, at which the gunners did on occasion shoot real artillery. Amy Johnson joined Rosemary at Portsmouth for a while, and eventually a few other women pilots also did the job. Throughout the summer of 1939 the air was thick with planes for the Army Co-op flying along the South Coast.

There were target planes flying over London, too. The 'ack-ack' – or anti-aircraft – gunners and searchlight operators practised in the dark in case of night-time air raids. Mona Friedlander, a capable night flyer, was working for an air taxi company when she was called on to fly as a target for the guns in London. Mona had taken up flying, she said, because she was bored of her life as a socialite in London's Mayfair. She was already known as an international ice hockey player and attracted a fair bit of press attention for her boisterous and athletic exploits.

One day a friend gave her a couple of gin and tonics and persuaded her to go up in an aeroplane. From the minute she went up she knew flying was going to be her life, and after that she did barely anything else.

Mona's father, despite being a wealthy banker, refused when she asked him to help with the entry fee for the famous King's Cup Air Race – not because he was mean, but so he couldn't blame himself if anything bad happened to her. Mona entered anyway, of course, and she became something of a London celebrity, taking part in air races with sponsorship from the *Daily Sketch* and flying banners over sporting events. She was treated as a glamorous aviation novelty, but she was also a serious and very capable aviator who helped out at one of the top flying schools, Brooklands in Surrey.

By 1938 the club had around 2,000 members, 30 per cent of whom were women. Leisure flying was becoming more popular, but getting a job as a female professional pilot was still very difficult. Mona tried to get paid work with an air taxi service, but because many people still wouldn't take a woman pilot seriously, she struggled to get anyone to come up with her for the night flying. Eventually she did manage it and got a job flying with Air Taxis Croydon, where, unsurprisingly, she was the only woman.

As well as offering the public '5-bob joy rides', the job also involved taking quite a few children up in the air who were suffering with whooping cough. It was thought to cure them if they flew at 8,000 feet for an hour, but many of the children were just sick when they got up there, and Mona wasn't sure it ever cured any of them. In the end, she and her fellow pilots were doing so much flying they had to fiddle their log books to get the hours within the safety limits. Even so, she didn't earn enough to live on – only about £3 a week – but she also had an allowance from her father. Air Taxis Croydon were eventually given a government contract for Army Co-operation, which was how Mona found herself practising dive-bombing gunning placements by night in London as they aimed their weapons at her. All around her, searchlights flashed across the sky.

On 31 August 1939 Veronica Innes was flying with a friend into Portsmouth Aerodrome.

'It's been camouflaged,' she remarked as they came in to land. 'It looks smaller than usual.' She thought for a moment she was going to overshoot, but she made it. After having tea at the aerodrome, she took off again at dusk for the airfield near Reading. By the time she arrived it was almost dark, and light was pouring from the hangars.

'Where have you been?' her instructor asked crossly. Tommy was normally very cheerful, but this evening he seemed on edge. 'Don't you know all civil flying has been stopped?' They had a few drinks and Tommy calmed down and explained.

'The balloon barrage'll be going up any moment.'

'How exciting!' said Veronica. 'It won't be long before I'm flying to France delivering all kinds of things and going on secret missions, probably.'

The next day she tried to find out more about what was going on.

'No idea,' said Tommy. 'Blackout curtains are up at the Falcon. Must be getting serious.'

All the planes were grounded, and it pained Veronica to see them sitting idle in the hangars while she was just hanging about twiddling her thumbs. Her enthusiasm for possible secret missions didn't last long – she was beginning to get the terrible feeling something awful was about to happen.

On 1 September German forces invaded Poland. Two days later, on an incongruously sunny Sunday morning, news came over the wireless from Prime Minister Chamberlain that Hitler had not pulled his troops out of the country. 'Consequently,' he said sombrely, 'this country is at war with Germany.'

3. Women to Fly RAF Planes

As if to signal the outbreak of war, almost immediately after it was declared, air-raid sirens started up in London. Margot Gore was at home with her father in West London when the news came over the wireless. There was a flurry of panic across the city as the klaxons sounded their eerie rising and falling wail. Margot looked out of the window and saw people running up Gloucester Road.

'Must be heading to Kensington Gardens, to the slip trenches,' said her father.

He and Margot stayed put, but others abandoned their Sunday dinner preparations and headed straight for public air-raid shelters or made their way down to the Anderson shelters they had dug in their gardens. Others simply hid under tables and stairs. Some did nothing at all. One man said he swore he saw a German plane flying up the Thames.

Giant silver barrage balloons began to rise up across the city, but there were no German planes and this was not an air raid. The continuous all-clear siren sounded and people began to emerge from their shelters to get back to their Sunday dinners. It had been a false alarm – for now.

For most people in Britain, the declaration of war in September 1939 did not have an immediate impact on daily life. The majority dutifully carried their gas masks. Some didn't even bother with that. Some children were evacuated. Others stayed where they were with their parents. There were no air raids yet, and no battles being fought close to home. The war still seemed something of a distant concept. The eight-month period that followed became known as the phoney war.

It was nevertheless a shock for people to see trenches being dug and sandbags piling up around the most vulnerable buildings. Margot had heard that hostilities were largely on hold for now, and she commented to her father, who had seen the last war, that it felt as if they were in limbo. Her brother was in the army in India, and he had told her that things would hot up before long. Although the war wasn't affecting them much directly, they sensed there was worse to come.

In Poland things were very much tougher. At 6 a.m. on 1 September there had been a German bombing raid on Warsaw, while the German Army invaded from north and south. Penned in by tanks, bombed from the air and eventually cut off from supplies, the Polish Army stood little chance. By mid-September Warsaw was surrounded and the Soviet Red Army, having signed a pact with Hitler, crossed the border. In two weeks of relentless bombardment, around 25,000 people in the city were killed, and Warsaw finally surrendered on 27 September.

Anna Leska had qualified as a glider pilot at the age of eighteen. She went on to get her balloon pilot's licence at the Warsaw Flying Club, but the authorities refused to let her become a fully-fledged powered-aircraft pilot. Anna was a fiery and determined character who wasn't likely to let something like that get in her way. She joined another club and eventually got her pilot's licence on a light aircraft in the spring of 1939.

With the outbreak of war, Anna was as keen as ever to continue flying and to do her bit for her country, particularly as many pilots at the civilian flying clubs were being swiftly incorporated into air force squadrons. Barbara Wojtulanis, who had been Poland's first female parachutist and licensed balloonist, was also keen to keep flying. She and Anna had both been turned down for the Polish Air Force, on account of their being female. But with the outbreak of war they were allowed to fly in a non-combat role and were assigned to Air Force Headquarters to fly liaison and reconnaissance missions. They became couriers for the Commander of the Polish Air Force, Józef Zając, and were also responsible for moving planes out of the way of approaching bombing raids.

At the beginning of the invasion, there was a wave of

Nazi propaganda claiming that the Luftwaffe had destroyed Poland's flying capacity in three days. That wasn't quite true. Although the attack was unprovoked, the Polish Air Force had mobilised a week earlier due to the political tensions, and had relocated many of its pilots to secret airfields. The Luftwaffe managed to hit several training planes and airfields, but many fighter planes remained safely hidden. Outnumbered three to one, the Polish pilots fiercely defended their homeland in the first six days of battle, and Polish Air Force bombers attacked the advancing German tanks. But the Panzers were gaining ground and making their way deeper into the country every day. As they ran short of fuel and supplies the pilots eventually had no choice but to evacuate their airfields.

Anna and her squadron were charged with carrying out vital reconnaissance missions. They made their way south as they tried to keep ahead of the advancing German Army. Every night the light aircraft they were using had to be hidden out of sight of the Luftwaffe bombers, with their wings tucked neatly away. A squadron of planes all lined up in a row would make a pretty obvious target from above. The pilots wheeled the planes anywhere they could to cover them up in the surrounding woodland. It was tiring and stressful work.

One morning, Anna Leska was wheeling her plane out from under some trees when she saw a bridge only a couple of miles away being blown up by German tanks.

She managed to unfold the wings just in time and jump in, but she didn't have time to run the engine for ten minutes to warm it up. She had to leave immediately, even though it meant taking off down a sloping potato field. Anna prayed the straggling potato plants wouldn't get stuck under her aircraft, and that she would make it over the approaching hedge.

With the outbreak of war, civilian flying clubs in Britain were shut down. Mona Friedlander was evacuated from Croydon to Manchester, where she continued to fly on a postal run to York. With war came rumour and speculation, and any overhead flying craft could be treated with suspicion. On one occasion Mona arrived above the aerodrome just as a thick fog was coming down. Her plane was not identifiable from the ground, and for one dicey moment the ground observers thought she could be a German spy attempting to land. Eventually clearance came through that she wasn't a danger and she was allowed in without any further trouble.

Even for the most experienced female pilots it was difficult to find a war job which involved flying. There was no hope of ever joining the RAF as a pilot, and women were not allowed to take part in combat. Margot Gore was advised by her instructor, Mrs Patterson, to get a job which wouldn't tie her down too much, 'just in case something does come up for us pilots'. Margot found work with MI5, which had moved its operations to Wormwood Scrubs Prison. It was her job to fetch files for the officers. She would be given a 'chit' to say which one they wanted, then she would fetch it, sign for it and cart it back. It was tedious work in practice, but it still felt quite exciting to be in this secret location handling all those important files.

Many of the younger men who could already fly joined the RAF straight away. For those who were unable to join, either due to age or infirmity of some kind, it was thought they could help in other ways. Leslie Runciman, the Director-General of the state airline BOAC (British Overseas Airways Corporation), had for some months been planning to set up a pool of civil pilots, an air transport auxiliary, who could fly light aircraft and carry out supply deliveries and other duties. Once this was approved, the job of forming and running the Air Transport Auxiliary (ATA) was given to Gerard d'Erlanger, an accountant-turned-aviator who had helped form BOAC. He was known in the industry by the affectionate nickname 'Pops'. He embraced his new job with enthusiasm.

Pops selected a group of amateur civilian pilots who had been deemed unfit to fly in the RAF. The stipulation was that they had to be men, between the ages of twenty-eight and fifty, with a minimum of 250 hours' flying experience. One thousand possible pilots were written to, one hundred responded, and just under thirty were initially selected.

The new ATA pilots were nicknamed 'Ancient and

Tattered Airmen', partly because they included among their number former First World War pilot Stewart Keith-Jopp, who had only one eye and one arm, and another First World War ace, Charles Dutton, who also had one arm, as well as a whole range of men from different walks of life, including stockbrokers, doctors, artists, shoe sellers, farmers, and even a conjuror. Rather than providing delivery or communications duties, it was decided they would be most useful to the RAF as ferry pilots, flying aircraft from factories to maintenance units and squadrons across the country when they were needed.

Female pilots were not permitted to join the ATA, even if they had been through the Civil Air Guard scheme or could already fly before the war. A prominent aviatrix, Lady Mary Bailey, who had flown solo from England to South Africa in 1928, made the bold suggestion that women might actually become fighter pilots. Unsurprisingly, she was met with scorn and hostility. The former Secretary of State for Air, Lord Londonderry, was adamant that women should not be exposed to the risk of combat. The Air Council completely agreed, firmly ruling out the possibility of women becoming fighter pilots. Londonderry was, however, open to the possibility of women pilots being put to use in other ways, although not everyone agreed with him. Charles Grey, the editor of the popular flight magazine *The Aeroplane*, said women would be 'incapable' of flying jobs. In spite of the general scepticism, there were several women who knew they would be more than capable.

Some of the most experienced female pilots in the country had been working hard behind the scenes for several years, lobbying for the possibility that they might fly in some capacity if war broke out. Spearheading the charge was Pauline Gower.

The youngest daughter of an MP, Sir Robert Gower, Pauline had taken a joy ride when she was a schoolgirl with a celebrity First World War aviator and test pilot, Captain Hubert S. Broad, who had been passing through her home town of Tunbridge Wells. She was sent to finishing school in Paris, from which she promptly ran away, and back in England she was 'presented' at court as a debutante, which she endured but found thoroughly boring. In 1930, not long after Amy Johnson completed her solo trip, and remembering her flight as a schoolgirl, Pauline enrolled at the Phillips and Powis School of Flying near Reading, without telling her parents. When she could no longer hide her new passion, her father cut off her allowance, so she gave violin lessons in order to fund it herself.

When she was seventeen Pauline had been seriously ill and nearly died at her convent school. She survived, somewhat weakened physically but determined to have a career and make something of her life. Her father wouldn't let her go to university, and when she took up flying instead, it was with an impressively focused vigour. Eventually her father came around to the idea of his daughter flying, or at least realised he was fighting a losing battle, and he put a down payment on a two-seater plane called a Spartan for her twenty-first birthday. It was about as basic as they came in those days and Pauline adored it.

Pauline Gower became the world's third and Britain's first female commercial pilot. She went into business with UCL graduate and engineer Dorothy Spicer, setting up the world's first all-female airborne business, giving joy rides from a field in Kent. They winged it, literally, and slept in a hut on the edge of the airfield, charging half a crown for a flight and 15 shillings for an 'aerobatic sequence'. In 1933 they did a tour with their plane of 185 airfields, and then a stint in 1936 with Tom Campbell Black's Air Display. Flying at these popular air displays could be dangerous. Pauline witnessed two fatal accidents of other pilots, and nearly got killed herself when she was hit on the head by a wheel from another plane she collided with on the ground. The same year, Pauline's mother committed suicide by gassing herself in the kitchen, thinking she had cancer. After a nerve-wracking and difficult few months, Pauline immersed herself in work, eventually becoming a commissioner for the Girl Guides, a lecturer on aviation, and a strong advocate for female pilots. By late 1939 she found herself busy drawing on every connection she had to persuade the powers that be that the ATA should hire women.

Often portrayed in the press as rather racy types, who smoked and drank and were altogether too privileged, the country's flying girls were thought by some to be merely chasing publicity. Twenty-seven-year-old Pauline, with her no-nonsense Girl Guide style, was perfect to allay these concerns. She had a trim figure, blonde bobbed hair, vivid blue eyes and a determined expression. She had an affecting blend of seriousness and spontaneous laughter, which lit up her face and reassured people around her. Pauline's ability to listen with a look of pure attentiveness on her face, particularly when talking to some of the more verbose VIPs and officials, was perhaps another of her great assets when it came to succeeding in this seemingly impossible quest, along, of course, with her more than adequate credentials. She had already carried thousands of passengers in her joy ride business, was a fellow of the Royal Meteorological Society, and even a member of a new parliamentary sub-committee reviewing safety regulations concerning 'low-flying banner pullers'. Pauline, who was very well connected in the world of politics, used every bit of diplomacy and charm she could muster, and in late 1939 she managed to persuade those in charge to allow a small number of women to fly. They also agreed that Pauline Gower was the best person to run this new women's section of the Air Transport Auxiliary.

Once word got out that women pilots were being considered, Pauline received numerous enthusiastic letters from hopeful pilots across the country. One of them was Elsie Joy Davison. Joy, as she was known, had been fascinated by flight since she was a child. She had moved to Britain from Canada with her mother and sister when her father died in an accident, and even as a little girl she could think of nothing but flying and puttering around in motors. She gained her flying certificate at the age of twenty and by the age of twenty-three she was a well-known flyer in her local area. In 1933 she married a man called Frank Davison, and the two of them ran a small aviation business in Cheshire, making Joy the first female director of an aircraft company in the UK.

The romance had developed while Frank was photographing tidal records from the air for the Liverpool Dock Board. Miss Muntz, as she was then, was the pilot. The marriage did not work out, though, and in 1939 the pair divorced. That year Joy was working at Portsmouth, Southsea & Isle of Wight Aviation Ltd, flying from Portsmouth Airport to Cardiff, Pengam Moors Aerodrome, and working for National Air Communications, a government organisation which directed civilian flying operations following the outbreak of war. Although she was lucky to have a flying job, when she heard about the ATA she wrote to Pauline Gower:

I have just this minute got wind of the W.S.A.T.A. [Women's Section Air Transport Auxiliary] . . . Could you let me know how much the ATA are offering as a salary, and whether (if you know yet) there will be any chances of promotion later, or will one stay for ever as a Second Officer? My experience at the moment is nearly 1,300 hours, of which about 600 is on twins and about 100 night. Normal peace-time occupation is Commercial Pilot; age is 29; not married any more (since 20/11/39!) 'B' Licence No 2567. Types flown: Moth, Avian, Puss Moth, Fox Moth, Cadet, Swift, Desoutter, Drone, Proga, Monospar, Tiger Moth, Klemm, Airspeed Courier, Airspeed Ferry, Miles Falcon.

She wrote again later.

My Dear Pauline,

Many thanks for your letter and dope enclosed, also for the further circular letter from BA detailing salary etc.

Sorry old thing, but I fear the dough isn't good enough, particularly considering one would be flying open-cockpit stuff for a large majority of the time! Afraid I'm getting soft or old or something, but when I've got a job which pays about twice as well and where one earns one's money in more or less comfort, the change offers no worthwhile attractions! Nevertheless I wish you all very well, and if any of you should happen to come to Cardiff for any reason do look me up. Of course I may be away, I can give no promises!

Let me know when you have time and things have progressed a bit further which of our flying females you have roped in!

Best of wishes to you, my dear, and the very best of luck to you. Awfully glad they picked you to be at the head of this thing. May it and you go far together!

One of those 'flying females' was Margaret Fair-weather. Margie, as she was known to friends, was the daughter of a prominent MP, Viscount Walter Runci-man. She learnt to fly at Newcastle Aero Club and got her certificate in 1937. She met and fell in love with a fellow pilot, Douglas Keith Fairweather, and they got married. He was a jolly and exuberant businessman from Glasgow, who was also a bit of an eccentric. He was a contrast to Margie, who was rather withdrawn and quiet, with green, somewhat faraway eyes. Perhaps it was this which led to her being nicknamed 'Cold Front', as she could appear a bit aloof. She was actually very loyal and loving to Douglas, who was devoted to her. He was once heard to say, 'I love Margie, better than any dog I ever had, or,' he paused for a moment, 'even a pig or a cat.' In the summer of 1938, Margaret's father, now Lord Runci-man, was sent on a mission by Neville Chamberlain to Prague to try and mediate between Germany and Czech-oslovakia. Margaret flew out to meet him, and she and Douglas also carried out a secret mission to photograph airfields in Germany. They were disguised as tourists and Margaret sent secret letters to her brother which contained coded messages. Margie and Douglas both became instructors with the Civil Air Guard, and Doug-las was one of the first to join the male section of the ATA when it began. By 1939 Margaret was one of the most experienced women pilots in the country, with 1,050 hours of civilian flying.

Also present on Pauline's list of eligible pilots was Mona Friedlander, Romford instructor Gabrielle Patterson and Rosemary Rees. They, along with another eight of the most 'air-minded' women in the country, were asked to attend a flight test at Whitchurch in Bristol in mid-December.

The test was carried out by a 'fearsome man', or so thought Rosemary, called A. R. O. MacMillan. He was the chief flying instructor at BOAC and had been loaned out to the ATA. Since all the women selected by Pauline Gower had at least 600 hours' flying experience, there wasn't really a question as to whether or not they could fly. But they had to pass the test anyway and the pressure was on them to prove the doubters wrong.

When Rosemary arrived at the aerodrome for her test she discovered she would be flying in a Tiger Moth. This was the RAF's elementary trainer made by de Havilland, and a type of plane that Rosemary loathed. It had an open cockpit and was a very draughty biplane with wings above and below the cockpit.

'It feels like being in a box kite,' she said to Mona as they waited for their test. She had got very used to the cosy closed cabin of her own sleek monoplane.

Of course Rosemary got in anyway when her turn came, and MacMillan asked her to do a circuit of the airfield. She then had to demonstrate a few spins, get out of them, and do a short cross-country, before coming in to land. After the test she handed in her log book and waited. MacMillan's face was inscrutable. After a while he said, 'You seem to be the sort that doesn't panic at least.'

Mona Friedlander had over 600 hours, including 100 hours of night flights. But that didn't stop her being frightfully nervous during her test. She got through it anyway and waited for the results.

Another pilot who was being tested that day was Joan Hughes. A petite 5 foot 2 inches, what she lacked in stature she made up for in skill and enthusiasm. She also had an impressive 600 hours in her log book, and had started flying when she was only fifteen. She had become the youngest girl in the country to get her licence at the age of just seventeen. After being in the spotlight for her youthful achievements, she also took an instructor's course and got a job as a flying instructor for the Civil Air Guard at Romford with Gabrielle Patterson and Margot Gore, which allowed her to gain a lot of hours. They all knew they had passed the flight test the same day, but since they had tested twelve people, and not everyone could be taken on, there was an agonising wait to find out who had actually got a place.

'What do you think we'll do? If we get in?' Joan asked the others as they left the airfield.

'Maybe secret missions! One can only hope,' said Mona.

'It'd be nice to do *something* with planes, though, wouldn't it?' said Rosemary.

They all agreed that if they were to have a job in this war, to do their bit, they would prefer to be flying, in whatever capacity. It felt like forever, but eventually the results came back. Rosemary was elated to have been chosen as one of the first. Mona Friedlander, Gabrielle Patterson, Margaret Fairweather and Joan Hughes had all been selected, too.

Just before Christmas there was a general announcement in the press that a small group of women were to be wartime pilots, with headlines such as 'Women Flying Aces' and, provocatively, 'Women to fly RAF planes'. These reports were a bit overblown, because the 'women' would only be flying non-operational aircraft – that is, not involved in any combat or military duties – for the time being.

'Women already well known in civil aviation' said one line in the papers, almost apologetically. The press release must have anticipated a backlash. Whatever criticism might be in store for them, a handful of women at least had earned their chance to prove they could do it just as well as the men.

4. Tiger Moths

In early January 1940, the first eight women ATA pilots and their Commander, Pauline Gower, arrived at Hatfield Airfield in Hertfordshire to begin their lives as ATA pilots. They were based in a small wooden hut behind the de Havilland aircraft factory, which produced the Tiger Moths they had been tested on. The group was a mixed, characterful and spirited bunch of some of the best pilots across the country.

There was Winifred Crossley, who had once performed aerobatics with Alan Cobham's and C. W. A. Scott's 'Flying for All' Aerial Circuses. In 1936 she was said to have provided 'one of the most amazing features of the display' after only two years' flying. As the only female pilot for 'Air Publicity Ltd' at Heston, she also towed advertising banners, one of which she flew over Whitehall with the message 'Give All Civil Servants Pensions'.

Also present in the group was Margaret Cunnison, a slight woman of 5 foot 2 inches, who was in her mid-twenties. She had been the Chief Flying Instructor with the Strathtay Aero Club. She was only the second woman in Scotland to get a commercial pilot's licence, and the first to become a flying instructor. Finally, there was

Marion Wilberforce. Tough and eccentric, she was one of seven children of a Scottish laird. She had had a strict convent upbringing and a French governess but was also a practitioner of the martial art of ju-jitsu and a member of the women's mountaineering team at Oxford University. Naturally sporty and active, she took up flying after being encouraged by her two brothers and flew all around Europe in her Cirrus and Hornet Moths. Among her early experiences was ferrying livestock to the family farm in Essex from places as far away as Hungary. By 1940 she had flown over 900 hours.

Many of the new ATA pilots already knew each other. Flying was a small world at that time, and some had already been courted by the press for their various feats and records. But this new job was a world away from the exploits of Cobham's Air Circus, or 5-bob joy rides.

When all the women were assembled, Pauline Gower outlined their duties:

'Your main job will be to clear out the Tiger Moths from here to the various units and squadrons around the country, as quickly as possible. We're only flying light aircraft for the time being.'

Rosemary's heart sank a little bit. *No doubt,* she thought to herself, *the chaps are more than happy to pass the job of delivering these draughty old Tigers over to us.*

It was mid-winter and flying at two or three thousand feet in an open cockpit wasn't going to be easy. Mona Friedlander was also a bit disappointed that they were only ferrying Moths, and nothing grander like Spitfires and Hurricanes. But they were all so excited to be there, and felt so lucky to be flying at all, they were really prepared to do anything. Pauline and her pilots still had a lot to do in order to convince those at the top that they could pull it off.

Not long after they had started there was another announcement to the press. It was thought that if the journalists, who were already hungry for a story, were given access to the women in a controlled manner the novelty of the glamorous female pilots might wear off and they could be left in peace to get on with the job. To try and contain the bubbling press interest, a general notice was put out that they could visit Hatfield. There would be a photo shoot and they could meet and chat to the pilots.

On a bright, chilly morning in early January they gathered on the airfield at Hatfield for interviews and a photo shoot. They had been issued with heavy fur-lined 'Sidcot' flying suits, flying helmets, goggles and furry black flying boots. The official photographer was very keen to get a shot of them next to their planes, kitted up in their flying gear, complete with parachutes weighing over 30 pounds.

'That's lovely, girls,' he said as they all stood in a row. 'Now if you could run to the planes, as if you're about to take off, and grab your parachutes.'

'He wants us to scramble for the planes like they're Spitfires or something,' whispered Rosemary to Joan.

'As if! In a Tiger Moth!'

But they did it anyway, and with a smile. They all duti-fully picked up their heavy parachutes and dashed towards the planes as if they were about to jump into them. When they got back the photographer smiled, then paused.

'That was ... lovely, ladies ...' he said. 'Now, just once more if you don't mind.'

They had to do it all again, until he finally got the shot he wanted. After that they demonstrated a short journey in some of the planes and posed for some more photos in their smart long ATA coats and blue forage caps. Some of the journalists asked the women a few ques-tions about their lives but the whole thing was quite carefully managed by Pauline. When the press finally drifted away, it was time for the real work to begin.

'We have an order. You're to ferry a group of Tiger Moths to an RAF training school in the Midlands,' said Pauline. One morning not long after the photoshoot, the pilots were in their cold wooden hut awaiting their instruc-tions. 'You will be flying in a gaggle. Four of you. You'll be easily recognised by the Observer Corps that way.'

A gaggle meant they'd all be flying together and arriv-ing as a group at the airfield. Despite her experience, Mona was quite nervous at the prospect of flying in a group. She was used to flying on her own and had never had any training flying in formation with other planes.

'Don't worry. Just watch the wing tips of the next

plane and you'll all be able to stick together,' Pauline reassured her.

With the help of the ground staff at de Havilland's, they pulled the Tiger Moths out of the hangars and on to the airfield. It was bitterly cold, and there was a layer of frost on the grass which hadn't yet melted. A dim stream of sunlight was breaking through the clouds.

In her Sidcot suit, furry boots, helmet and goggles, Mona climbed into one of the planes.

'It'll be nippy up there,' said Rosemary as she walked over to her own aircraft.

'Brace yourselves!'

Mona flicked her ignition switch, up for on. One of the ground crew spun the propeller and the engine started. The wooden chocks were removed from in front of the wheels, and they all began to taxi into a line on the airfield, facing into the wind for take-off.

An icy blast hit Mona's face as she checked the instrument panel. It was fairly rudimentary, with an rpm gauge, air speed indicator to show the speed of travel, a cross lever which kept the plane on an even keel, an altimeter which showed how high the plane was, and a small oil pressure gauge on the right. In the centre of the cockpit was a large joystick, or control column, which moved in any direction, and at the feet a control for the rudder on the tail which directed the turns.

Rosemary was ahead of Mona, who watched as she took off. Next it was her turn to bump along the airfield and when she got the plane up to 40 mph the Tiger Moth lifted gently off the ground with a small wobble of its large double wings. They were on their way. Behind Mona another plane followed, and she kept her eye on Rosemary as best she could.

Mona was used to flying, even at night, but now that she had to keep an eye on the planes around her as well it was a lot harder. She checked below for landmarks but risked losing sight of the other aircraft. As she flew higher, her face got colder, and after a while, in spite of the furry flying boots they had all been given, she could hardly feel her toes. It was a clear day and they soon reached the cruising height of around 2,000 feet. The English countryside was spread out beneath them, with the tiny railway lines and rivers like veins across the landscape, a godsend for navigation. Dotted around them were clumps of trees and fields, then villages, church spires and rows of houses appeared and disappeared. Tiny worlds whizzing by. Every now and again Mona could make out the small figure of someone looking up and pointing as the group flew over, or a little motor car puttering along on its own up a country lane.

Despite the new challenge of flying in a group, and the possible dangers it presented of crashing into one another, they managed it and in a couple of hours Mona noticed that Rosemary was preparing to land and followed after her into the wind. One by one they came down with a gentle bump. The delivery had been a success. The ground crew came out to bring the planes into the hangar, and when the four women got out the men looked quite shocked to see them.

'So, you're the new girl pilots, are you?'

The women couldn't answer, their faces were so numb with cold. The men were all quite charming, even a little pleased to be seeing this novel group of women at their aerodrome. They insisted on helping them down out of their aircraft. The pilots were delighted to hear the words, 'Come in out of the cold. You're just in time for lunch.'

After a quick stop in the officers' mess, where they compared notes from their journey, the reality struck that they now had to make their way back to Hatfield, without the luxury of a plane. The trains were running, thank goodness, but it was going to take a good few hours to get back. They just managed to get seats but were all so tired from the cold and excitement of the journey that they dozed off on the way. It was late evening by the time they arrived back at Hatfield Station. They made their way in the icy darkness back to their digs. Rosemary and Joan were staying at a local hotel in town called the Stone House. They slept well that night, but it seemed as though barely any time had passed before it was morning again, and time to report back once more at Hatfield for duty.

In Poland, Anna Leska had prayed as she taxied down a gently sloping potato field that she would be able to take off in time to beat the advancing German tanks. Her aircraft just about cleared a hedge, and she swept into the air. On the ground below her, she could see the tanks rumbling their way on to the road at the edge of the wood where they had just been hiding. It had been a narrow escape.

On the orders of General Zając, the head of the Polish Air Force, Anna made her way to Czerniowce in the south-east of Poland, in what is now Ukraine. The aim was to move the remaining air force pilots out of the country and reassemble in Romania. From Czerniowce, Anna jumped into a tiny light aircraft and made her escape. She had four passengers squeezed in with her as she flew across the border and arrived just as the plane ran out of fuel. But Romania turned out not to be the safe haven they had been hoping for. Many of the Polish refugees who were also pouring across the border were detained and interned. Some were shot in the mountains as they made their way over. The Gestapo had infiltrated Romania. No one knew who to trust.

Anna arrived at an airfield where many other Polish aircraft were crammed in, along with a lot of exhausted and desperate pilots and civilian refugees. They slept in the hangars, all piled in together. Many of their planes were confiscated and in due course most people were interned. Some were sent to camps, some died. The lucky ones were billeted with local families. Anna was taken in by a police chief and his wife, where she remained until she was contacted by her squadron commander and told to move out. A rumour circulated that the Red Army was marching their way. Anna's leader, Major General Zaremski, sent a message for her to meet him by a nearby crossroads at seven in the evening to make their escape. The plan was to make their way to Bucharest by car.

Anna bought a skirt for the occasion to try and look more like an ordinary civilian and less like the daring undercover pilot she actually was. It took a week to reach Bucharest. It was a nerve-wracking time during which Anna had to hide their revolver under her blanket, in case they were searched. She, they thought, would be the least likely to be given a difficult time if caught. Once in Bucharest it took seven months for Anna and her compatriots to achieve their final goal, of getting visas and travel documents for their ultimate destination, France, where the Polish Government had relocated.

Anna's father was a general in the army. She had no idea what had become of her mother or her sisters, and whether they had survived the bombing and invasion. Staying at a hotel in Menton, she got the shock of her life when she saw familiar handwriting scribbled in the guest book. Her own father had stayed there just two nights before on his way to England. A sign, she dared hope, that things might just be all right.

5. A Harsh Winter

'"Ace Girl Pilots"!' laughed Rosemary Rees. '"Three hundred and fifty mph fighters"! Hardly. More like eighty in those Tigers.'

'"Out to show the RAF",' said Mona Friedlander. 'Well, they won't like that.'

'Oh heavens, look at this one: "How d'ya like the togs, girls?"' laughed Joan Hughes, picking up one of the newspapers. They were all sitting in the little office at Hatfield with a pile of newspapers.

'Look at you, Mona, with your parachute draped over your shoulder!'

'"We like you flighty!"' said Mona. 'Well, really! This is supposed to be serious stuff. But I'm used to all this, from when I first started flying. They made out my father was a millionaire, which he's not. And called me the Mayfair Minx and all sorts.'

'I'm sure they'll get bored and it'll be something of a seven-day wonder,' said Joan, who was well used to all the attention, having been the youngest female pilot in the country and often in the press. 'They'll soon find somebody else to gawp at,' she sighed.

When the pictures and the story of the 'ATA girls' hit

the press, and it got around that these women had been audacious enough to fly, not everyone was pleased. Some said they were taking jobs from the RAF, from men, when they most needed the work. Others thought women pilots were racy creatures, over-privileged social butterflies, thrill-seekers larking about when they should be doing much more important things like housework, child-rearing and preparing their husbands' dinners.

William Joyce, aka Lord Haw-Haw, who had taken to delivering propaganda broadcasts for the Nazis from Hamburg to Britain, sneered over the airwaves that the rich men of England, having been ruined by the war through taxes, had found a way to get their money back by putting their wives and daughters into planes. A thing, he said, that these depraved, unnatural women would no doubt enjoy. He exaggerated the wages the women were getting, claiming it was £8 a week when it was in fact 20 per cent less than their male counterparts and closer to £6. For some people, the mere fact that the women were earning more than some junior RAF recruits, who were being paid £4 a week, was too much to bear.

From the moment they started there was an enormous pressure on the women pilots not to get anything wrong. It was still thought it was better for women, if they were going to insist on flying, to stick to light, non-operational trainers. It certainly never occurred to many people that they could fly big bombers or fighters. Some thought women were simply not built, or physically able, to fly fast or large aeroplanes. The result was that they were absolutely terrified of breaking anything or mucking up. After having been put under such a public spotlight, they knew if anything went wrong there would be screaming headlines about women smashing RAF aircraft, and questions about what these women were doing being allowed to fly anyway. Even in the light Tigers, the big horror for everyone was the prospect of having an accident, not so much for their own safety but in case it jeopardised the future of the experiment.

'If we prang one, there'll be hell to pay, of course,' said Mona one day as they were waiting for the next order. 'If the men break one, that's just part of the job, but if we do, they'll all say it's because women aren't fit to fly.'

The Aeroplane's editor, Charles Grey, had barked while the debate was still raging in 1939 that while women could indeed do 'useful jobs', the trouble was that 'so many of them insist on wanting to do jobs which they are quite incapable of doing'. The 'menace' he continued, 'is the woman who thinks that she ought to be flying a high-speed bomber when she really has not the intelligence to scrub the floor of a hospital properly, or who wants to nose round as an Air Raid Warden and yet can't cook her husband's dinner'.

Others who wrote in to his magazine asked when the RAF would realise that all the good work they were doing was being 'spoiled by this contemptible lot of women', these 'overpaid show-offs'. The National Men's Defence League weighed in, asking for the issue to be raised in Parliament about the problem, as they saw it, of women encroaching on men's work. It wasn't just men complaining, either: some women thought it was all rather disgusting, their kind trying to be like men for the sake of a hobby, when there were men who needed jobs.

Pauline Gower made a valiant effort to keep the public on side. She spoke on the BBC in a typically straight-talking, practical fashion. 'We are a small group of women pilots with a job to do. We are just helping, along with others, to win the war,' she said. 'Our job will be unobtrusive. But it is going to be well and efficiently done.'

Along with the women at Hatfield, there were two male test pilots, John and Geoffrey, who worked for de Havilland's, and lots of ground staff – cleaners, fitters, riggers and cooks – attached to the factory. In the ATA office there was also an adjutant, who helped Pauline run the office and saw to anything else the pilots needed to keep things running smoothly. Every morning the women came in to find out what deliveries were required that day. They picked up their 'chits', pieces of paper which told them what their destinations were. These included short runs locally, and various training squadrons and aerodromes in places like Wiltshire or the Midlands, as well as further afield.

'There's an order from Wales,' said Pauline to the pilots one morning. They were to fly in a gaggle, four of them, all the way. They checked the Met weather report and a little fog was predicted, but nothing that seemed too dangerous. The planes were brought out of the hangar and they all took off. The group stayed together for a while, the cold wind once again biting at their increasingly numb faces. They weren't allowed to fly above the clouds because they had no radio in case it could be intercepted by the Germans to locate them. This meant they needed to see the ground for navigation at all times. If the clouds got too low and they were fly-ing blind, it became dangerous to go any lower, because of hills, tall chimneys or unexpected barrage balloons.

They were flying at about 2,000 feet when a cloud of fog suddenly descended. Mona lost visual contact with the plane in front and could no longer see the ground to navigate. She breathed in deeply and kept the aircraft steady. The fog lifted for a moment and she saw the dark outline of a plane to the left below. She banked and adopted that course, taking her plane lower to drop below the clouds. The fog continued to thicken and her face was wet with the fine freezing droplets. They all wanted to do well, with no mistakes, and deliver the planes on time, but Mona felt in her gut that it was get-ting dangerous. As the cloud dispersed slightly she saw the other planes getting lower. She guessed they must be going in to land on what looked to be an area of farmland. Luckily all four planes saw what was happening and, as the cloud was getting thicker by the minute, it was a relief when they all managed to land one after the other, as if it had been planned all along.

'Weather clamped down,' said Rosemary as she switched the engine off and climbed down. 'Had to stop. It was getting far too dangerous up there.' Her face was freezing and her hands had gone completely white and numb, even with big furry gloves on.

'I thought so too. It was getting a bit thick,' said Joan, rubbing her hands together and shivering. 'But what are we going to do with these Tigers? We won't be able to take off again today. It'll be dark soon.' In the end they had no choice but to get the police to come and put a guard on the planes and they put up at a pub in a nearby Shropshire village.

They had been told to try and avoid doing this kind of landing unless it was absolutely necessary. There was a lot of pressure for everything to be perfect in these first few weeks, with the spotlight of criticism still on them. But this time, they all agreed, it would have been too risky to keep going.

They made it to Wales the next day when the weather cleared, but they had to make the arduous journey back to Hatfield, via London, again by train. This time there were no seats at all and they sat on their parachutes in the unheated corridor. It was not a comfortable journey. Rosemary still had her chocolate ration and they shared it between them. It was a small mercy. It was gone midnight by the time they pulled into Hatfield station. They were relieved to have delivered the aircraft intact but thoroughly exhausted. As they walked back to the Stone House Hotel, slipping with every step on the crunching ice, hauling their heavy parachutes over their shoulders, Rosemary turned to Joan and said, 'If this is what it's going to be like all the time, I don't know if I can take it.'

No one could force the ATA pilots to fly or stop them from going up. It was up to them whether or not they took off, after listening to the weather report. Pauline was careful to discourage the flying from becoming a competition, because in the end the aeroplane was the prime concern. It was about using common sense, deciding how low it was safe to go; and they had to work out, if they did hit fog or low cloud, whether they should land or whether they could fly down a valley between hills. They knew that it was better to stay safe and leave it for a few days until the weather lifted, than crash the precious commodity they were flying. On the other hand, if they were to get the job done at all it inevitably meant taking some risks in order to keep things moving.

The furthest deliveries were to Scotland, to aerodromes in Lossiemouth and Kinloss, which meant a put-down on the way to get fuel, and an overnight stay. Trips like this could take up to two weeks if the weather was very bad. If they could get a ticket in these busy times, they got an overnight sleeper back from Glasgow.

More usually they had a horrible night sitting up stiffly on a seat, or on their parachutes again in the corridor. At times they even resorted to bedding down in the luggage racks on a really crowded train. They always packed an overnight bag and had money for a hotel if they needed it, as well as their emergency chocolate bar, which in that cold winter was very welcome indeed.

The male ground staff they met at aerodromes displayed varying reactions to a bunch of women landing on their turf. Some thought they were something of a bore, and that they were just getting in the way. There was not much of a WAAF presence yet, and very few, if any, amenities for females at the aerodromes. They couldn't stay there on site as that would never do in that all-male domain, so they had to stay in local hotels if there was an overnight put-down. At some aerodromes women were not allowed in the officers' mess at all. In those situations, they could be left feeling self-conscious and awkward at lunchtime as a tray of food was brought to them in the 'Ladies' Room' to eat alone. Going to the lavatory could be awkward too, with no female 'facilities'. If there were two of them, one could stand guard while the other used the men's. If you were alone, it was all very well risking going into the enclosed cubicle, but if timed badly, coming into the 'outer' area could be embarrassing for both parties if a man was engaged in minding his own business and a woman emerged.

Sometimes they got the distinct feeling from the men

that it was a bit tiresome having all these females around suddenly, and there was always one who would ask, 'What are these blessed women doing here?' Others just found them something of a novelty and a joke. It was, after all, also a bit of fun having a few girls around their usually all-male environment.

When they arrived at one aerodrome, Joan Hughes and some others were sent for by the RAF Commanding Officer, who was quite intrigued, he said, because he hadn't seen any 'lady pilots' before. They stood awkwardly in a line while he inspected them up and down. What he was looking for exactly they weren't really sure, but he seemed satisfied.

The ATA was a civilian, not a military, organisation, and the uniform was a distinctive navy blue with shoulder lapels in the shape of wings, gold stripes and braids, and they wore a forage cap and black silk stockings. Initially, the head of the ATA, Gerard d'Erlanger, stipulated that his girls had to wear their skirts at all times. Trousers were not the 'done thing' for women in those days, and having his girls parading about the place in slacks wouldn't do at all. However, the women all knew that it would be impossible to fly in skirts, indecent even, and they thought it was a ridiculous idea from a purely practical point of view. In the end they usually wore their flying suits and boots when they flew. D'Erlanger relented and they were eventually issued with regulation ATA trousers, though he still tried to insist they wear their skirts if they were out of the aircraft, and especially if they were in London or anywhere they might be seen by someone important. So they had to carry their skirts in their bags and pull them out all crumpled and rumpled, ready to change when they were expected to be on show for inspection by the curious. Without any changing facilities, they often had to find an out-of-the-way corner and hop about on the aerodrome as they tried to slip discreetly into more 'ladylike' attire.

Because the ATA was a civilian organisation, there was no military-style formality and they were not required to do drills or marching or saluting to the CO, or things of that nature. But they were under Air Force secrecy and discipline and weren't to do anything the RAF would disapprove of, or which would bring them into disrepute. There were also matters of security, and they were not allowed to give away any sensitive information about the locations of balloon barrages or secret aerodromes and other sensitive sites.

The winter weather of 1939–40 was the harshest in decades. With temperatures into the minus twenties, icy rain and heavy snowfall, January was the coldest month since 1895. Over the months the women delivered more than 2,000 Tiger Moths without a single accident. There was snow on the ground at Hatfield right through until April. When the grass began to appear and daffodils and spring flowers began to peep tentatively through, the snow was swiftly replaced by driving rain. Temperatures were rising slightly, but flying the open-cockpit Tiger Moths was beginning to take its toll physically and psychologically. Summer still seemed an age away.

'I couldn't feel my face,' said Joan after one trip. 'I had to stop and refuel, and my face was so frozen I could hardly speak. I couldn't even smile. My hands were that cold, you know, thawing them out in the mess was actually painful. They practically had to lift me out of the cockpit, like an Egyptian mummy.'

While the eight pilots got used to their new job, Pauline Gower maintained a firm but fair grip on operations from her office at Hatfield. She had to keep a fine balance between command and friendliness, discipline and good humour. She would be met with a steady stream of questions and requests and 'Pauline, can I have a moment' when there were things to sort out. She always had time for the pilots and was very patient, despite having quite a nervous energy. If a word was needed about a mistake or a problem, she didn't shy away from giving someone a strong ticking off, but she was also ready with a joke or a smile to soften the blow. It could be a lonely position at the top. Sometimes she would have loved to do something silly with the girls, but had to assume a position of ultimate sensibleness. Nonetheless, her office at Hatfield was welcoming and she seemed to take the job in her stride. It was easy to forget she was still only in her late twenties after everything she had already achieved.

The phoney war seemed to be dragging on and there wasn't much happening on the home front in early 1940, but news of the war filtered through on the wireless. In January a ship called the HMS *Exmouth* was escorting a merchant ship north of Scotland when it was sunk by a German submarine, with the loss of all on board. In March an air raid on Scapa Flow led to the first UK civilian casualties. Rationing was being brought in bit by bit, and restrictions on certain foods were beginning to bite. The conflict was starting to feel closer to home.

In the early winter of 1940 two more women joined the ATA. Lady Mary Bailey, who was fifty years old, and Lois Butler, who, as many were eager to point out, was a grandmother, both joined the ranks at Hatfield. Lois Butler was married to the Chairman of de Havilland's, and unsurprisingly they were both very experienced pilots. In 1928 Lady Mary Bailey had been, at the age of thirty-eight, the first person to fly solo from London to Cape Town and back. She had five children and had taken up flying, she said, in order to 'get away from prams'. Her appointment with the ATA led to a flurry of negative publicity. There were claims that she got the job because her husband was a millionaire, and that she was, in any case, too old, although there were men in the ATA who were older. Concerned not to bring any negative publicity to the group, she stepped down within a fortnight.

In 1938 Amy Johnson had escaped from her turbulent marriage to fellow pilot Jim Mollison and gone through a difficult divorce. She had also been deeply affected by the mysterious disappearance the previous year of another celebrated female pilot, Amelia Earhart, over the Pacific. In need of money and desperate for a flying job, she found work as a pilot with the Portsmouth, Southsea and Isle of Wight Aviation Company, providing a ferry service and acting as a target for anti-aircraft gunners. Amy was glad to be flying and earning a wage, but she was frustrated that men with less experience were flying to France, while she was working only a few hours a week. She knew Pauline Gower from flying together at the Stag Lane club and she respected her down-to-earth approach. When Pauline was given the top job, however, Amy was a little put out at being overlooked for the position herself, saying that if she had 'played her cards right and cultivated the right people' she could have done it. In truth she didn't really want the job and was a bit dismissive about the women pilots she thought had been given a few 'crumbs to keep them quiet'.

Pauline wrote to Amy in January 1940 to sound her out about joining, but she was hoping for something a bit more exciting than transporting Tiger Moths and so declined. Amy really wanted to work in commercial aviation, but the war, and her being a woman, made these opportunities somewhere between scarce and non-existent. She looked on as the women of the ATA were splashed across the pages of the newspapers. When the Portsmouth, Southsea and Isle of Wight's fleet was requisitioned by the government in March and Amy lost her job, she swallowed her pride and sent in her application to the ATA. But she was too late. The places had filled up and she suffered the indignity of being put on a waiting list. Amy continued to pursue a job in aviation. She wrote to the Finnish Embassy about the possibility of flying their planes, and even considered a job in Kenya. She tried Allied Airways, the BBC, anyone and everyone she knew. At every turn she was accused of trying to take valuable war work from the men. When Pauline got permission to hire some more women, she thought of Amy Johnson again, and after a bit more soul-searching, Amy finally agreed to take a flight test for the ATA.

Given her existing apprehensions and perhaps a bit of nervousness about being tested, it's perhaps not surprising that it didn't take much to put Amy off. She arrived at Hatfield in early May, but when she saw another applicant waiting to fly, 'all dolled up in a full Sidcot suit, fur-lined helmet and goggles', as she wrote later to her father with more than a hint of snobbery, 'fluffing up her hair etc., the typical C.A.G. Lyons waitress type', she turned tail and ran. She telephoned in to Hatfield to say she had the flu.

In April Hitler invaded Norway and Denmark. Parliament was losing faith in Neville Chamberlain's peace efforts. He had, it seemed, underestimated Hitler's ambitions. A decision had to be made, whether to appease or to fight and accept the prospect of a bitter war with Germany. As the situation in Norway worsened there was increasing pressure on the Prime Minister to resign. Things came to a head when MP Leo Amery made an impassioned attack on him in the House of Commons. Chamberlain stepped down on 10 May. The same day, Nazi forces began their invasion of the Low Countries, the Netherlands, Luxembourg and Belgium. Winston Churchill seemed to be the only candidate to form a coalition wartime government, a role he relished, promising to 'fight them on the beaches'. Despite the bombast, almost the entire British Expeditionary Force at Dunkirk looked as if it was about to be wiped out by the advancing German tanks. Many thought that Britain didn't stand a chance.

In the secret corridors of MI5 at Wormwood Scrubs, Margot Gore was glued to the wireless. Churchill had ordered that civilian boats with a shallow enough draft should be requisitioned to help the navy rescue British troops in the audaciously risky Operation Dynamo. Margot was gripped as she waited to hear the outcome of the Dunkirk evacuation, thinking of all those little boats crossing the Channel and wondering what the outcome would be. Fortunately, the weather held. Operation Dynamo was a success and most of the troops were evacuated. When her brother arrived back from India he told Margot that the war was now on. On 10 June, Italy allied with Hitler, and not long afterwards Germany invaded France. Britain, many feared, would be next.

6. New Planes, More Pilots

The Polish pilots who had fled the Romanian capital Bucharest arrived in France homesick, hungry and frightened by the prospect of what might happen next. Four women had escaped and, wearing their full Polish Air Force uniforms in Paris, they turned quite a few heads in the city. Anna Leska had made her way to the capital, but with German troops advancing on France, the Polish Government once again decided to relocate, this time to London. After the invasion, French Vice Premier Marshal Pétain formed a new government and made a deal with Hitler. In return for demobilisation and armistice, Pétain gave Germany control of part of the country, including Paris, while he became chief of a French state with Vichy as its capital. With France effectively surrendered, the Polish Air Force made their plans to evacuate.

On 21 June Anna Leska and Barbara Wojtulanis climbed on board the passenger ship *Batory*, which had docked in the fishing port of Saint-Jean-de-Luz. Along with several thousand of their compatriots, they were ferried out to the ship by French fishing boats in choppy waters. The journey across the Channel was short but dangerous, although it was actually the bad weather that probably helped prevent an attack by the Luftwaffe. They managed to avoid the fate of the RMS *Lancastria*, which had been sunk just a few days earlier packed with thousands of troops and civilians. The *Batory* docked safely at Plymouth and Anna made her way to London, to the Polish General Staff building on Buckingham Palace Road. She eventually got a job as an interpreter with the Forces Ministry at the Foreign Office. When she heard about the ATA's women's section she was eager to get back to flying as quickly as possible.

Veronica Innes found a job as an ambulance driver in London, earning £2 a week. The shifts were gruelling, especially at night, and with the phoney war dragging on she hankered after some excitement. As soon as she heard about the ATA, she wrote to them at once, but was told that she didn't have enough hours, so her name would be kept on file. Her single-mindedness was such that when she saw a woman in the distinctive dark blue uniform with glistening gold wings through the window of a London bus she hopped off the moving vehicle in order to pursue the unsuspecting pilot up Oxford Street. Startled at being accosted by a complete stranger, the woman told Veronica kindly she was sorry but there was nothing she could do to help. Veronica had nearly got herself killed trying and she was no closer to her dream of flying again.

With the war escalating rapidly, Amy Johnson managed

to overcome her initial reluctance to join the ATA. Perhaps she also got over a few nerves at the prospect of a flight test. She returned to Hatfield in late May 1940 and was accepted. Amy was a household name and had been the centre of publicity and adulation during the 1930s. Going from that to the gruelling business of delivering open-cockpit planes for little reward on a relentless schedule must have been quite a shock. Amy had said she was joining only 'for the time being', and she hated it at first. She thought it was being run too much like a girls' school and felt like something of an outsider. She watched with envy as the ATA boys flew overhead in the fast Hurricanes and gritted her teeth in the face of all the Tiger Moths. However, as the magnitude of the conflict became clear, Amy soon saw the value of her work with the ATA and began to settle in as one of the girls. It was easy for the other pilots to forget the enormity of her fame, until they were at an RAF airfield, where Amy would often be immediately surrounded by half-apologetic, very determined young airmen demanding her autograph. Amy would then be led regally into the CO's quarters and treated, as she had been nicknamed in the press, like the Queen of the Air.

Behind all the fame and glory, Amy was thoughtful, sensitive, determined and hard-working. She could be very funny at times, and at others quite maudlin and sad. She was kind and offered the younger pilots advice.

Her flying motto before the war, probably to stop her mother worrying, had been 'Be Careful', but she wasn't that keen on sitting out bad weather either, and she would rib the girls who had cautiously 'put down' or landed to avoid the rain if she had made it through.

Pauline Gower was all too aware of the rumbles of discontent when the pilots were faced with yet another slog to Scotland and back in the draughty training planes. She knew they could do a lot more and wrote to the head of ATA, Gerard 'Pops' d'Erlanger, about the prospect of being allowed to fly other types of aircraft as the men were doing. Pops was non-committal. Preoccupied by the growing need for more RAF pilots and with Hitler seemingly on the doorstep, he had a lot to contend with. Pauline was persistent. She took matters into her own hands and met up with some aviation high-ups, including the Director-General of BOAC, Leslie Runciman, who duly arranged for Pauline to dine with the Air Member for Supply and Organisation, Air Marshal Sir Christopher Courtney. The pair got on well. Over dinner Pauline explained the plight of her pilots, stuck on those blessed Tigers, unable to make full use of their skills and having to watch while young men with no experience got into Spitfires and Hurricanes, while they, with hundreds of hours, had to sit back and do nothing. 'I'll see what I can do,' replied the Air Marshal.

*

Instructions for flying summer 1940:

(a) Avoid interference with or confusion amongst the active or passive defences of the country
(b) Avoid the risk of false air-raid alarms
(c) Avoid the risk of being shot down by our own defences

'Shot down!' said Joan Hughes as she read the rules which had been posted on the notice board at Hatfield.

'Ships can get quite trigger-happy too, you know,' said Pauline, 'if you fly over a convoy. Best to avoid them if you can.'

The ATA pilots had to fly within sight of the ground at all times, by the Observer Corps. They also had to keep strictly to special routes in areas which were defended by balloon barrages and avoid areas sensitive to ground defence, as well as dangers from hostile aircraft. They were issued with flare guns – Verey pistols – and got 'colours of the day' before each flight, but it was not really possible to fire the colours while flying for the ATA, which was why they had to fly in gaggles in order to be identified by ground defence.

Winston Churchill was eager to get behind the expansion of air power, and eventually Pauline got the welcome news that she could select a group of pilots to be trained on the single-engine trainers used to teach the RAF to fly fighter planes. They were one step closer to flying the Hurricanes and Spitfires they dreamt of.

The RAF fighter pilots were trained at Central Flying School at Upavon. Despite their misgivings, Pauline had managed to persuade them to let women convert to fighters there, 'What? Can't the men there handle our women?' she said cunningly, and the reverse psychology seems to have done the trick. They were told they could send a group of women to train on the Miles Master and the Airspeed Oxford, which would then clear them to fly other easy twins and single-engine fighter trainers.

They were also told they could take over ferrying another non-operational aircraft, the Percival Proctor, a single-engine monoplane used for radio training and communications, and Pauline got the go-ahead to expand the group. She wrote to a number of other experienced pilots about the urgent need for more women to join.

Veronica Innes was beyond excited when she got the letter asking her to go for a flight test. She hired a car and drove to Hatfield, where she looked in awe at all the Tiger Moths taking off and landing. She hadn't seen a plane that close for ten months. She made her way tentatively to the ATA hut and found a group of equally nervous-looking hopefuls waiting for their encounter with Miss Gower. One of the current pilots walked past the open door, complete with parachute and flying gear. They all looked at this Amazon striding purposefully towards the airfield and felt pangs of envy. It broke the ice and they began to chat about what had brought them to these hallowed doors. Among their number were Bridget Hill, Mary Hunter and a girl who introduced herself as an Austrian princess. While Mary was having her test, Veronica and Bridget larked about, trying on a forage cap they'd found in the room. A figure appeared at the door and they quickly put down the cap and sat back in their seats, suppressing their giggles.

'V. Innes,' said a small Scottish woman. It was Margaret Cunnison. She handed Veronica a parachute and they walked together towards the airfield. Veronica chatted nervously to try and break the ice. She looked down at the parachute.

'If I want to bail out, do I –'

Margaret cut her off briskly. 'We shan't be going nearly high enough for any of that sort of thing today.'

Veronica wanted to dissolve into the ground. She promised herself to try and avoid at all costs asking any more stupid questions.

Things didn't improve much once they were in the aircraft. Veronica had convinced herself she had already failed anyway, after the parachute comment. Then when Margaret taxied to the take-off point and handed over control to her, the aircraft started to swing as it left the ground. She was mucking it up. She tried desperately to control the plane. As it reached 2,000 feet she started to get hold of it and did a few turns. Margaret suddenly closed the throttle. 'Your engine's cut,' she said. 'Now forced land.'

Veronica looked around wildly for somewhere to put down without her engine. She made out the vague shape of a small field in the distance. It might just be big enough, but she didn't know which direction the wind was. Fortuitously she saw a train coming along the railway line and with a bit of quick thinking she checked the wind direction from the way the puffs from its chimney were blowing. She made the landing and the journey back was problem-free. When she got out of the aircraft, Margaret's face was unreadable.

'I'll take you into Miss Gower's office now,' she said. They walked back to the hut in silence. Pauline was charming and kind in the interview, but she told Veronica that although she had done well in her test there wasn't yet space for someone with so few hours. She felt deflated. After all that excitement, effort and nerves she had to go back to driving ambulances in London.

Hitler had stepped up the pressure on Britain by attempting to create an economic blockade. Luftwaffe dive-bombers started to attack merchant ships in the English Channel and air attacks were carried out on British ports, food and materials warehouses and aircraft manufacturers. His hope was that that Britain would 'see reason' and agree to a last-minute peace deal. When Churchill refused to co-operate, Hitler decided to implement the suggestion made by Hermann Göring, the Commander-in-Chief of the Luftwaffe, that they should destroy the RAF. This was a prelude to the bigger plan, Operation Sea Lion, aka invasion. The phoney war was over.

There was a panic among Veronica and her ambulance colleagues that the Nazis would descend on Britain at any moment by parachute, or maybe they were already moving about among the population in disguise, dressed as nuns or chambermaids. They hoped that London would be safe under its vast balloon barrage, for the time being.

A young South African pilot called Jackie Sourer was also tested at Hatfield that summer. She was only eighteen. As a child growing up in the military town of Pretoria, Jackie had been so timid she wouldn't even climb a ladder or go in a rowing boat. She, as she put it, dreamt her way into aviation, having told people she would be a pilot as something of a joke after watching the planes landing and taking off from the local airstrip. The first time she went up in the air as a passenger she was sick. When her mother offered to pay for flying lessons she felt unable to say no, having told everyone she was going to be a pilot. On her sixteenth birthday she had her first lesson and was sick again, all over her instructor. 'She'll never make a pilot,' he said wearily to Jackie's mother when they landed. This made Jackie more determined than ever to jolly well show him, even if it killed her.

Officially she was too young to go solo, but her mother told them her daughter was already seventeen and Jackie began to make her jokey dream a reality. After her initial terrifying flight, the once-timid girl developed a remarkable tenacity, a natural instinct for aviation and an extraordinary amount of pluck. While still a schoolgirl she became the first woman in South Africa to perform a parachute jump. On something of a whim, and with no instruction, she decided to jump from a plane but, being too light for the parachute, she plummeted to the ground and broke her ankle badly. Jackie landed in a field of polo players, who watched on bewildered as she was carried off to hospital.

This didn't stop her flying, and in 1938 her mother allowed her to travel to the UK to train for her flying licence at Witney Aeronautical College.

In the early days of the war, Jackie joined the WAAF and they put her on domestic duties for the officers. Not used to the military etiquette, on one occasion when a warrant officer saluted at her commanding officer as they passed by, *she* saluted back. She was very embarrassed when she realised the faux pas. Her job with the WAAF consisted mainly of cooking. Jackie was not a cook. In fact she had never cooked in her life. In the end she was sent to a radar station and trained as a radar operator. The secrecy around the job was such that she still had to tell people she was a cook.

The radar operators were based on an out-of-the way

island. They sat in cubicles where they had to monitor a radar screen, a bit like a television screen. Jackie watched wiggly lines across the middle and her job was to wait for an 'echo' or V shape on the screen. Then she had to 'DF', or Direction Find, and note down the direction and height of the object and whether it was approaching. If there was a long line, it was one of ours. If not, she had to call up on headphones and say, 'We've got an echo.' It was all so top secret that at first the operators didn't know what they were actually looking for. Eventually they found out it was enemy aircraft. As Jackie became more highly trained she became more useful, and less dispensable.

When she got a letter from the ATA, Jackie jumped at the chance to try out for a job, but on the day of her test, her nerves were high. She had not been in a plane for several months. She pressed her WAAF uniform, polished her buttons and strode through the RAF security gates at Hatfield. She was a bit surprised at how unassuming the ATA offices were, tucked right behind the de Havilland factory. But the energy of the place brought back all the excitement and anticipation she remembered about flying. The rumble of aircraft landing and taking off, the smell of engine oil, the buzz and business of ground staff and engineers. Seeing it all again made her even more anxious to join the ATA as soon as possible.

When she got into the Tiger Moth Jackie felt all of a sudden clumsy and awkward. Would she remember everything? She listened intently to the voice of the pilot through the speaking tube. 'Three circuits and landing,' said the voice in a kind of high-pitched squeak which seemed to her in that moment vaguely absurd. She pulled herself together and did what she was told. The first time she went around she really thought she had messed it up. Everything seemed to go wrong, swinging about all over the place. The second time she managed to pull off something half reasonable. She hoped the third would be enough to salvage her chances. The plane climbed to 1,000 feet, then at 60 mph she closed the throttle and trimmed for a glide. She gently pulled back on the control column and prayed this final landing would be a success.

Jackie went home that day buoyed up with triumph and relief. She had passed. She was in for a horrible shock, however. It transpired that senior figures at the WAAF were not inclined to lose their radar staff. She had told her immediate boss that she was leaving, but during inspection on the parade ground when her officer told an inspecting Commanding Officer that Jackie was about to join the ATA, the CO informed her: 'Your work here is of the utmost importance. We need all the operators we can get.' Jackie felt as though she had been punched in the stomach. There was a military-style discipline in the WAAF, and absolutely no answering back. She had to keep her mouth shut and left the parade ground fighting back tears. There must be a way to get out. But they were short of operators and it wasn't easy to train them. Someone was fighting her corner, though. Pauline Gower was adamant that flying had priority. Behind the scenes, unbeknownst to Jackie, there was a battle being waged on her behalf.

Several other pilots did manage to join that summer. They included Philippa Bennett, a fun-loving and boisterous pilot. Philippa had been flying since she was seventeen and had gained a great deal of experience at Heston, and she was very popular because she had an open-top MG car. There was also Lettice Curtis, a bright, athletic Oxford graduate with a first-class degree in maths who had been in the tennis, fencing and lacrosse teams. Then there were Audrey Macmillan and Audrey Sale-Barker, who became known as 'the two Audreys'. Sale-Barker, nicknamed Wendy, was a tall, slim and graceful skiing champion who mingled in high society. She had made a daring journey to Cape Town in 1933 with another female pilot and they had crash-landed in the jungle near Nairobi. According to one account, they were saved by a Maasai tribesman who took a note to the nearest available help. It was scribbled by Audrey in lipstick and read: 'Please come and fetch us. We've had an air crash AND ARE HURT.'

Margot Gore also received a telegram for a flight test. She had 280 hours and with the requirement now reduced to around 300 she was just about in the running. Margot was softly spoken and quietly assured. She was the type who only says something when there's something really worth saying, which gave people around her a sense she must be wise and capable. Although she had only just enough hours, she did her test and was accepted and swiftly issued with her passes. She was sent off with Philippa Bennett for the routine visit to Austin Reed, the BOAC tailor, to be fitted for their regulation navy blue skirts, slacks and tunic.

When they arrived to be measured up, they discovered to their great amusement that the male tailor in charge was not at all used to dealing with the female of the species and would have to 'see what could be done' about these two. He reluctantly agreed they could fit them out but sent for two older gentlemen to take over the actual measuring, while he retreated to a back room and occupied himself with some folding, stealing occasional furtive glances at the proceedings. The two older gentlemen did everything humanly and physically possible to avoid any contact with Margot and Philippa as they measured them up. One of them threw the tape measure around Margot's back and caught it before looking away in an attempt to carry out the procedure without actually looking at her or getting too close. He whispered his findings in the other man's ear, who scribbled them down in a notebook as though it was secret information. When they discovered there were trousers as well as a skirt to measure for, they swapped jobs, and the whole procedure was carried out so reluctantly and with such embarrassment that when Margot and Philippa got their suits back they discovered that the seat of the trousers was hanging down 4 inches too low.

Audrey Sale-Barker shunned the usual tailor altogether. She and a few others insisted on getting their uniforms fitted at their own tailors on Savile Row, with the addition of a scarlet or green satin lining sewn into their jackets, a minor rebellion which caused something of a sensation to those who got wind of it, including the press. When Audrey let slip about the scarlet lining to an eager visiting journalist, he pounced on the image with the subsequent headline 'Scarlet and Gold . . . Golden-haired pilot would not fly without her scarlet-lined tunic'. The papers loved to make much out of anything that showcased the glamorous side, or the general female-ness, of the ATA girls. When Pauline objected to this tendency to one journalist, they ran the headline 'Woman CO Says Please Don't Glamorise Us'. But they loved to latch on to any mention of lipstick or tea or flowing locks, or knitting or grandmothers – anything which reminded the public they were not just pilots, they were *women* pilots.

Joy Davison, who had flown with Rosemary Rees and Amy Johnson for Army Co-operation in Portsmouth, had turned down the chance to join the ATA when she found out what the salary would be. She also wasn't overly keen on being stuck with a whole lot of Tiger Moths. As the ATA expanded, however, Joy thought it might be more exciting than what she was currently doing with National Air Communications in Cardiff. By June she was ready to join and wrote to Pauline:

Dear Pauline,

Herewith the dope about me. Since chatting on the phone, I've managed to get some extra petrol to cover the trip to Hatfield by car, so think maybe it would save time if I were to come through while the contract's going through official channels – what do you think? If you agree send me a wire, and I'll pack up and come pronto. Point is, the posts here are awful and I didn't get your letter till this morning so a whole day was wasted which in these times is the devil!!

What sort of digs accommodation is there around Hatfield? Pretty crowded I reckon.

Am looking forward to coming a lot and so glad I can be of assistance. I'll tell you more about what's kept me out of it since N.A.C. cracked up, when I see you!

She subsequently wrote enthusiastically to her cousin about her new job, but added a hint that her work was about to get a lot more dangerous.

At the end of June Hermann Göring gave an order to draw the RAF into battle. 'The British Air Force must be eliminated,' he railed, 'to such an extent that it will be incapable of putting up any sustained opposition to the invading troops.' On 16 July Hitler called for preparations to be made for a British invasion.

Joy Davison was experienced enough to be sent on the conversion course to learn how to fly fighters almost as soon as she joined the ATA. She went to Central Flying

School, at Upavon, to learn on a Miles Master with an experienced instructor called Sergeant L'Estrange. The lesson got underway and they were flying over Wiltshire. As they neared the aerodrome things started to go wrong. The aircraft made a 'spiral dive' at about 600–700 feet. It continued nose down in a fast and terrifying spiral. Those watching from the ground, some of whom were experienced Upavon pilots, said they had no reason to believe the plane was out of control as it fell. But for some unknown reason the aircraft remained in the dive until it hit the ground.

There was horror and confusion. Ambulances were sent to the scene of the mangled aircraft. Sergeant L'Estrange was exceptionally experienced and was well acquainted with the Miles Masters. Joy was also very experienced on many different types of aircraft. There didn't appear to be any explanation. It was too late to save them and both Joy and Sergeant L'Estrange lost their lives. Joy's sister, Hope, and all the women at the ATA were deeply saddened by the loss. Joy's friend Jennie Broad, who had also applied to join the ATA, wrote to Pauline the next day:

Dear Miss Gower,

I would appreciate any information you are able to give me of Mrs Davison's accident. We were old friends and if there is anything I can do please do not hesitate to let me know at once.

I have written to Mrs Davison's mother, but as she will probably be in Hatfield before she receives my letter, will you be so kind as to give her, or anyone else representing her, my address and ask them to get in touch with me?

Pauline wrote straight away to Joy's mother:

I should like you to know how we shall miss your daughter. She was a most kind and cheerful member of this Section, and a first-class pilot. May I offer you our most sincere sympathy in your bereavement.

The theory soon got around that carbon monoxide had leaked into the enclosed cockpit. It was thought this had left the two of them unconscious and the plane had simply spiralled out of control. Despite the rumours, the cause of the crash was never confirmed.

Joy was the first woman to lose her life in the ATA. A dark cloud hung above the Hatfield airfield that week. But life for the other ATA pilots had to go on.

1. Pauline Gower (*far left*) and the first eight women ATA pilots at Hatfield: Winifred Crossley, Margaret Cunnison, Margaret Fairweather, Mona Friedlander, Joan Hughes, Gabrielle Patterson, Rosemary Rees and Marion Wilberforce.

2. Pauline Gower and Dorothy Spicer with a de Havilland Gipsy Moth. They were the first to run an all-female joy-riding business, Air Tours Ltd.

3. Dorothy Spicer and Pauline Gower working on their plane.

4. Mona Friedlander during her time at Brooklands Flying Club.

5. Pioneering aviator Amelia Earhart, the first woman to fly solo across the Atlantic. She disappeared in mysterious circumstances in 1937.

6. De Havilland Cirrus II Moth.

7. De Havilland Gipsy Moth.

8. Amy Johnson at Stag Lane before she became the first woman to fly solo from England to Australia.

9. Amy Johnson and Jim Mollison in their de Havilland biplane just before their transatlantic trip.

10. Amy Johnson before her great solo flight to Cape Town, South Africa.

11. Pauline Gower, Winifred Crossley and Margaret Cunnison.

12. Margaret Fairweather, Mona Friedlander and Joan Hughes.

13. Gabrielle Patterson, Rosemary Rees and Marion Wilberforce.

14. De Havilland Tiger Moth – which the pilots flew in all weathers.

15. Mona Friedlander and Joan Hughes in their 'Sidcot' suits with parachutes.

16. ATA pilots at Hatfield with their parachutes and the Tiger Moths they would become very familiar with.

7. Battle of Britain

The women continued to be trained on the Miles Masters and the Airspeed Oxfords. Philippa Bennett, a new recruit, Mabel Glass, and Margot all went to Upavon for their conversion courses. The Oxford was a twin engine, the like of which many of the pilots had never flown before. It was a more difficult aircraft because it had two throttles and more controls, and there were flaps and gills to contend with, resulting in quite a checklist before take-off. These monoplanes were much faster than the Tigers and it was quite a thrill to be in them after the creaky biplanes. After two hours on the Master, and two and a half on the Oxford, they felt a lot more confident.

From that point on more Oxfords started appearing on their chits. These new aircraft were taken mostly to aerodromes in the Midlands or Scotland ready to train the next batch of RAF fighter pilots. They also had another new aircraft called a Dominie, a passenger transport and radio navigation training plane, which was also made by de Havilland. With these new planes on the books, operations were steadily becoming more complicated. But the office at Hatfield was still a fairly ad hoc affair. Often it would be one of the pilots who took the role of organising the chits, acting as an unofficial operations officer, with the help of an adjutant in the small office. It would be their job to collect the information about the weather from the RAF Met Office, get the location of all the balloon barrages and highlight any areas which were prohibited for flying. Pauline Gower took down the details of what was to be delivered where by phone from Central Ferry Control in Andover, which had become the organisational hub of all ATA flying across the country. She often scribbled the orders down on a bit of paper before allocating the pilots to each job. But the system always worked and no planes went astray.

The Tiger Moths built at the de Havilland factory were mostly now all successfully delivered, and there were secretive plans at the factory for building a new, powerful bomber. There were new Tigers being built at a different location, in Cowley, Oxfordshire, so a lot of journeys started from there. They also had access to some taxi planes, including Fox Moths, open-cockpit biplanes, with an enclosed cabin below which could seat four passengers, and an Anson, a large taxi plane which could carry a bigger group of pilots.

The Avro Anson was developed by the RAF as a twin-engine reconnaissance plane and was also used during the war to train bomber pilots, navigators, wireless operators and air gunners. It was affectionately nicknamed 'Faithful Annie', and was a well-loved aircraft which was strong, reliable and handled nicely. There was space for nine pilots to be carried, along with their parachutes and overnight bags. Rosemary Rees loved the Anson and spent many a trip snuggled up in her layers of fur and blankets when she was piloting it. One day when a planeload was coming in to land, she remarked wryly that people on the ground must think it was a load of bomber boys coming back from an operation, when in fact it was 'just a load of women knitting'.

The Anson was a great workhorse and it was also fun for the women who flew it to have control of a larger, enclosed plane. It sometimes took an extra pair of hands to help the pilot with the manual retraction of the undercarriage, which was state-of-the-art but took around 150 turns of a heavy hand crank to bring down the wheels for landing. The crank was awkwardly placed to the right of the pilot's seat and could be very hard work. Winding that thing certainly strengthened the arms of the pilot and her 'stooge', even as they shared the load, each taking twenty or thirty turns a time after take-off, getting the gear legs safely tucked away under the aircraft. They then had to be lowered again for landing.

Coming back by train was increasingly impractical and wasted valuable flying time, so taxis were integrated more and more into the operations. The Fox Moths and the Anson, and an American plane called a Fairchild Argus, took them to their pick-up destinations, and were also used to pick up pilots who found themselves caught out, which meant they could be ready sooner for the next trip. For shorter trips it meant they could drop off a plane and be taxied to another, carrying out several deliveries in one day.

Summer 1940 brought more new recruits, more new planes and more bearable weather. It also meant the days were long and tiring. As long as there was light the girls flew, and they often found themselves working late into the evening.

Amy Johnson lived near the ATA Headquarters at White Waltham, near Maidenhead. She rented a room with some friends called the Hofers, who looked after her pet St Bernard, Christopher, while she was working. She flew a Fox Moth taxi, or took the Anson taxi plane in to Hatfield every day, along with fellow pilot Margie Fairweather, whose husband, Douglas, was in Number 1 Pool at White Waltham and often piloted the Anson. Most of the other pilots lived in digs in and around Hatfield, so they could walk or take a bicycle to aerodrome. Each morning when they arrived there was a rush to see who had got what on their chits. Amy was disappointed if she got a Tiger Moth again now that they had other options and were one step closer to the fighters.

If the weather was bad and they couldn't fly, the pilots played bridge or darts and drank coffee and knitted, or chatted in the mess until it cleared up. One day Rosemary Rees found an article about the ATA girls in the paper and was cutting it out for her scrapbook. 'Do you want one?' she asked Amy, who replied that she didn't really need yet another picture of herself from a newspaper. Amy was well used to press interest and it wasn't always welcome when you just wanted to get on with the job.

Although many of the girls admired her and had even been inspired by her to take up flying, Amy didn't make a big deal of her fame, and gave out autographs and kind words of advice about flying to any inquisitive newbies. She was funny and serene, and the other pilots liked being 'stuck' with her if they had to put down in bad weather as she could be very entertaining. Alison King flew with her one day to help pick up some equipment and she found her to be very kind, not leaving her out when they went to the mess and Amy was crowded with fans. A male ATA pilot they both knew had been killed in bad weather and on the way out of the aerodrome Amy suddenly turned to Alison, and said 'You know, that'll be me one day.'

Pauline had managed to win her battle with the radar operators and South African pilot Jackie Sourer extricated herself from her job with the WAAF. She arrived at Hatfield in July, feeling nervous and quite intimidated to meet this supremely confident collection of characterful women who made up the Hatfield Ferry Pool. Some of them were very well-connected socialites used to mingling in high society. Jackie marvelled at their tapered fingernails and meticulously applied make-up and wondered how they managed to look so glamorous while flying in the open air. By comparison, she felt timid and unremarkable.

The British weather and terrain were very different from what Jackie had experienced in her home country. There it had been possible to fly in open cloudless skies for miles over endless desert roads, without meeting a single obstacle. She was used to being able to navigate by memory, virtually without thinking, and without a map. This was just as well, because one of her first deliveries was to Scotland, and the ATA were so short of maps they only had one between five of them. It wasn't given to Jackie. She was put at the back of the gaggle and could only pray that whoever was in front knew what they were doing. As she watched the other planes take off, she had to try not to get dangerously close, while maintaining visual on it the whole way.

After two hours of flying they landed to refuel and Jackie was relieved to have a break. They took off again, then landed again for another stop-off. There was no accommodation at the aerodrome and it was rather late, so they put up in a local hotel. The following day the weather was bad and they were all a bit frustrated about having to wait as they were losing valuable daylight hours. Eventually they got the all-clear from the Met and eagerly jumped to their planes. Jackie got into her kit, straps and helmet, again with no map. She was at the back of the gaggle again when they stopped at Carlisle. It had taken them eight days just to get there. This was the last stop before their final destination of Prestwick.

It was a misty late afternoon as they approached and Jackie could hardly see the airfield down below. She just made it through but as her plane hit the ground, she saw the other four aeroplanes taxiing out again for take-off. She hurriedly strapped herself back in and took off to follow the fourth plane. She was rather confused because they hadn't arranged to do this. She looked at her gauge anxiously, wondering if she would have enough petrol to get all the way to Prestwick. Then she looked around. She had lost the gaggle. With no map she would have to follow the railway line and river and fly amongst hills to avoid going too high.

When she approached what she thought must be Prestwick she could not see anywhere to land. Her petrol was registering nearly empty. She eventually managed to make out the airfield. Somehow, she had managed to get ahead of the others because they all came in to land just after her. She looked at her gauge again and saw there was about 1.5 gallons left in her tank. This would have lasted a few minutes. When she got out of her plane to meet the others she got the shock of her life. It wasn't Rosemary and the gang she had left with, but four completely different pilots.

'How did you end up with us?' they laughed.

She explained what had happened, and it turned out

that her own gaggle were still stuck at Carlisle in the bad weather. They didn't make it out for another four days.

Operation Sea Lion, the planned invasion of Britain by Hitler, was scheduled for mid-September. The first move that summer was to attack the British Navy in the English Channel, and then gain air superiority by damaging key infrastructure such as radar stations, airfields and fighter planes. Göring was swaggeringly confident the RAF could be defeated within a month. Since the fall of France, and with German squadrons now located at French bases, the Luftwaffe's fighter aircraft were alarmingly close to Britain – just six minutes by air from Dover.

The ensuing air raids over Britain destroyed aircraft and damaged airfields, making it difficult for aircraft to operate, but the RAF fought back and did their best to mitigate the damage being done across the country. On 24 July 1940 Brooklands Airfield was bombed. Mona Friedlander had learnt to fly there, mingling with the glitterati of the flying world, but its carefree peacetime atmosphere had been transformed to one of camouflage and barbed wire.

The RAF did their best to defend the country against the incoming Luftwaffe fighters. The public were presented with hair-raising spectacles of dog fights between Spitfires and Hurricanes and the Nazi planes with swastikas on their wings. The sight may have been exciting for the civilians, who had never witnessed anything like this before, but the reality was that the RAF was outnumbered and the battle, raging in mid-August over the skies of Britain, was diminishing them further. The fighting reached its peak on what became known in Germany as 'Eagle Day', *Adlertag*, when the Luftwaffe launched its main raids on British radar stations and fighter airfields. Delayed at first by bad weather, it eventually opened with a series of attacks on coastal airfields and progressed further inland during the week that followed. Both sides saw their greatest losses of the Battle of Britain in what became known as 'The Hardest Day' towards the end of August when the Luftwaffe tried to destroy RAF fighter command.

Despite the losses, the newsreels continued to try and boost morale. They claimed that the RAF had 'mastery' over the Luftwaffe and congratulated RAF Fighter Command's fresh glory at every alarm, giving confident assurances to the nation that the Hurricanes and Spitfires were shooting down Nazi planes 'by the score' and returning in triumph to their bases.

The images seen by the public on cinema screens were generally triumphant pictures of German bombers hurtling to their doom and mangled Nazi planes in flames having been brought down by the daring and gallant actions of our brave boys. Images of Hurricanes and Spitfires returning from successful hit-and-run raids became a familiar and morale-boosting image for the general public on cinema screens across the country. There was even the odd bit of macabre humour as the fallen Luftwaffe aircraft were shown being collected for scrap, to be turned back into RAF planes, something the Nazis would doubtless not have appreciated.

With their eight machine guns on their wings, the iconic Spitfires fired imaginations across the country. They were almost like something from the realms of science fiction with their ability to 'pierce steel', move at 110 yards a second, and 100 mph faster than a bomber. As they took cover in cloud they could climb above bombers and lay waste to Luftwaffe planes, leaving their hulks strewn about, shattered by the RAF's tactics, courage and machinery.

With all this bombastic propaganda, it's hardly surprising the fighter planes piqued the public imagination. Eventually, the propaganda began to resemble something like reality. The German losses of the Junkers 87, or 'Stuka', the main Luftwaffe precision-bombing weapon, were eventually so bad that the Nazis were forced to stop flying them.

The RAF, when they could not replace the number of British pilots being killed, were bolstered by several Polish fighter squadrons which had evacuated from France and became operational in August 1940. Anna Leska watched the battles overhead as her compatriots fought it out in the skies and wished she could be flying herself. The ATA's women pilots could only look on too as the

Battle of Britain raged above them. They watched the sky trails blazing and occasionally saw the mangled wreckage of Nazi planes. They weren't allowed to fly the fighters or bombers, but they had the odd close encounter with one from the other side.

Oxford graduate Lettice Curtis was delivering some Tiger Moths to Kemble one morning that summer. She stood on the airfield with fellow pilot Ruth Lambton and watched the outline of a plane making its way across the blue sky.

'Is it one of ours?' Lettice asked. Just then a man came running over, waving his arms.

'There's something dropping from it! Get to the shelter!'

'Do you know, I think they're bombs,' said Lettice. But they just stood there watching. It seemed too absurd that they could be at risk from bombardment in that field in the middle of nowhere. They *were* bombs but they landed in a field nearby and thankfully not on the airfield itself. Lettice and Ruth were in any case hustled away into a nearby ditch to shelter in case there was another attack.

'I'd rather go and have some lunch instead of scrabbling about here in this ditch,' said Ruth.

But they had to play it safe.

The Luftwaffe continued to bomb towns, cities and airfields across the South Coast of England, the Midlands and the North-East. On 20 August Winston Churchill acknowledged his enormous gratitude to British and

Allied aircrew in a rousing speech. 'Never in the field of human conflict was so much owed by so many to so few,' he said, immortalising 'the few'.

London remained largely unaffected for a while, apart from sporadic air-raid warnings and the usual strict blackout controls. Residents of London suburbs did hear the roar of engines and watch as the vapour trails of the fighter planes in the skies criss-crossed above them, the planes like silver fish darting between one another as the two forces vied for air supremacy.

Attacks on RAF airfields began in earnest in late August, and bombs began to be dropped over residential areas of London. In early September the Luftwaffe targeted the London docklands. The wharves and warehouses were set ablaze with incendiary and bomb attacks and nearly 500 civilians were killed.

Daylight raids on London shook the population. Amy Johnson got a taste of the Blitz when she took her ATA uniform to be altered by a Savile Row tailor. The shop took a direct hit and was badly damaged. Fortunately, her trousers survived. On the train back from a delivery with Rosemary Rees one day, Amy talked with her about life and the war. Rosemary, who was a cheerful, jolly type, listened patiently as Amy told her about her worries, concerns which to Rosemary seemed quite trivial. But Amy took it all in and felt things deeply. She wrote to her father that the only way to survive the war was to be 'fatalistic'.

Mona Friedlander had been returning home to London once a fortnight that summer. By this time she was utterly worn out from flying and really just wanted to sleep. With London now being bombed, there was too much noise and tension and confusion, so she decided to stay at Hatfield instead.

In retaliation for the attacks on London, the RAF launched a bombing raid on Berlin. The Luftwaffe in turn attacked British cities and ports, aiming to knock out major trade and economic centres, and batter the morale of the population. Hitler was still hoping that Churchill might go for a peace deal, and that this would persuade him. A massive attack on London on 15 September saw a major fightback by the RAF, and the Germans suffered huge losses. The tide was beginning to turn in the Battle of Britain. But the war was far from over. The Blitz was about to begin in earnest and mass bombing raids were launched against London and other major British cities.

In late September the Luftwaffe succeeded in hitting and destroying the main Supermarine Spitfire factory near Southampton. The factory sirens began just after 4 p.m., which gave the workers enough time to evacuate. About two hundred bombs were dropped but only seven actually hit the Woolston factory and another hit the works at Itchen. Unfortunately, a large number of bombs did hit the residential areas and shelters around the factory and several people were killed and wounded in the attack.

The destruction of the Spitfire factory led to the establishment of various secret 'shadow factories'; parts were built all over and assembled by a secret workforce of men, women and children at requisitioned premises in the surrounding counties. One was situated in a bus depot in Salisbury, and others were at unassuming places like garages and small furniture workshops.

Airfields were also targeted. One of the male ATA pilots landed a fully armed Hurricane at North Weald in Essex just ten minutes after a 500-pound bomb had been dropped there. An airman waved him in wearing a tin hat, pyjamas and sea boots.

'This war's getting brisk, isn't it?' he said. He had got a bullet through the front of his tin hat and the explosion had torn the seat of his trousers.

The aircraft hangars were burning, and all the buildings had been partially demolished. There were bomb splinters all over the aerodrome, although remarkably few aeroplanes had been damaged. One Hurricane did catch fire in the air and landed with its wheels up, in flames. Neither ambulance nor fire tender could get out to it. In the end the ambulance was on its side and the tender's tyres all burst. The pilot of the Hurricane managed to escape and there were fortunately few casualties. Thousands of machine-gun bullets went off for hours afterwards and a few delayed action bombs blew up at intervals, so the taxi could not come and collect the pilot. The operations room arranged a lift to Hatfield in a Blenheim. Amy Johnson, who gave the pilot a lift home from Hatfield in her Anson, heard the story at first hand.

It wasn't long before Hatfield itself became a target. In late August a bomb was dropped at a nearby village, with no recorded fatalities. In September three bombs came down at a house just south of the town. The de Havilland factory where the ATA girls were located was developing the prototype for a fast new bomber called a Mosquito. With this top-secret work going on behind the closed doors of its hangars and workshops it was a prime target. The threat felt closer than ever to the site of Ferry Pool Number 5. Air raids were familiar routines by then. During the Battle of Britain many an hour was lost traipsing to the shelter at the de Havilland factory. On the morning of 3 October 1940 an unexpectedly low-flying plane was heard from within the factory.

'Sounds like Jerry,' said one of the fitters. But the siren didn't sound, so he and his friends thought nothing of it and carried on working. The plane was so low in fact that spotters who were on the look-out for enemy aircraft thought it was one of Hatfield's own. The anti-aircraft gunners stationed to protect the important factory didn't open fire.

To their alarm, they soon spotted the swastikas on the tail and realised the aircraft was in fact a Junkers Ju 88, a fast and deadly German bomber. As it flew over, several explosives were dropped from the undercarriage on to the factory. The air-raid warning finally started up, and Pauline Gower and the other ATA pilots began heading briskly towards the shelter. The plane was only about 100 feet above them, and as they ran a bomb dropped right next to them. Fortunately, it failed to explode on impact and the ATA women were able to make it to the shelter.

Four more bombs landed directly on the metal workshop of the de Havilland factory and the building caught fire. The gunner from the plane machine-gunned people running towards the shelter. An anti-aircraft gun on the administration building roof managed to hit the Junkers, and it flew away, tail blazing in flames, before crash-landing a few miles away in a field.

The crew of four airmen managed to get out of the plane and they ran off. A horse guard was put on the aircraft and the Luftwaffe pilots were picked up a few miles away and taken to Hatfield police station. After the devastating bombing, a decoy factory and airfield were built a few miles away, complete with decoy aircraft, in an attempt to lure bombers away from the real thing.

Twenty-one people were killed and seventy injured in the Hatfield bombing. Eighty per cent of the work in progress on the new Mosquito plane was also destroyed. The 'wooden wonder' as it became known, because it was built entirely from plywood, was delayed for several months. It was eventually rolled out the following year as one of the most celebrated British bombers, and the women of the ATA would become very familiar with it.

They weren't quite flying two-engine bombers yet, but since converting at Upavon the pilots were now seeing some light bomber training planes on their chits. One of these was the Hawker Hart, a two-seater biplane. Lettice Curtis picked one up on her morning delivery chit.

'Hart from Silloth to Sealand,' she said with a smile. It was still nice to get something which wasn't a Tiger Moth.

'You can cadge a lift to Silloth with me in the Master,' said Amy Johnson, who was also flying something more powerful, the Miles Master. This was already familiar from the conversion training at Upavon and was one of the fastest trainers of its day. A two-seater monoplane, it was largely used as a target tug trainer, pulling drogues for gunnery target practice, but it had been modified for use as a fighter during the Battle of Britain.

Lettice thanked Amy and they jumped in, but although this plane was fast and convenient, she soon began to regret it. She noticed that the petrol gauge seemed to be dropping dangerously low. Amy didn't look worried at all, but Lettice couldn't take her eyes off it from the back seat. It made the whole journey quite stressful, and by the time they arrived at Silloth she was in quite a state of nerves.

When she went to show her chit, she was even more shocked to discover that it wasn't a Hart she was picking up, but a 'boosted' Hawker Hind, another kind of bomber being used as a training aircraft. She had never flown a plane with a 'boost gauge' before. It was faster and more powerful than the Hart and she had no idea how to handle it.

'Would you mind going over the cockpit for me?' she asked one of the ground staff, who was inspecting the chit. He said nothing of any use, before sending her off to the aircraft. She tried to work out whether there was a way she could get out of flying the thing but nothing came to mind. The weather was fine, if a little overcast, and there were two hours of daylight left, just enough to make the delivery. There were no excuses. Although she had been very excited about flying all kinds of new planes, the Hind seemed alarmingly enormous compared to the Tiger Moths she had flown so often. They now seemed rather cosy and familiar compared to this vast beast. As she climbed into the large open cockpit she asked the fitter a few things and he offered some advice about how to use the mixture lever for the boost gauge. Then she was left alone to settle into the roomy cockpit, hoping she could handle it.

The first thing she noticed was that it felt much higher off the ground than the Tiger. She carried out all her cockpit checks, then one of the ground crew cranked the engine and she taxied to the take-off point. She felt a huge kick from the engine as it started and she somehow managed to get it up to speed and make it into the air. She had a shock when she looked down at her instrument panel and it was already at 150 mph. The Tigers only managed about 80 mph at best. Uncertain what to do to enable the boost gauge, Lettice pointed the nose towards the sea. As advised by the fitter, she inched open the mixture lever. The engine began to splutter and shake. She pulled the lever back and tried it again. It spluttered again. She looked down and saw the forbidding rocks of the Cumberland coastline and the swirling, white-tipped breakers around them.

This is no place to put down, she thought. *But I might not have any choice if I can't get this lever to work.*

The weather was worsening. Maybe she would have no choice but to land wherever she could and take the consequences. Flying much faster than in a Tiger, she soon found herself crossing the Wirral and closing in on her destination. There was a steady drizzle and she saw that the airfield was not yet complete. High up in the cockpit, she was amazed when she managed to make it on to the ragged airstrip with only a bit of a bump, into the wind. She breathed a sigh of relief as she taxied to a stop and clambered out of the aircraft. She was greeted by one of the ground crew.

'Hello! This one's not for us, it's for the Maintenance

Unit at Little Sealand. Do you mind awfully taking it over?'

Lettice's heart sank. Nothing would have persuaded her to get back into the Hind that drizzly evening as darkness approached. She was relieved when a test pilot agreed to do the delivery instead.

With all the bombing and chaos of the Blitz, rumour and speculation were rife. Word went around that the Germans had landed on the east coast, and that others had parachuted in. Mona was on her way to an airfield in the east, and as she approached it she looked around for any signs of invasion. *Well, they haven't arrived yet*, she thought. She could hear German planes bombing airfields some way off, but she kept her distance.

Most of the time they didn't worry much about encountering enemy aircraft, or it wouldn't have been possible to carry on. They had to take each day as it came and not get panicked or imagine things which hadn't happened yet. Mona was very strict about not going above cloud, though not everyone was if they wanted to get somewhere quickly and didn't want to land.

'I'd rather hop across telegraph lines than go above cloud,' she said to Rosemary in the mess one afternoon. 'At least you know where you are.'

From her home in London, Veronica Innes could see that the city was protected by a huge balloon barrage during the

Battle of Britain. She had caught a glimpse of an air battle on the South Coast and made out the comforting shape of a Spitfire projected against the blue sky. She craned her neck to get a good look, but in a few seconds it was gone again. That same day a German plane was nearly brought down on top of Victoria Station.

Throughout October and November London was bombed without let-up. In the Blitz's first month several thousand Londoners were killed and nearly ten thousand seriously injured. The sounds, sights and smells of air raids became very familiar. The stomach-tightening buzz of an enemy aircraft approaching would soon be followed by the all too familiar whistling of high explosive bombs dropping. The whistle meant they were close and would inevitably be followed by a deafening explosion. If incendiaries were dropped, they gave off a flash of light in the night followed by the creep of flames if they set fire to whatever they had hit. There was the relentless crack and boom of anti-aircraft guns. Although they were supposed to boost morale, they actually added to stress levels for some people, and along with the constantly ringing bells of auxiliary firefighters it all made for a cacophonous experience.

The aftermath the next day would bring more piles of rubble and brick, glass and dust. Whole streets were suddenly gone, or the odd single collapsed house would be surrounded by its still-standing neighbours. Half-rooms were exposed to the open air, revealing shattered bathroom fittings and flapping wallpaper. But people also continued with their lives as best they could and tried not to let it damage morale. After all, many had jobs to do and were keen as ever to get on with them.

Veronica had found it quite exciting at first. The usual parties went on and there was every effort to maintain morale and keep going. There was a stoicism among Londoners, who refused to let anything dampen their mood. Veronica found that the nonchalance of Londoners alarmed anyone who came in from outside the city. She and her friends continued going to parties in ballrooms and dance halls, or in the cellars of hotels, while Bofors guns and exploding bombs could be heard above. The whistling and tearing sounds cut through the sound of the band as a bomb fell not far away from where there was laughter and dancing. But it didn't seem to stop the fun. One evening, after a dance, Veronica was walking through the streets with a male friend from outside London. As soon as the air raid started up he fell down head first to the pavement and clasped his hands behind his neck.

'What on earth are you doing?' she asked. She had grown so used to it that she had barely flinched.

'That was what we were taught to do,' he said, gathering himself together and looking rather embarrassed. It turned out that this was his first raid.

'Of all the people in London, it would be supremely arrogant of us to think the bombs should choose to drop on us, don't you think?' said Veronica. Her friend did not seem so convinced.

That night Veronica slept in her bed while the bombing continued nearby. She was reluctant to sleep in an air-raid shelter and felt quite cosy and invincible within the strong walls of her flat near Park Lane. But a bomb did drop, right beneath her window. The force of it shattered the window and her bedroom mirror, and the lights went out. She jumped up and immediately cut her feet on the broken glass on the floor. She grabbed her dressing gown and a flashlight and made her way outside.

'Bomb on Edgware Road,' said a passer-by. There had been another explosion nearby which had caused a gas main to catch fire. Veronica walked down the road and looked at the fire as it raged a bright orange against the dark shapes of the buildings. People were rallying around to help, and she was asked by one of the firefighters to gather water in leather buckets. She got stuck in, hoping that nobody had been badly hurt. The bomb outside her own building had damaged the water supply and, with the windows shattered in her bedroom, she had to sleep on a mattress in the hall. In her youthful naivety and craving for excitement, she had wished for something to happen. Now that it had, it had all begun to feel rather too real for comfort.

8. Above the Clouds

As the dramatic events of the summer unfolded in the air, the ATA had grown into an efficient machine, led by Central Ferry Control, where a team of men and women manned telephones and relayed the complex web of deliveries to the various pools.

'Turning them out like sausages,' said the CO responsible as he surveyed the blackboard with its list of pilots and aircraft, their names and numbers, all to be allocated into the busy schedule. The RAF were taking on more and more planes as each day went on, from factories and maintenance units around the country, and they all needed to be ferried.

A small training school was set up at Hatfield which consisted of circuits and bumps, take-offs and landings. An increasing number of women were also being converted at RAF Upavon to the Miles Master and Airspeed Oxford, the trainers for the Spitfire and Hurricane fighter planes. It was an exciting time and they felt as though they were really making progress.

Lettice Curtis stayed with fellow pilots Connie Leathart and Audrey Sale-Barker when she converted. They had a house on the River Avon, and they walked together each morning up the hill to the aerodrome and exchanged chat about their lessons on the new planes.

'It's the take-off I find most dastardly,' said Audrey. She was wearing her flashy jacket with the red silk lining. 'When you get caught by the wind.'

'For me it's landings. Every time,' said Lettice. 'My stomach still heaves up like it doesn't know what's going on.'

They had a lot of new information to take in on the course – all the different instruments, new retractable undercarriages, constant speed propellers. Words and phrases whizzed around in their heads, and they had to remember it all when it came to flying, without any written notes.

Lettice was a bit shaken when she was asked to do some aerobatic turns on her first flight in a Miles Master. It was a terrifying prospect, but she got through it, and after a few hours and some solo flights on the Master it was on to the single-engine Oxfords. It was a little taste of what was to come.

The joy of flying, especially as the planes got faster and sleeker, never diminished. If the pilots had no problems on their flights, they could relax into the journey and take in the ever-changing light and colour of the sky, and the shapes of the constantly shifting clouds could be quite breath-taking. Some formations looked like fantastical lands rising up out of the cloud base. Some were dense, some light and airy. When the sunlight came streaming through and around the clouds it was as though the heavens had really opened. The sunsets were awe-inspiring from this high-up perspective, and even the rain clouds were always different and mysterious, like great creatures. They had never seen so many shades of grey.

Although the delivery orders were increasing, the staff numbers at Hatfield were still quite low. There were a couple of drivers for transport, and a typist who helped in the office with Pauline's letters. There was someone to pack the parachutes, an assistant and an adjutant who was a sort of general dogsbody, willing to do just about anything no one else wanted to do when it came to operations.

In October 1940 there was a bit of an emergency because the adjutant was having appendix trouble and there was a lot of work coming in. It was all getting a bit much. Marion Wilberforce, who had been working as deputy CO with Pauline Gower, was currently in charge of the operations side, and she had been forced to stop flying to cope with the increasingly demanding job of working out the programme and dealing swiftly with any hitches and hold-ups. With the departure of the adjutant, Marion's workload increased and she was getting quite desperate. Margot Gore had a suggestion. Her friend Alison King, from the flying club in Romford where they had got cheap lessons before the war, was working for de Havilland. While Margot had paid for extra lessons and gained her licence and a lot of hours, Alison hadn't become a qualified pilot, but she was still very keen to be involved with the ATA and the world of flying in some capacity.

'I'm certain she'll be up for doing anything – typing, making the tea. Whatever we need,' said Margot. The next day Alison King was hired. Her job mainly involved dealing with equipment, petty cash, accounts and anything else the pilots required. She was so efficient right from the start, taking note of how the flying side of things worked and mastering the great Operations Book, which laid out every daily detail about who was to fly what, when and where in the complex schedule. Marion was only too glad to hand over some of this work and get back to a bit of flying. Alison kept a watchful eye on what Marion did, and what it took to keep operations running smoothly.

As the weather got colder in the winter of 1940, the German bombing intensified. It was not uncommon for the ATA pilots to be away for several days as they ferried between different airfields. Among the new planes they flew, alongside the Tiger Moths, were the Airspeed Oxford training planes. When Lettice Curtis took an Oxford she usually worried about landing, which was still a scary moment even for experienced pilots. On a typical day, she might fly an Oxford to somewhere like Prestwick and get another plane back for the return journey, instead of relying on the slow and freezing trains.

One day Lettice and Philippa Bennett tried to get a return journey and were given a pair of rickety old Gipsy Moths, one for Philippa to take to St Athan, and one for Lettice to take to Llandow, both in Wales and about five hours away.

'A bit ropey, aren't they?' said Lettice as they approached their aircraft. But it was still better than the prospect of a freezing train carriage.

They both took off, and stopped to refuel at Blackpool, where they parted on their separate ways. On the next leg of the journey Lettice was beginning to worry about whether she had enough fuel to make it all the way to Llandow when she heard a strange noise above the roar of the engine. She looked up and saw great billows of smoke coming from an unidentifiable source. She had the shock of her life when she heard anti-aircraft fire whizzing past her head.

ATA pilots rarely worried about encountering any Luftwaffe planes, but once in a while they experienced a close shave. Lettice throttled back and landed as quickly as possible, not wanting to hang around for longer than necessary in the line of fire.

'Jerry plane just spotted flying over the airfield,' said one of the crew on the ground when she had come in to land. The German plane must have been flying directly above her.

'What a terrifying prospect,' she said.

Having narrowly avoided being hit, Lettice arrived at

Llandow in one piece and dropped off her aircraft. She and Philippa met up back at St Athan where they hitched a ride home in a taxi plane. Lettice regaled her friend with tales of her close shave with the enemy, before sinking into bed that night exhausted and relieved to be home.

As winter returned, it brought with it bleak and sad memories of the last war. On 11 November there was a sombre mood as people remembered those they had lost and thought of those who were now out there fighting. There was a man selling red poppies on the tarmac at White Waltham HQ.

Three days later, news came over the wireless at the Stone House Hotel that there had been a heavy raid on the city of Coventry.

'The BBC says a thousand casualties,' said Rosemary to Joan Hughes when she arrived back from a delivery.

'It's so awful. The Cathedral's been completely destroyed.'

They spent the evening in quiet contemplation. They didn't have much time to dwell on such things, but their job, and their small part in the grim machinery of war, began to feel ever more urgent. ATA deliveries continued as the RAF was training more and more new pilots. Throughout November there was a lot of rain. By the end of the month, much of the country was flooded and many aerodromes were muddy quagmires, barely serviceable for use. One night, at White Waltham, someone left a light on. Able to see their target more clearly as a result, the Germans dropped a bomb within 100 yards of the aerodrome. It left a 30-foot crater not 20 yards from the main railway line. Events like this were no longer surprising. They all knew that as pilots they, and their airfields, were ready targets.

In December Amy Johnson wrote enthusiastically to her mother about the exhilaration she felt on stepping out of one of the larger planes and catching the look of surprise on people's faces when they saw that it had been flown by a woman pilot. But Amy was also feeling rather angry that winter. Her ex-husband, Jim Mollison, had joined the ATA and, as a male pilot, he was earning more than she was for the same job: £700 a year, compared to her £450 annual salary. The Treasury had deemed women's work to be worth 20 per cent less than men's – something Pauline Gower was eager to set about rectifying.

Marion Wilberforce was keen to get back to more flying. As she took on more short flights, Alison King had a greater workload in the office. 'Do you think you'd be up for taking this over?' she asked Alison one day. 'All the time, I mean?'

Alison didn't hesitate. She would love to take on more responsibility and jumped at the chance. She was delighted to be able to tell Margot Gore that evening that she was now Operations Officer at Hatfield.

The lead-up to Christmas 1940 was not pleasant for many people. There was a big raid in London. Luftwaffe bombers dropped over 380 tons of high explosive and many thousands of incendiary bombs across the city, causing houses and buildings to catch fire. Two hundred and fifty Londoners were killed and six hundred others were seriously injured. In the West End, a parachute mine hit BBC Broadcasting House, taking the attack right to the beating source of British morale.

Unsurprisingly, something of a sombre mood pervaded many houses that festive season. Friends and loved ones had been killed or were missing. The Blitz, although with a temporary let-up on Christmas Day itself, was proving relentless. Houses had been destroyed and people had been displaced. There was a covering of snow across the country, and a bitter easterly wind.

Amy Johnson was stuck in Scotland, away from her family and friends over Christmas. Work as a ferry pilot didn't stop, although the bad weather had grounded many pilots. Amy passed the time knitting for her sister's daughter and feeling rather low thinking about things with Jim. With the weather no better, she was unable to bear it any longer, and ended up taking a dank and crowded night train back south. She arrived back at Hatfield on 29 December, ready for work.

That same night the city of London suffered its worst night of the Blitz to date. St Paul's Cathedral was severely hit by incendiary bombs and, in what became known as the Second Great Fire of London, the city became alight with flames. The Home Secretary admitted the severity of the event over the radio, calling for 'compulsory service for firebomb-fighters and fire-watchers'. The Cathedral was partly destroyed, saved only by the huge efforts of auxiliary firefighters fighting over a thousand blazes across the city. The Guildhall and eight Wren churches were gutted in the flames, and five of the big railway stations were directly hit.

Veronica Innes was out on the town that night. She was off duty from her ambulance duties, at a party at Grosvenor House. At 1 a.m. she saw the sky glowing a blazing red and felt a new kind of unease as the reality of the war crept its way into her consciousness. She could smell acrid smoke, and as the night-time raiders used the fires to guide them, she realised she was witnessing the true horror of the Blitz. A lucky change in the weather, along with the valiant efforts of the firefighters, eventually stopped many of the fires.

In spite of the cold, the ATA women still had to deliver open-cockpit biplanes. These included the Queen Bee, a Tiger Moth which had been converted to be flown remotely as a target aircraft for gunning practice, a sort of early drone. There were more Masters to deliver, and a new lot of Harvard American trainer planes which needed delivering. As the new year broke, the weather worsened, but the flying continued.

Among the worst hazards for ATA pilots were balloon barrages, which were supposedly to protect the main cities from aircraft. The most hazardous of these was the Liverpool barrage, through which they had to fly almost every day in the first year, with so many deliveries to the North and Scotland, where there was another important ATA pool at Prestwick.

Liverpool was submerged in the thick smog of industry and visibility was often bad. They were not supposed to fly above cloud and had a strict visibility limit of 2,000 yards. It wasn't always easy to stick to, and although they rarely saw them, the pilots knew the balloons were there, like giant sea creatures waiting to tangle them up in their tentacles. They had to fly through a pre-arranged corridor, which was supposed to be balloon free, although it was not very wide. The route was marked out to go up to Sealand, then they were supposed to follow the road to the Mersey, then cross Speke, where they should look for the railway line before heading north and hoping for success. If they didn't hit the balloons after that, they usually made it without any problems.

There was also a continuing risk of snow, which was harder to fly in and predict than rain. With rain clouds, it was quite often possible to see them approaching from miles away in great grey clumps. With snow, it seemed to come from nowhere out of the whiteness. In the first few days of January it snowed a lot, making flying particularly hazardous. The weather was so bad one day that Philippa Bennett, who was flying a Tiger Moth bound for Prestwick, was forced to came straight back to Hatfield.

'The weather's just too dicey,' she told Pauline, and she headed for the lounge to play cards and wait it out.

A few days later, things were not much improved, but some people were risking it.

'There's an Airspeed Oxford to Prestwick,' said Pauline Gower. 'And another to take on to Kidlington from there.'

Amy Johnson was relieved to have something to do again after her lonely Christmas so she took up the job with enthusiasm. She stopped off on the way because of the continuing bad weather but she made it the following day to Prestwick. While she was there, she met an old friend and fellow ATA pilot Jennie Broad, who had just delivered a plane herself.

'Could I cadge a lift back down with you?' asked Jennie, who wasn't keen on taking the dreaded train.

'Of course,' Amy said, packing up her parachute. She would enjoy the company. As the pair were about to depart, Jennie got an urgent telephone call from Pauline Gower.

'She wants me to pick up a Priority One,' said Jennie when she came back from the office. A Priority One meant the aircraft needed to be delivered urgently to a squadron that required it straight away. 'She said I should get the train back down now so as not risk the weather up here.'

Amy decided to take the Oxford to Kidlington anyway. It meant she could drop in and see her sister Molly, who lived near Blackpool, on the way. 'Stay safe,' said Jennie, and she got a lift to the railway station, leaving her friend to make the journey by air alone.

South African pilot Jackie Sourer was in South Wales that dismal day. She had also been given a job ferrying an Airspeed Oxford to Kidlington. Her take-off was fine but when she got to cruising altitude she hit a sheet of low drizzle. *I could fly low through the South Wales valleys and cut through that way*, she thought. It was a risk, but it was either that or turn back. She decided to keep going and made her way through the sleet and snow, keeping an eye when she could on the ground below. Eventually she could make out the dark shapes of the hills surrounding the valleys ahead. She could see a gap through the centre large enough to fly through. She banked left and headed into the valley, expecting to find a clear path. Just as she levelled up, she hit an area of low cloud and, all of a sudden, she couldn't see anything around her except a mass of white-grey cloud.

I'll have to go over the top, she thought, starting to panic. This was strictly forbidden by the ATA because the pilots were not in touch with the ground by radio. There was no way of communicating, and she did not have the instruments for navigating blind that the RAF used. Many planes had not been fitted with them yet, and in any case they were not trained to use them, to discourage them from flying too high. On the other hand, if she stayed in this thick cloud, unable to see anything ahead or below, she could hit a hill at any moment. She didn't dare drop below the cloud because she had already taken the aircraft quite low to get through the valley.

Jackie pulled the control column towards her and took the nose of her Oxford up. She increased the throttle and it climbed steeply through the cloud with a roar of the engine. In a few minutes, she burst out of the cloud. A bright stream of sunlight came in through the cockpit window. She squinted, brought the nose level and straightened up the aircraft. The tension lifted from her shoulders when she saw the blue sky stretching out all around. The clouds were spread out below like a land of white mountains. It was a relief to be out of the stifling weather. A few minutes later she felt a churning in her stomach. *I'm completely alone*, she realised. There was nothing familiar. No landmarks to orient herself. She had left everything earthly down there beyond the cloud. It was timeless, liberating and absolutely terrifying.

She breathed in deeply to steady her nerves and gripped the control column tightly, searching for any signs of a gap. As the plane whizzed on she could see nothing but the tiny, vague shape of the aircraft, her own shadow, with a hazy rainbow glow around it reflected on to the cloud below. She began to feel giddy. *I'm circling!* she realised, feeling sick. With nothing to navigate by, it was impossible to keep a straight line. Her fuel gauge was dropping. She would have to drop lower but had no idea whether she would come into hills, or barrage balloons, which would mean a dreadful crash landing. If she was lucky, she would see the wide-open space of the west coast and the sea. To her relief she caught sight of a tiny break in the clouds ahead and through it a glimpse of water.

Must be the Bristol Channel, she thought, and banked towards it, taking the nose down sharply. This was her only option. With twenty minutes of fuel left and the gauge ticking down every minute, she urgently needed to find somewhere to land. Coming down over the Channel would mean she could avoid any low hills and reorient herself. With barely any time left, she made it over the Channel and saw a small aerodrome in the distance. Her landing procedure kicked in, almost as though she was on autopilot, and before she knew it she was coming in gently on to the airfield and slowing to a stop. Her face and hands and whole body were clammy with sweat under her Sidcot suit. She took off her goggles and wiped her eyes, then climbed out of the plane. As soon as her feet were back on hard ground she realised her legs were shaking. As she handed in her delivery chit, she tried not to think about how close she had just come to possible disaster.

Amy Johnson checked the weather at Prestwick. It was foggy. She decided to continue on the journey to Kidlington as planned, found her aircraft and checked the engine. It was running fine. She put on her helmet and goggles and wrapped herself up in her furry leather flying coat. The ground staff waved her off. The weather had lifted a bit here and there and she could navigate her way towards her refuelling stop near Blackpool. She managed to avoid the barrage balloons, and just over an hour later she came in to land at Squire's Gate Aerodrome in Lancashire. She gave her sister a big hug and they exchanged Christmas presents. It had been a while since they had seen one another and they had a lot to catch up on. Though the day was no doubt tinged with sadness at the memory of the other sister they had both lost, it was welcome contact for Amy.

'I thought the compass was out slightly on the way over,' she remarked casually. But she didn't think too much of it. The following day, 5 January, the weather was foggy and freezing. 'Are you sure you should go?' her sister's husband, Trevor, asked. 'Perhaps leave it another day? Or I could phone Squire's Gate and ask them to check the compass at least.'

'Don't worry,' said Amy with a smile. 'I'll be fine. If the weather clamps down, I'll smell my way to Kidlington!'

At Squire's Gate the duty pilot was also concerned about Amy leaving in such bad weather. Visibility was very poor and the whole country was covered by a thick layer of snow.

'Do you want to wait it out?' asked one of the riggers anxiously.

'I'll go over the top if I have to,' she replied with a grin and taxied off down the airstrip.

At Hatfield Aerodrome, Pauline Gower was getting ready for the first anniversary of the women's ferry pool. She had organised a small party to celebrate the success of the year, and all the things they had achieved. There was a festive and excited mood about the place. Amy was looking forward to the party as she headed off in the direction of Oxfordshire. She might just make it back in time. She kept below the cloud and picked out the familiar landmarks. Across the Midlands a layer of snow had formed and covered and blurred all the usual colours of the landscape. It was a magical scene, but rather like trying to navigate with a black and white aerial photograph. The snow made everything a lot harder to pick out.

Exactly what happened next remains something of a mystery. Amy was due to arrive at RAF Kidlington about an hour after take-off. When she had not arrived after two hours people began to wonder what had happened.

Amy was no longer heading towards Oxfordshire. Her plane had drifted off course. Possibly because of the faulty compass, she was several hundred miles away above the Thames Estuary, near Kent. She had most likely gone above the cloud, as Jackie Sourer did, to avoid the fog, and headed towards the coast looking for a break in the cloud in order to reorient herself and find a landing spot. With the Blitz a constant threat, anti-aircraft gunners along the coastline were trigger-happy and ready to fire at any German bombers heading towards London. Either out of fuel, or believing she was above land, Amy attached her parachute and bailed out of the Airspeed Oxford. She had been in the air for just over three and a half hours.

Just off the coast, HMS *Haslemere* was in a convoy sailing from Southampton to the Thames, escorted by barrage balloon vessels. The convoy was flying its balloons at 1,900 feet. Amy may have seen these floating above the low cloud and thought she was flying over land. In any case, a lieutenant on the bridge of the ship saw the small figure bail out of the plane and the parachute drifting down. The ship, along with an escort vessel, altered its course to try and reach the pilot. Before they got there Amy had landed in the freezing water. The captain gave the order to manoeuvre the *Haslemere* closer and away from the fallen wreckage of the plane, but the ship ran aground on a sandbank. The figure in the water had drifted towards the vessel and as Amy came along the stern side of the ship the crew heard a voice calling out.

'It's so cold, so bitterly cold. Please be quick. Hurry, please, hurry.'

'It's a woman's voice,' said one crew member, and he clambered down to throw a line out to the figure struggling to keep afloat in the choppy waves and the driving snow and sleet.

Amy could not grab hold of the rope. Her face and fingers were white with cold. The stern of the ship was rising in the swell and crashed down on top of Amy. Some crew members reported later that the ship, which was still resting on the sandbank, was ordered into reverse to shift it free. The engine fired up and the propeller spun, churning up the water before Amy disappeared from view.

The captain of the ship, Lieutenant Commander Walter Fletcher, ran down from the bridge and threw off his coat and boots. With a rope around his waist he jumped into the freezing water. His search for a survivor was futile and after about twenty minutes in the water he was pulled unconscious on to the deck of another vessel. The Airspeed Oxford sank nose-first into the Thames Estuary. Neither the plane nor Amy was ever found. At 9 p.m. that evening a report came over the wireless.

'Something happened to celebrated pilot Amy Johnson's machine . . .' said the newsreader. 'She was seen to bail out; a launch searched for her for some time without success.'

Later that evening Pauline Gower came into the operations room at Hatfield and reported the worrying news from the Admiralty that they had found a bag in the Thames Estuary marked with the initials AJ and Amy's log book. Alison King feared the worst but went through the procedure of checking if and when Amy had departed from each airfield, just in case she had put down somewhere. She and Pauline sensed the inevitable but, as if led by a natural coping instinct, continued to hold out for any glimmer of hope. They had not yet confirmed the number of the aircraft. The phone rang. A nasal voice asked if he could 'please speak to Miss Johnson'. Alison's hand tightened on the receiver. She felt sick. It was, she sensed, a journalist who had already got wind of Amy's disappearance and was hungry for a story. Alison got rid of the caller and the pilots at Hatfield waited for any news from the Admiralty.

The following day it was revealed to the public that Amy had got lost and run out of petrol. With only low visibility, and icing conditions at all heights, some pilots remarked that they would not have flown in those conditions. Pauline Gower, ever efficient, sent an official, unsentimental telegram to Amy's parents informing them their daughter was 'missing believed killed'.

It now seems most likely that Amy was sucked underwater by the force of the *Haslemere*'s propeller as it reversed. In a horrible twist of irony, she was probably chopped to pieces by the ship which was trying to rescue her. What her flying colleagues did know was that they had lost a brilliant pilot and a true friend. Amy Johnson was the second woman in the ATA to lose her life. She wouldn't be the last.

With the drama of her disappearance came the inevitable rumour and speculation. Some of the crew of HMS

Haslemere thought they had seen another body in the water. It was even officially announced that she had a passenger with her, although that was quickly retracted. A rumour spread that she must have been carrying someone – a mysterious 'Mr X' – who was a German spy, or a secret lover.

'I think she was on a secret mission,' said Alison King. 'I can feel it in my bones,' she added, convinced there had been something fishy about the whole enterprise.

It's more likely that the mystery 'passenger' was either Amy's pigskin bag, which she took with her as she bailed out and, bobbing in the water, could have resembled a second body, or the door of the aircraft which she could have detached on exit. The bright yellow undercarriage of the Oxford, for easy identification from below, made it an unlikely aircraft for a secret mission, and all reports indicate she had left Squire's Gate alone.

Having been pulled from the sea exhausted, freezing and unable to save Amy, the ship's captain, Lieutenant Commander Walter Fletcher, died later in hospital. The press and public mourned the nation's favourite Queen of the Air. The day after she disappeared, a piece of plywood covered in yellow fabric featuring the letters 35 was found in the water by a passing vessel. It was part of the identification number of her aircraft. A week later, Amy's chequebook, secured in a small plastic bag, was washed ashore on the mudflats opposite Shoeburyness.

9. The Blitz Continues

Having made their way from Poland, via Romania and Paris, to London, Anna Leska and Stafania, or Barbara as she was known, Wojtulanis finally joined the ATA in January 1941. After their arrival in Great Britain Anna had initially worked at the HQ of the RAF and after that, at the Air Ministry. Having passed a flying test intended for those with 250 hours of flying, even though she had one tenth of the requirement, she was recruited by the ATA.

Anna was well-loved but a fiery and forceful presence who very quickly established herself as one of the characters at Hatfield. She told the women about how she had evaded the Germans and dodged shots from guards and driven night and day to escape. Since the Polish fighter squadrons had reformed, she looked forward to flying over the east of England because that was where many of them were based. While she was in Paris she had met a flight lieutenant navigator called Mieczysław Daab, who had also come to England. She was hoping to meet him again and found any excuse to drop in at the Polish aerodromes – the weather, for fuel or to have lunch. It was always a pleasure to see her compatriots and reminisce about their time in Poland and all they had been through.

On 1 February 1941 Veronica Innes finally saw the brown envelope on her doorstep she had been waiting for, marked 'Hatfield'. She tore it open and to her joy read that she had finally been accepted into the ATA. She was to report on 1 March. Veronica had been writing begging letters to Pauline Gower for several months, and her persistence had obviously paid off.

Veronica reported at 9 a.m. for the start of a month's trial and refresher course at the new training school at Hatfield. There was a group of other new girls there too, and they were known among the more experienced pilots as 'sprogs'. They were all nervous because they would not be fully accepted until they got through their refresher course. Veronica was pleased to see the girl she had met at her flight test, Mary Hunter. Another new girl that day was Honor Pitman, who was heir to the Pitman family who had invented shorthand. She was a likeable character who got on well with everyone.

Honor originally learnt to fly in 1927, apparently at the age of fourteen, which was even younger than Joan Hughes had been when she started. Honor had become a driver with the ATS in 1939. When she found out about the ATA she wrote:

*I am an 'A' pilot & have only done about 120 hrs flying in
small club planes – Swallows, Cadets and Aroncas, but I am
prepared to take any training in any line if I could help you.*

Eventually she was invited to do a flight test, which
she passed, although the assessment was that she lacked
experience and would need to be carefully supervised
during her development. She found it exhilarating,
though:

*Monday was a wonderful break to this humdrum war life for
me. I thought everyone was so kind.*

She didn't have enough experience and wrote again:

*I am of course very disappointed to hear you now cannot take
me, but I am still buoyed up hoping one day you may call me up.
In the meantime, I have a very interesting job and am trying to
persuade myself that I am lucky.*

She started her probationary month with the ATA in
March 1941, after her brother Peter had died in Libya on
17 July 1940, and she was keen to do everything she
could for the war.

The sprogs were taught by Margaret Cunnison and
Joan Hughes. After their month-long trial, they were
sent for another test at White Waltham. After another
attack of nerves, Veronica, Mary and the others made it

through, and could finally get their longed-for uniforms and, most pleasing of all, to indicate their rank as second officer, a single gold stripe on their lapels.

There were now about twenty-five pilots at Hatfield, and Veronica got the feeling the more established ones weren't altogether in raptures about having a load of less experienced pilots swanning into their domain showing off their new uniforms. But they had no choice. The deliveries were coming thick and fast and they needed to get more pilots ready to take on the workload.

Britain still ostensibly 'stood alone' in early 1941. In February, Churchill pleaded with Roosevelt over the airwaves asking the US for help: 'Give us the tools and we will finish the job.' On the home front, the Luftwaffe did not let up and continued with its attack on key cities and on the nation's morale. Shortly after Churchill's begging broadcast, parts of Swansea, a major port, were almost completely destroyed in three nights of aerial bombardment, and 7,000 people lost their homes. Portsmouth and its docks were badly hit in January and again in March, and Southampton was so badly struck the authorities at one point began leading people out of the city en masse. Glasgow, Belfast, Hull and Plymouth followed, and these few months also saw the worst raids on London to date, including many incendiary bombs causing not only destruction of buildings but also fire. On 8 March a Luftwaffe bomber flew over Buckingham Palace and dropped a single bomb. The Café de Paris nightclub on Coventry Street was hit, killing swing dance band leader Ken 'Snakehips' Johnson and thirty-four others.

During this period Margot Gore was making her way to London by train after a delivery of Tiger Moths, with the gaggle she had flown with. They had to pass through the capital in order to get back to Hatfield, but before they arrived word spread around the train that Paddington Station had taken a direct hit.

'We could be stuck here for hours,' said Margot, resigning herself to an uncomfortable delay sitting on her parachute again. As the train approached Watford someone had a bright idea and shouted, 'Let's jump out!'

Margot and her fellow ATA colleagues scooped up their parachutes and overnight bags, opened the door and flung them from the slow-moving train, before leaping out themselves. Margot was the last one out and only just made it on to the platform as the train passed through Watford station. On days like this it was tough going, and they were very relieved when Pauline sent a car from Hatfield to pick them up.

With compulsory military service in place, friends, husbands and brothers were sent abroad. News began to arrive by telegram that they had been 'killed' or were 'missing in action' or had been taken prisoner in Germany. Death and disaster were now visiting the cities and ports being bombed on a daily basis, and food shortages and the rationing of butter, sugar, meat, eventually tea and jam, and even clothes, were damaging the nation's morale.

RAF pilot Tom Lockyer woke up one wet February morning at his base in Oxfordshire. He looked out of the window and saw the low cloud and felt a horrible dampness in the air. His job was high-altitude photographic reconnaissance. This meant flying in unarmed Spitfires into dangerous enemy territory to photograph key strategic sites. 'We won't be flying in this weather, surely,' he said to a fellow pilot. They needed a clear sky for their work and low cloud meant being grounded. Tom felt a moment of relief. He had a lurking bad feeling about the thought of flying that day.

He had not long been engaged to Irene Arckless. They had been young sweethearts in their home town of Carlisle, where they had both been keen civilian flyers before the war. Tom was looking forward to seeing her again soon to catch up on all the news from home. With no operations on, he made his way to the nearby site where his aircraft was based and gave his Spitfire a good scrub and polish.

'Always good to have the bus clean,' he said to one of the ground staff there, who heartily agreed.

'It would do no good to get caught out with a dirty plane.'

Every second counted when flying at high altitude alone, unarmed, with no radio or armour. It paid to be as shiny as possible if you had to get away quickly from enemy aircraft.

'Weather's on the mend,' said a Met officer back at the base.

'Narks want some pictures of the barges building up in the Low Countries,' said an operations officer. Ops were on and it was his job.

Tom still had that uneasy feeling in his stomach, but it would do no good to call it off for an uneasy feeling. He checked the cameras on his plane then plotted his course and prepared his cameras for use. After take-off the stripped-down aircraft climbed swiftly to 10,000 feet and beyond. Before he could get his cameras going, on the approach to Ostend he could make out a dog fight between some Spitfires and a group of the Luftwaffe's Messerschmitt fighters. Tom turned away from the mob of planes, not wanting to get involved in any brawl. He looked back in the rear-view mirror as he flew away and saw a faint vapour trail. A plane was nearby. He dropped to 1,000 feet and reached an area where he could begin to photograph the canal as instructed. All of a sudden, a Messerschmitt dived past with a horrible roar of its engine. Then a few more appeared. Tom was a sitting duck. With no 'teeth', or weapons, he could be attacked easily. His only chance would be to ram one of them, but then they had their pals to back them up so he thought better of it. He turned and headed back towards England. They weren't going to give up that easily.

The yellow-nosed Messerschmitts pursued him, then attacked from left and right, above and below.

Tom could see the tracer bullets, or 'red fireflies' as they called them, followed by a whoosh and an explosion. His fuel tanks were hit and petrol was pouring into the cockpit. A moment later the whole thing went up in a ball of flames. Tom had no choice but to bail out or be incinerated. Before he could get out of the door, which was jammed stuck, there was a huge explosion from underneath. Seconds later he was free-falling. The bottom of the plane had completely disappeared. Tom's clothes were burning. He didn't pull the parachute cord in the hope the cold air of the fall would put the fire out. After about 20,000 feet he pulled the chute and hoped for the best.

The chute opened with a jolt and he was sucked back up into the sky again. As he drifted back down he was pursued all the way by the Messerschmitts and finally came to land near a canal. He was badly burnt and in shock and was almost immediately apprehended by some local Nazi soldiers. They gave him treatment and, remarkably, seemed quite concerned for his welfare. Tom was eventually taken to a hospital where there was concern about his face and eyes, which had been severely burnt. He was then returned to the local HQ, where he was told that the following day he would be sent to Dulag Luft, the RAF prison camp in Germany.

Irene was shocked by the news of her fiancé's

imprisonment, and she was deeply worried about what might be happening to him. She had heard all kinds of horror stories about POW camps. She stayed tuned at all times to any news of the war in Europe. She was restless and fidgety and desperate to do something useful for the war and for Tom. One day, as she turned the dial and the radio hummed and warmed up, out came a man's voice making an urgent appeal for 'more pilots required to join the Air Transport Auxiliary'.

'Lord Londonderry,' said her father. 'He wants more people to fly those planes for the RAF, I suppose.'

The cogs whirred in Irene's brain. Tom had joined the RAF to continue his flying. Although she couldn't join in any military capacity, Irene had notched up 50 hours solo before the war, which was a remarkable achievement for someone of a fairly humble social background.

'I must write to them right away,' she said, her eyes gleaming. Knowing there was nothing he could do to curb his high-spirited daughter's enthusiasm, her father didn't try to stop her. Irene immediately got down to applying to the ATA in her hasty scrawl. Her pen could barely move fast enough to convey all the thoughts whizzing through her mind.

'I wish to put forward the following for your approval,' she wrote. 'I was studying for my 2nd class navigator's certificate and intending to take a "B" licence but the war stopped all that I'm afraid.' She noted down her particulars: '25 years of age, height about 5 ft 4', and said she would most like to get into the ATA because her fiancé, as a prisoner of war in Germany, was 'no longer able to fly his beloved Spitfires'. She was keen as mustard to carry on his good work.

Irene concluded that she was swotting up all the information she could get hold of 'with regard to v.p. airscrews, superchargers and boost pressure, as we did not have any of those on our poor old gypsy moths, hornet moths etc.! Hoping I can do my bit for our dear old country.'

Every minute of waiting to hear back about her application was agonising for Irene. She had firmly set her heart on this as being the only thing worthwhile doing. Finally, a telegram arrived. Flight test 8 April. She would finally get to fly again.

'But I wonder what the test'll be on,' she said, suddenly pausing and looking worried.

Irene had only flown light aircraft, although quite a few of them, and every plane had its little quirks. It would certainly be useful to know in advance which one she would be tested on. She took pen to paper and wrote again, this time to a Mr Wood.

First of all I better give you an explanation of this letter! What I want to know at the moment, and before I go to Hatfield next Monday – I am travelling down to London on the 7th instant, is – I might as well come straight to the point! – do you know what kind of machines they are using at Hatfield for the flight tests? [. . .]cause I want to be as well prepared as possible. I have handled Gipsy II, Hornet Moths, Fox Moth, and several of the ultra-light types, such as Pragas, Taylor Cubs etc. I am hoping I don't have to do the test on a completely strange machine – if they have Tiger Moths there I shall be quite happy, as they are very similar to Gipsys as you know. If it will be in order for you to inform me what I will be most likely to take the test on, I shall be most grateful to you.

In his telegram, Mr Wood told Irene all she needed to know: 'Tiger Mothers for initial test'.

She laughed at the typo from the telegram as she told her father.

'Tiger Mothers should be no problem. At least it's not on a Hurricane or anything.' She paused. 'Although what fun that would be! But the Tigers are not so different from the old Gipsies we flew at the club.'

The day before her test, Irene wished her father and mother goodbye with a hug and made her way by train towards Hatfield via London. She sat in the packed compartment with a sense of excitement and nervousness. This was her chance to do something really worthwhile for the war and for her beloved Tom. *Maybe I could even go and rescue him*, she thought for one wild moment. The train guard called out her station, and she leapt to her feet and off the train.

When Irene woke up in the morning and made her way to the aerodrome, she was captivated by the row of Tiger Moths all lined up outside the hangars. She smiled to herself. She longed to be in the air and free again. She felt, at that moment, as though anything was possible.

10. Letters from Home

For over a year the women had been permitted only to fly non-operational aircraft. They had carried out the task diligently and without a single accident. But the argument that women were not 'conditioned' to fly larger and faster aircraft was becoming harder for them to stomach. More men were also joining the RAF to fly Spitfires and Hurricanes with fewer hours than the women had. Their Commanding Officer, Pauline Gower, had been busy behind the scenes negotiating with the powers that be for more equality with their male counterparts for months.

She had already convinced the head of the Air Ministry to allow them to fly the fighter trainers. She continued to press the matter with the head of the ATA, Gerard d'Erlanger, and other influential decision makers, including Margaret Fairweather's brother, Leslie Runciman of BOAC, who was also d'Erlanger's boss. Her persistence was beginning to pay off and in April 1941, it was agreed that the women at Hatfield could fly *obsolete* operational craft. These were planes which had been used actively by the RAF but were now being used for other, non-combat roles.

This meant some new and interesting planes appeared on their chits, including the Westland Lysander, or the 'Lizzie' as it was known by the RAF. This high-winged monoplane had been used by Army Co-operation for reconnaissance, message-dropping and artillery spotting, and later as a light bomber and for delivering supplies. By 1941 the planes had been deemed unsuitable for most operational flying and too vulnerable as a bomber. But some UK-based Lysanders stayed in use for air-sea rescue, and even in covert operations, as well as for target towing and training.

Audrey Macmillan, an experienced pilot who had a little white Pekinese puppy named Wun Wing she carried around in her parachute, was given a Lizzie to fly, and amused the other pilots when she described this sinister hulking beast of a plane. 'My dears,' she said to them in her best King's English, 'it makes me feel just too feminine!'

Other planes they added to their list included the notorious Fairey Battle, a light single-engine bomber which had suffered very heavy losses in 1940 during the invasion of France. Although it had the claim to fame of having been the first British aircraft of the war to shoot down a German plane, and the first to have the powerful Rolls-Royce Merlin engine also used in the Spitfire, the Fairey proved too vulnerable as a bomber and, after severe losses, was withdrawn from operations to be used for training.

While the women were getting used to the quirks of these new planes, Hatfield received an important visitor. Lieutenant-Colonel John Moore-Brabazon had been an aviation pioneer and something of a legend in aeronautics as the first resident Englishman to fly a plane in 1909. A lively and likeable character, he once put a pig in a bin attached to one of his aeroplane's wings. The reason, of course, he said, was to prove that pigs *can* fly. The following year Brabazon became the first licensed pilot in the UK.

By 1941 he was an MP, with the much more serious role of Minister of Aircraft Production which made him effectively the political head of the ATA. Brabazon greeted the women at Hatfield like old friends, which indeed many of them were, having known each other through the small world of air races and flying rallies. Pauline Gower, Ruth Butler and Winifred Crossley all took lunch with the minister, and it's likely that high on the agenda was the possibility of her girls flying operational aircraft. After lunch they posed for a photograph. There were smiles all round.

Not long afterwards, Pauline Gower was at a party when she bumped into the head of the ATA, her old friend Gerard 'Pops' d'Erlanger. She mentioned again the small matter of her women pilots and the operational aircraft they were all longing to fly. Perhaps weakened, or simply feeling generous in the convivial atmosphere,

Pops finally relented. Pauline jumped in before he could change his mind. 'Fine,' she said. 'When can we start?'

Irene Arckless could barely contain her nerves and excitement before her flight test. But once in the air in a Tiger Moth, she felt at home again, with the rush of the wind and the sunlight streaming across the fields and tiny houses below. By the time she had finished her test, she felt sure she had passed. 'It all went perfectly,' she said to her father when she got home. 'They were ever so nice. You should have seen my landing. Not a foot, or a wing wrong.'

'We're so pleased,' said her mother, but she looked anxiously at Irene's father. They were bound to be nervous about their daughter's flying, but they knew there was nothing they could do once she had set her heart on something. That night Irene took pen to paper again, writing to the adjutant at Hatfield, Kitty Farrer.

Dear Madam,

First of all I would like to say how pleased I am that I was successful in passing my flight test yesterday, and that I am looking forward very much to coming down to take up duty. I already feel I shall be very happy with you all . . . I do sincerely hope it will not be long before you send for me – you know I am honestly very anxious to get down to what I term 'a real job of work'.

There was one thing I forgot to ask you yesterday, a rather important one as well! The question of salary!!

I know the rates as published in 'Flight' but whether these apply to male and female, or only the former, I do not know, will you be kind enough to tell me exactly what the scale is?

From what you said yesterday, I gather I shall be at Hatfield 'under training' for about a month, & during this time I take it flying pay will not be applicable. I should like to know just how I shall be fixed as regards salary, so that I can make necessary arrangements here before I leave, i.e. (so that if necessary I will have sufficient cash to last me until I draw my first pay).

I am asking you this because I have recently transferred my Bank balance to War Bonds, & naturally do not want to have to 'cash in' on these if not necessary. I think you will quite understand my asking – I hope so anyway. Further, if there are any special subjects I can 'swot' meantime, will you send me a list? I am swotting up Met: Navigation, etc., and also my Morse – I don't know whether the ATA ever have need to use the latter, but it may be useful at some time or other.

Believe me Mrs Farrer, this job of work I am going to do, & I shall do my utmost to do it well, means an awful lot to me, I told you my fiancé F/Lt Lockyer is a prisoner of War, & to me now, every 'plane we can deliver to the Great Lads of the RAF, means one day nearer to the time he will be home, & everyone carefree & happy again. You don't know Tommy, but he is a grand fellow, & a damn good pilot, he has over 3,000 to his credit! My record is a mere detail beside that isn't it?

To me, however, his 3,000 hours means an awful lot, & whenever I fly, I always try my best to do it well, I've his good reputation to uphold you see. You'll probably think that a very sentimental reason, on the other hand, maybe you'll understand what I mean.

By the way, I think I could get off with a fortnight's notice, so if perchance I could start with you in May, will you let me know. Here's hoping I can start then.

Forgive me for taking up so much of your time with this letter please; I started it with the intention of being very business-like! but I'm afraid it's got to be a personal letter in the end — hasn't it?

Hoping to be with you all very soon.

Irene

Irene also wrote back to Mr Wood to thank him and let him know that she had

passed the flight test successfully — in fact, I did very well indeed, so I was told by the Adjutant afterwards — she said 'Your test was excellent'. So you may guess I felt quite proud of myself!

Actually I surprised myself I must admit, because after being 'off' flying since the outbreak of war, I thought maybe I'd have forgotten a few things — however I hadn't, thank goodness! because this job means rather a lot to me as I told you.

Her outpouring of confidence and enthusiasm elicited no response from anyone at ATA, and a resounding silence followed. It was not, it seemed, to be just yet for Irene Arckless.

By April 1941 Pauline Gower had been instructed to bring her numbers up to forty women. Having tested quite a few possible candidates there was now a long waiting list of potential pilots to choose from. One of the new recruits, Betty Sayer, joined with only 37 hours solo on her log book. With the extra demand, the hours required had been substantially reduced from the original 600.

That month the Blitz reached its most destructive phase. Coventry was badly bombed again. Birmingham and Liverpool were hit. The RAF retaliated with heavy bombing raids on several German cities. All this tension and destruction increased Irene's anxiety about Tom. She wondered what he had been doing since his last letter, whether he was getting enough to eat, whether he was being well treated, whether he was just plain bored, and whether he was thinking of her.

Over the wireless came the news of a naval battle between key German and British warships. When British Navy ship HMS *Hood* was sunk, all but three of her crew of around 1,400 were lost. The *Prince of Wales* counter-attacked and hit the pride of the German fleet, the *Bismarck*, which subsequently sank with the loss of over 2,000 lives. The sinking of the *Bismarck* was a potent propaganda victory for the Allies. But with the loss of so many people on both sides, it was also a symbol of the tragic reality of war.

In London May saw the worst bombing of the war so far. Guided by the light of a full moon and with over 500 bombers, the Luftwaffe dropped high explosives and incendiaries. Nearly 1,500 Londoners lost their lives, and 2,000 others were badly injured. The let-up came only when Hitler turned his attentions east and began executing his plans to invade the Soviet Union in Operation Barbarossa. The attack plans drew the German aircraft away from Britain and, for a moment at least, the people let out a tentative sigh of relief.

By the time Irene was trying out for the ATA, her fiancé Tom Lockyer had been taken to a new POW camp in Barth, between Stralsund and Rostock. He was put in a compound where there were four people per room, each room measuring about 14 by 9 feet. They slept packed in together on double-tiered bunks. The window was fitted with a thick wooden shutter and a steel locking bar. There were three huts, each with about thirty-six of these rooms where groups of RAF pilots found themselves crammed in together. About 20 feet away from the hut was a low, single-strand tripwire fence, which was a foretaste of the real fence beyond it, which consisted of double barbed wire about 15 feet high and about 8 feet wide, with a tangle of barbed wire in between it.

Anyone who dared go beyond the first tripwire was shot immediately and without warning.

The days were long and bleak and monotonous. First there was roll call, or *Appell*, and parade, where they were all counted to check for any escapees. Breakfast was black bread with margarine and jam, and tea. Then came cleaning of rooms, then a bit of walking in the limited space, and if they could talk, mostly planning their escape. In the evening was a second roll call, followed by a meal of potatoes, tinned meat or fish and cheese and biscuits with tea or coffee from the Red Cross food parcels, if they had arrived. As the sun set on the camp the bleak wooden shutters came down firmly over the windows and the doors were locked for the night. Inside their sealed, chilly rooms the men passed their time playing cards, reading, writing, mending clothes and plotting possible escapes, until it was time to sleep.

Letters from home took about a month to arrive, and it was a similar story getting correspondence out. This meant there was a horrible delay in contacting Irene, or Renee as he called her. Tom looked forward to any word from her, and he kept nearly all his ration of post for writing her letters. He occasionally wrote to his parents if he had something particularly urgent to ask them. He had for some time known about Irene's plan to try and join the ATA, although she hadn't had enough hours at the beginning. Tom heartily disapproved of the idea. He knew all about the dangers of flying, even over Britain, as he had been a ferry pilot for the RAFA for a time, and had met many ATA pilots. He felt their training wasn't sufficient for the job, and had dissuaded Irene from the idea before their engagement. Or at least, he thought he had, but fearing the worst again, he wrote to his parents and asked them in strong terms to steer her well clear of any notion she had of joining. He was relieved when he got a letter from his parents assuring him they would make sure she didn't. He rested a bit easier that night in the belief that Irene had put all thoughts of joining the ATA firmly out of her mind.

11. The First Hurricanes

There was a buzzing and chattering around Hatfield aerodrome. It was almost a year to the day since the Battle of Britain had begun and it was a clear and sunny day. News had got around that one of the aircraft which had played a key role in the air battle was sitting out on the airstrip.

'Captain Henderson, a test pilot and chief instructor from HQ at White Waltham, has arrived and he's brought a Hawker Hurricane,' announced Pauline, 'which a few of you will try out today.'

There were a few gasps and some excited whisperings.

'This is of course with a view to taking on more operational craft in due course.'

As the news drifted through the factory almost the entire staff of de Havilland's wandered over to the edge of the airfield, abandoning their work to witness this historic moment.

'Good morning, ladies,' said Henderson. 'She's quite something, this one. Be sure to brace yourself for the kickback when you engage that throttle. Who's the first victim then?' They knew he was joking. They were far from being victims, and everyone was desperate to have a go.

Winnie Crossley stepped forward. As one of the most experienced pilots, she had been chosen to fly first, along with four others. She climbed up on to the wing and into the cockpit and was given a quick tour with Captain Henderson. As she started the engine and taxied to the take-off point everyone craned their necks to get a good look. The plane lifted up gently and then soared up into the bright blue sky. Some people were standing on the roofs of transport vans to get a good view as Winnie and her Hurricane whizzed overhead. After a few minutes of turning and circling she banked, then levelled up. It couldn't have been smoother, with barely a bump as she did a perfect 'three-point' landing. When she had taxied to a stop, Winnie climbed down and addressed the waiting crowd.

'It's lovely, darlings!' she said with a debonair smile. 'A beautiful little aeroplane.'

Margaret Fairweather was up next, followed by Joan Hughes, who was the youngest pilot that day, Rosemary Rees, and finally Margot Gore, who had the fewest hours of them all.

Margot was not without a good dose of nerves as she watched the others take off and land perfectly, one by one. *What if I'm the one to mess it up?* she thought as she pulled on her helmet. A lot was riding on these first five flights being flawless.

For Rosemary Rees, who had already done a lot of ferrying on the Master and Harvard training planes, it didn't feel like too much of a jump. Sure enough, she sailed through her flight. As Margot's turn approached she was getting more and more nervous. She hadn't really flown anything with that much power before. Although flying the Miles Master was supposed to prepare them for the Hurricane, for Margot at least it didn't stop it being altogether terrifying and nerve-wracking. She needn't have worried. Margot did her circuit, landing without too much of a bump, and found the whole thing thoroughly exhilarating.

The Hurricane wasn't all plain sailing. Away from the glare of the crowd, they compared notes. Margot said she had found it a bit awkward changing hands on the stick to lift the wheels with the right hand. The Master had everything to hand on the left behind the throttle. These were the little differences that you had to be on top of as a ferry pilot constantly changing planes.

'I wasn't sure whether to approach with a good deal of throttle,' said Joan. 'When the machine is already in landing attitude, do you think it's necessary to stick back before touching down?'

'If you do land tail first or power off at a slightly higher speed, when the nose is well down you have to get the stick back to make a three-pointer,' said Winnie.

But they all agreed, whatever the technical details, it was thoroughly exciting.

'A real fighter,' said Margot. 'I can hardly believe it. We watched them so often, their sky trails, all the dog fights. I never imagined we'd be flying one of those that actually took part.'

'Well, we are now,' said Joan, who also couldn't keep the smile off her face.

'And not a moment too soon,' said Rosemary.

Pauline came in and clapped them on the backs. 'Worth a celebration, I'd say.'

'Why don't we pool our petrol rations and take a motor car to London?' suggested Alison King, who loved organising things. They could all have gladly driven to London right there and then.

'Dinner in St James then,' said Pauline. 'And at least a glass, or two, in honour of our Hurricane girls.'

They were finally cleared to fly operational craft. From now on Hurricanes would be on the books and they had been given the chance to prove that they could do the same job as the men, and just as well. But with responsibility came immense pressure. Margot was all too aware of it.

'Now we really can't muck it up.'

'Have you got Prestwick too?' Joan Hughes asked Lettice Curtis one morning as they gathered round to collect their chits.

'Yes, Magisters. A pair, I think.'

They thought nothing of flying Magisters, lightweight

elementary trainers, now that they had experienced planes with extra power. Joan and Lettice were taken to Cowley in the Anson, where they were to pick up the aircraft and head on, via two refuelling stops, to Scotland.

After delivering the Magisters with no problems, they spent the night in a nearby town. It felt to them like the middle of nowhere and very far from home.

'I don't much relish the idea of taking the train back, do you?' said Lettice to Joan over dinner.

'Nor I. Shall we try and get a delivery back?'

It wasn't yet that common to take another plane back all that way. But after a year of air raids, the railway system had become increasingly unpredictable and time-consuming. There were numerous lengthy hold-ups, and trains were often packed to the gills with service personnel. There would be no chance of a seat or a sleeper carriage. Remarkably, when they enquired, there was a pair of Hurricanes which needed collecting from an RAF airfield at Silloth in Cumbria.

'We can take a Hudson part of the way,' said Lettice, having made the enquiry. 'Then we'll have to find a lift on from there.'

They were bundled into the Hudson and managed to get a lift in a small passenger biplane, a Dragon Rapide, to the pick-up point at Silloth.

'Where is everyone?' asked Lettice as they climbed down out of the Rapide and looked around what seemed to be a completely empty airfield.

'It's lunchtime. They've probably all gone off to the mess,' said Joan.

'I could do with something to eat myself. I'm half starved.'

Eventually the ground staff returned from lunch and they were shown to their aircraft.

'They're Canadian built,' said the fitter. 'Should be just enough fuel in there for two hours. About enough to get you there.'

Just enough was no joke. They hadn't been flying Hurricanes for long and nerves were still high.

'Should we stop off somewhere, do you think?' suggested Joan. 'The Met said there might be some low cloud and rain. We might not make it all the way on one tank.'

'If we cross the Pennines, we could refuel at Finningley,' said Lettice, pulling out her map and tracing the line, 'via Penrith towards Doncaster.'

'Good idea,' said Joan, feeling relieved. 'Better to be safe than sorry with these Hurricanes. Wouldn't want to prang one already!'

They pulled on their helmets and goggles and bundled their overnight bags in the lockers, before jumping into their respective planes. Joan settled into her seat and ran through the checklist. She tried to remember all the quirks she had been warned about by Captain Henderson. The fitter hadn't mentioned any snags, so once she settled in she wasn't too worried.

'Contact!' she shouted to the fitter once she had checked the engine. He removed the chocks and she was away.

Joan pulled the nose up and the plane lifted. As she got higher she tried to raise the undercarriage, which should have been a simple operation. To her surprise she found the lever was stuck. She tried not to panic and pulled hard on it, all the while keeping an eye on the height and level of the plane. After much heaving, she managed to move the selector lever and the undercarriage and wings folded up under the plane as they were meant to. But when she tried to return the lever to the neutral position, it wouldn't budge. She tried a few more times then had to get on with the business of flying.

I'll have to leave it, she thought. But she was far from happy about it. As she reached cruising height and speed Joan started to enjoy the flight and forgot for a moment about the stuck lever. It was still a novelty to be flying this fast fighter. As she headed over the Pennines the weather held enough for her to stay beneath the cloud, and she enjoyed the view as it whizzed by below, with the shapes and colours of the light cloud around her. As she approached Doncaster and could see the airfield she tried to move the lever again but it simply would not shift.

They'll think it's because I'm just a little girl, she thought. *A useless female. We may never be allowed to fly Hurricanes again if I can't get this blasted thing down.*

She tried to stay calm because it would do no good to lose control of the plane. She saw Lettice fly past and her undercarriage drop easily as she went in to land. A panic started to rise up as Joan circled the airfield once, and then again. She tried to move the lever again, but it was absolutely no use. The flaps were also useless as they worked on the same lever. She circled a couple more times trying to decide what to do. She looked down. The airfield was grass. It would be a risk, but it didn't look like she had any choice.

I can't stay up here forever, she thought and braced herself to bring the nose down for a flapless belly landing. Her whole body tensed as she lowered the throttle. She tried not to imagine the impact, visions of the plane being destroyed, and all the awful things they'd say if women were no longer allowed to fly Hurricanes because of her breaking this one. The ground got closer and closer.

'Too late now,' she said, and the tummy of the plane came down with a heavy bump and proceeded to slide along the grass. Joan gripped the control column and braced herself.

Eventually the Hurricane slid to a halt. She lifted her hands away and they were completely stiff. She managed to climb down out of the plane and Lettice came running over.

'We wondered what you were going to do. What happened up there?'

'Couldn't get the undercarriage down,' said Joan, still

shaking. 'I hope there's not too much damage. Oh God, what if I broke it and they say it's because I'm just a girl?'

'Hello,' said one of the ground staff who was standing by to refuel the aircraft for them. 'Doesn't look too bad,' he said, inspecting the aircraft. 'Quite remarkable really.'

'Thank goodness it was grass!' said Lettice. 'If it had been concrete, it would have been quite a different story.'

'Bent the prop a bit,' said Joan as she inspected the front of the aircraft. 'But yes, not much else. Let's hope they don't take it too badly.'

'We'll take it for you and you can have a lift back in the Hampden if you like,' said the man.

'I'll see you back at Hatfield then,' said Lettice and she went back to her own refuelled aircraft for the final leg of her journey.

Joan was relieved she had landed the Hurricane unscathed, and that she had got a lift back, but the whole journey in the Hampden she was worrying about would happen next, not just to her but all the women who were now cleared to fly Hurricanes. Every accident, no matter how minor, had to go through the Accidents Committee. She had no idea what the outcome of the investigation would be, and this time the stakes were higher than ever.

Fortunately for Joan, after something of an agonising wait, she was exonerated of all blame for the accident and they were allowed to continue flying Hurricanes.

*

While the more experienced pilots were flying the fast fighters, the 'sprogs' were just starting to convert to the lighter trainer aircraft at White Waltham HQ. Veronica Innes was called on to go on a Harvard conversion course, which would mean she could fly Hart Variants and Proctors, in addition to the many Tiger Moths that they had now inherited from the more experienced pilots.

Veronica was on the course with some other relative newcomers, including Margery Spiller and Mary Hunter. Margaret's husband Douglas Fairweather, who was an instructor at White Waltham, took charge of some of the training.

'I'll take you to Newton where you're to pick up some Audaxes,' he said one morning. 'It's a variant of the Hawker Hart. You can take it to Kemble and see how you go solo. That should test your mettle.'

They bundled into the Anson taxi plane and Douglas flew them to the airfield, where there was a row of Audax planes waiting to be collected.

'They look ancient,' said Veronica to Mary, feeling a bit dismayed.

'Ginormous compared to the Tigers, though,' said Mary.

As Veronica climbed in, the cockpit felt much roomier than she was used to, but to her horror, when she sat in the seat she couldn't easily reach everything.

'This is . . . awkward,' she told the fitter. 'But do you by any chance have a cushion I could use? To boost the seat a bit.'

He looked rather confused by her request but was kind enough to go and find an old cushion for her. Veronica settled down into her new seat, now able to reach everything.

As she opened the throttle she was amazed by the surge of power. It was quite a jump from a Tiger Moth to a Hart. Even though it was still a biplane it went almost twice as fast.

'It's like being kicked in the back,' she shouted to the fitter, as she readjusted herself from the impact and the engine roared.

'You'll get used to it,' he shouted back. 'They all do eventually!'

Once she was in the air, she settled in and began to quite enjoy this new, more powerful plane. She noticed how much more quickly she flew over the land below and she made it to Kemble without any problems. But when she went inside the aerodrome she couldn't find Mary anywhere.

'I hope nothing's happened,' she said to Margery, who had also arrived.

Back at White Waltham, Mary appeared, looking a bit distressed.

'Engine cut out. In mid-air!' she said. 'As soon as I took off. Damn scary, too. Had to do a forced landing.'

'Blimey! A good bit of experience, I suppose,' said Veronica. 'If you're being philosophical about it. And so long as you're still intact.'

As their skills and confidence grew they were also asked to ferry Hawker Hinds, light bombers which were even more powerful than the Harts. As the sprogs got the hang of flying more aircraft they longed to get back to Hatfield and begin the real work of ferrying.

When they weren't flying, the students had to do a stint as duty pilot. This involved standing on a roof with a Verey pistol, a kind of flare gun. They were based in what was nicknamed the 'ice cream cart', which was actually a caravan, overlooking the aerodrome. Veronica took her turn watching as all the Harvards, Oxfords, Blenheims and the Anson taxi came in and out of the aerodrome, landing and taking off with the deafening roar of their engines. Some planes had nervous pupils at the helm, led by their instructors. Others were doing their first solos in a new aircraft and there were a few bumpy landings. With all this traffic, if it looked as though any were about to collide it was Veronica's job to fire the Verey pistol's red signal rocket as a warning to the pilots.

They also had technical courses to get through, which filled Veronica with dread. They had to learn about engines, new and complex instruments, the theory of flight – all of which Veronica would have been fine with, if it hadn't been for the fact that the instructor had taken a severe dislike to her.

Nothing seemed good enough for him, and the more pressure he put on her the more she seemed to flounder and dry up in class. He took to employing a nasty kind of sarcasm every time he spoke to her and he seemed to delight in embarrassing her in front of the class, asking bizarre trick questions and putting her on the spot at every opportunity. As she was only a junior second officer, Veronica could never answer back and had to bite her tongue as the humiliation increased. One particularly gruelling day, the instructor had been sniping and barking at her all lesson. She tried not to reveal her disdain for him, but it must have shown on her face because he finished up the class with a vitriolic outburst, aimed directly at her.

'I've got a list of people in the ATA who are going to kill themselves,' he said with a cold sneer. 'And your name, Veronica, is right at the top.'

Veronica's hands began to shake. She clenched her jaw, trying to suppress all the emotions and thoughts she had been bottling up over those two weeks. But she couldn't hold it in any longer. She let out a stream of angry words right back at her instructor, laying out in no uncertain terms exactly what she thought of him. The instructor, who was not used to this kind of insubordination, went bright red, and unsurprisingly she was put to the bottom of the class. It was now all down to her performance in the air as to whether she would pass. She was more determined than ever to prove his ghoulish prediction wrong.

Veronica put all her energy into surmounting the next challenge, flying a new American plane, the Harvard. It was a single-engine trainer, and one of the types which had been dragged by horses over the border into Canada by America, in order not to violate the US Neutrality Act which did not allow the USA to export aircraft to Britain. She wrote everything down on postcards to try and memorise what she needed to know about it. How to do a circuit, climbing approach speeds, boost and rev settings. She could not afford to fail.

Her grafting paid off and she conquered the Harvard. She was on a roll, and it was time for the Fairey Battle – the obsolete light bomber. Finally she got a go on the school's own Hurricane. Having watched in July as the other women had taken the notorious fighter into the air, she was nervous and excited to be following in their trails.

She did the cockpit checks she had learnt in class: HT2MP2FG2: Hydraulics, Trim, Tension, Mixture, Pitch, Petrol, Flaps, Gills, Gauges. Then that kick in the back and, whoosh, up into the air, which nothing could prepare you for. As she rose and fell Veronica enjoyed the new-found freedom of whizzing through the sky at such a speed. For a brief moment, all the problems, even the image of that devil of an instructor, her nemesis, seemed to fade away.

'It's like an Audax with about five hundred times more guts,' she said to Mary later that day, still hyped up by the energy of it. 'I suppose it's a bit like, well, a . . . skittish horse at first. But then it's like a dream. Seems to land itself, really. Perhaps I'll prove that horrible man wrong after all.' They celebrated with a night out on the town in London.

Veronica passed her conversion course. The training was over. It was time to go back to Hatfield for the real business of flying.

When the weather was uncertain, the pilots could decide for themselves whether or not to fly. If it was touch and go, they were advised that they could fly if they wanted, and if they couldn't get through they should come back.

Because the rules were a bit tighter for the RAF, sometimes they would land at Air Force aerodromes where they weren't flying at all, and the ATA pilots would land and take off again. But the RAF couldn't stop them because they had a special pass, so the control tower couldn't tell them not to fly, even if they advised against it. Sometimes the ground staff and maintenance people thought they were mad going up, but often they were quite charming and helpful, giving the pilots tips about new planes, telling them where the throttle and petrol were and so on.

Things didn't always go perfectly, even for the most experienced ATA pilots, particularly when they were asked to fly old and barely airworthy planes.

Mona Friedlander was horrified one day when the engine cut out on an old Hart she was flying in mid-air. It was being taken for scrap and was on its last legs. She had to carry out a forced landing and was relieved to find a suitable field, but was not expecting to come down right on top of a Jersey cow.

'The poor creature didn't make it,' she said to Rosemary in the mess afterwards.

'I'm sure there was nothing you could do, flying that ropey old thing.'

'You're right, I suppose. Only good for scrap. And it went right up on its nose. I was lucky it didn't flip right over.'

After the investigation Mona was exonerated, but the ATA had to pay the farmer £150 for his loss.

As the number of planes the women were able to fly increased, the sense of anticipation grew. Each morning they arrived first thing to collect their chits. The planes were also scrawled on a blackboard with names alongside them. When they had first started they knew pretty much they would be flying Tiger Moths, with the odd ride in the Anson taxi, or a Fairchild. Now the doors had finally opened to a whole new world of aircraft, they didn't always know what they would end up with. Having flown most of the non-operational aircraft, and quite a few Hurricanes, by the summer there was one plane on everyone's wish list.

12. Spitfires

Margaret Fairweather arrived in style on the Anson from her home in White Waltham one clear and balmy July morning. She went to the office to collect her chit as usual with a light heart. There was a buzz of conversation: some were happy with what they'd got, and had a Hurricane or something they liked; others who had an old Proctor or something a bit ropey were grumbling. Margaret greeted the adjutant and took her delivery chit. She had to read it twice to be certain what it said.

Spitfire. Pilot: M. Fairweather.

There was none of the fanfare that had surrounded the first flight in a Hurricane. Margaret simply smiled and told the girls, who were of course all green with envy. She then picked up her bag, goggles and helmet and went to find her aircraft. She climbed up on the wing to get in and settled into what was a very snug cockpit. After all the checks and a few notes from the fitter, she fired up the powerful Merlin engine. The plane was a bit nose-heavy on the runway and she realised it was near impossible to see ahead because of the huge engine blocking the view. The brakes were touchy and to be used sparingly on taxiing. As she pulled the throttle and released the brakes, the plane issued a sharp kick from the engine right into her back and there was a huge roar in her ears. Although she had heard it many times from a distance, it was quite another thing being right next to it.

Almost imperceptibly she left the ground, accelerating into the air much faster than she had experienced before. She shot up into the sky, soon reaching 250 mph, and took note of how sensitive the controls were. It was like no other feeling. Once airborne, the Spitfire was smooth and cosy and natural as it swooped and soared with ease. The central control column, or stick as they called it, moved gently back and forth, allowing her to climb at will with barely a movement of the hand.

Margie's delivery went without a hitch and when she arrived back she was characteristically low-key about having been the first woman to fly a Spitfire. She was of course proud of her place in aviation history and mentioned it in a letter to her father some weeks later.

When they heard more about the pleasure of flying such a well-designed aircraft, the other women couldn't wait for their turn, and that summer more of them did indeed find the Spit on their own chits.

Jackie Sourer, who had added an extra gold stripe to her lapel and been promoted to first officer, made her first delivery of a Spitfire in August. She found the whole thing exhilarating, as she dived and climbed, amazed by how easy it was in the air. Being of a slight build, she actually found it a benefit to be in such a compact cockpit where everything was right there where you needed it. When she came in to land at Tern Hill, Jackie climbed down from her plane ready to present her chit. She was greeted cheerfully by a group of fighter pilots at the aerodrome and, as she smiled back, she almost felt for a moment she was one of them.

Irene Arckless was still waiting anxiously for any word about when she was to join the ATA's own lucky Spitfire pilots:

Dear Mrs Farrer,

Yes, it's that Arckless pest again! I am going to ask you something point blank, and leave it to you to decide what happens!

As so far there seems no possibility of me coming down to join you in the immediate future on the flying staff, I wonder if in the meantime there is any chance of a Ground appointment, either as a typist or clerical staff.

If there is any opportunity of work of this nature in the meantime, I would be perfectly willing to come down, and then later, when a vacancy exists for a pilot, I could be transferred to that vacancy.

I feel sure that I could make myself quite useful if there are any openings in this direction, but of course, as you will understand, I naturally want to start on flying duties as soon as possible.

I am sure you will think I am an awful nuisance, but as you

*have been so kind, I hope you will forgive me troubling you
again. To be perfectly honest Mrs Farrer, this is between you and
I entirely – I am sitting in the office here doing practically
nothing all day and I don't like it!*

*You see, as Mr Brown, our Accountant, knows I am leaving
to come to A.T.A. sometime, he has taken on someone else who
is taking over my job, and the point is, that I am left without
anything to do, except to watch that my job is done correctly by
someone else!*

*Well, there you are, that's the position, and if you are able to
help me, I shall be most grateful to you.*

Thanking you in anticipation of your reply,

Very Sincerely,
Irene

Not hearing anything back again, Irene had almost
given up hope when she got marvellous news: 'Report at
Hatfield.'

Irene completed her training – she couldn't exactly say
without a hitch, as she bumped into another aircraft
when landing. It was put down to 'bad airmanship'. But
she was given a chance to prove herself and join the team.

In May 1941 a young woman with striking black hair
and dark eyes arrived, exhausted and bewildered, alongside thirteen of her Chilean compatriots, into Liverpool
docks. Their hoped-for destination was the Headquarters

of the Free French Forces. Margot Duhalde was born in 1920, the second of twelve children. She started flying when she was only sixteen and got her licence two years later in 1938 by talking her way into an all-male flying school and becoming something of a protégée of the maintenance chief there. When war broke out she had a kind of instinct that she wanted to become involved in it, and her French ancestry led her to try to join the Free French. She was not alone: 139 Chileans left the country in April 1941 with the same idea.

After making her way by car and train to Buenos Aires, Margot boarded a freighter for the long journey to Liverpool. Against a background of paranoia about a possible fifth column of enemy agents entering Britain, Churchill had become suspicious of those claiming allegiance to the Free French, believing it might be the perfect cover for spies. On her arrival on British soil, Margot, who didn't speak much English, was promptly arrested by the police and taken to jail. She eventually managed to make herself understood and when her story checked out she was released. She was disappointed in her hope of being able to fly for the Free French. It seems they hadn't realised she was a woman and had put her up in a hotel in London while they decided what to do with her.

Unable to find much to do with her time, Margot spent a lonely three months with the shock of the Blitz going on around her. While she was in London she met a

French military chaplain and told him her story and her hopes to be a pilot. Before anything could come of it, she was sent to the Midlands to work as a kitchen assistant at a home for convalescent pilots. It was a far cry from the heroics she had pictured before she left. Then, out of the blue, she discovered the chaplain she had met in London had told a French pilot about her story and, amazingly, the pilot had been to Chile, and he had even heard of Margot's flying exploits there. Margot was keen to meet him, and when she did, he told her all about the ATA, and how they were hiring women. Of course she wanted to sign up straight away, and through the French pilot's flying connections she was able to secure an interview with Pauline Gower and a flight test at Hatfield.

Despite the language differences, Margot must have impressed Pauline with her flying abilities, because on 1 September 'Chile', as she was nicknamed, joined the ATA. But things didn't go that smoothly. Her first solo flight resulted in yet another encounter with the local constabulary. Margot got lost and made an emergency landing in a field full of posts belonging to a local anti-aircraft battalion. The plane upended. When the police discovered her, she had no papers and was promptly arrested, despite being covered in blood. She was eventually rescued once she had made herself understood to the police, but Pauline Gower began to worry that perhaps Chile was not quite the pilot she had originally thought.

Margot Duhalde very nearly lost her place in the ATA. That is, until the chief flying instructor, MacMillan – who had turned out not to be as fearsome as Rosemary Rees had thought, but actually a bit of a softy – came to her defence. Margot told him her story and, as she put it, 'cried like the Magdalena' in his office. MacMillan persuaded Pauline to allow Margot to stay at White Waltham and work in the hangars for a while, where she might also learn a bit more English.

Back at Hatfield, Pauline summoned the other Margot, Gore, to her office for an urgent chat.

'We're getting a bit too big for this place,' she said, shuffling some documents on her large wooden desk. 'We've decided to break up the pool, to set another one up near Southampton, at Hamble. I wanted to know, well, how you'd feel about taking on a small pool of your own, running the operation there?'

Margot was flattered to be asked but aware that it would be a daunting undertaking to run a whole pool herself.

'It might be rather a challenge, at first, I'll admit,' said Pauline. 'You could choose twelve of the best pilots here to take with you. Anyone you like, within reason. You'll form the nucleus of the thing. Then some sprogs will join you later as things expand. It'll be a lot of Spits, probably, being near the factory at Eastleigh. I have every confidence you can do it, otherwise I wouldn't have asked.'

Margot was ready for a change and willing to step up. She felt, in that moment, supremely confident she could form a happy and efficient team.

'I'd be honoured,' she said and they shook hands.

As she left the office, though, Margot began to weigh up the enormity of the task. She would be running an entire pool. She started to list everything involved, setting up in a completely new location, and her confidence began to waver.

I hope I'm up to it, she thought. She began planning which pilots to take.

'Some of us are moving to Hamble,' Rosemary Rees told Lettice Curtis, who had just arrived back from delivering her second Spitfire. 'You're on the list.'

'Gosh, really? Well, I suppose things are bound to change. We can't stay here forever.'

Rosemary had been asked by Margot to be the Deputy Commanding Officer. Alison King was to be Operations Officer, and they would be going with several others, including Jackie, Anna Leska and Barbara Wojtulanis. Before they could move to Hamble, the pilots had to go on another conversion course at White Waltham, this time on a Blenheim, a British light twin-engine bomber. That would mean they could fly all types of twin engine in that class.

'You know, now we're leaving, I'll miss this old place,' Margot commented to Rosemary as they packed up their things from the wooden lockers. Hatfield was where it had all started. But things were changing and the ATA had to adapt accordingly.

They made a final visit to the operations room and thought fondly of all the chits they had collected here and all the successful deliveries they had made. They remembered the scary moments, the amusing and boring and downright terrifying moments.

'Do you think they'll trust us girls with any of those heavy four-engine beasts?' Rosemary asked as they made their way home for their last night at their cottage. 'I'd love to get my hands on a Lancaster.'

'We can dream!' said Margot, who also had a hankering to try one of the heavier four-engine bombers herself. They walked in silence for a while, thinking about the people they had lost, and the uncertain future which lay ahead of them.

'Do you even miss those blessed Tigers?' said Rosemary with a wry smile. 'You do, don't you?'

Margot looked at her and they both laughed. 'Even them.'

13. Hamble Ferry Pool

Diana Barnato was mad about flying. She had learnt at Brooklands and gone solo after only six hours in the air at the age of twenty. Her father was a millionaire motor-car racer, her grandfather was a South African diamond merchant, and she mingled in the highest of social circles. She had been given a Bentley as a twenty-first birthday present. She was jolly and funny and quite fearless. She was also a brilliant horse rider, and a couple of her friends, Dick Fairey and Bobby Lowenstein, who were already ferry pilots, hatched a mad plan to arrange for Diana to bump accidentally on purpose into A. R. O. MacMillan, the chief flying instructor of the ATA, who they knew liked to ride in Windsor Park on a Sunday. The friends set off together on their horses and after a while they did indeed bump into MacMillan. Diana must have impressed him, because after a bit of cajoling from all sides by her friends, he agreed to give her a flight test. MacMillan knew Diana had flown before, but he didn't know she had only flown ten hours.

Diana asked everyone she knew in the flying world to fill her in on all the gen about the Tiger Moths she would be tested on. They set up a big sofa at Diana's house as a mock-up flight simulator. For days before her test she sat on it in a flying position, pretending she was in the air. All the while Dick and Bobby shouted instructions at her from their easy chairs.

'OK, your engine's cut!' shouted Dick. 'Forced land.'

Diana imagined the procedure and really felt for one daft moment that she was in the air.

'Now take off again. What's the take-off speed?' asked Bobby.

With all this and more she did her best to memorise all the take-off and landing speeds, where all the controls were and everything else she needed to know for her test.

After a painful wait, and all the cramming she could possibly fit in, the day finally arrived and Diana found herself in a real Tiger Moth with not Bobby or Dick but A. R. O. MacMillan calling out his squeaky instructions at her through the Gosport Tube, the speaking tube through which instructors could communicate with the pilot from the rear cockpit. Amazingly, although Diana had never flown over a railway line and didn't even know what they looked like from above, when he asked her to follow one towards Reading she somehow managed it. It was all rather a blur, but before long she found herself coming back in to land at White Waltham. As usual MacMillan gave nothing away. Then there was another agonising wait for the result.

*

Deciding that some horse riding would take her mind off things, she accompanied Bobby up to Leicestershire, where he had a point-to-point course they could ride on. They had a wonderful day's jumping but they must have taken the horses round one too many times, because Diana's horse finally missed a jump. They crashed through the fence and Diana was thrown off and smashed her face very badly. In a blur of pain and shock, she somehow managed to ask the housekeeper to collect her broken teeth from the ground for the dentist to copy. Bobby was distraught, saying it was his fault and he should never have taken her on that course. He sat with her as she was rushed to hospital and he was in floods of tears the whole way, saying he felt truly awful about the whole thing. In the midst of the drama he blurted out that he loved her and asked her to marry him, declaring that he'd have her 'whatever she looked like'. Diana didn't know what to say. She was in agony. Her jaw was smashed up and her mind was whizzing with all kinds of strange thoughts about Bobby and her face and teeth. *Whatever I look like . . .* she thought. *Oh dear. Is it really that bad?*

Diana was taken to the London Clinic, where she then suffered the additional agony of being wheeled down on a shaky hospital trolley to the shelter during the nightly air raids. Staff and patients sat huddled and cold, before she was wheeled back up again with just as much pain. In the end she told the nurses she preferred to stay in her room upstairs and risk the prospect of being bombed rather than make that godawful jolting journey again. It transpired that Diana's face was very badly damaged and she had to have her broken jaw wired up and a tooth extracted.

Bobby, who was still feeling terrible about the whole thing, came dutifully every evening after his ATA flying to sit and chat with her for an hour before driving back to White Waltham for flying the following day. After ten days of this intensive schedule he crashed his Bentley into a wall. He wrote the car off but continued flying. The following day, perhaps due to exhaustion, he pulled the wrong lever coming in to land in a Blenheim. The plane flipped over. Poor, dear Bobby Lowenstein was dead. With her face still a mess of bandages, scars and bruises, Diana got a letter not long afterwards to say she had been accepted into the ATA.

There is something about getting into an aeroplane which divorces you from everyday problems. There is a unique feeling of freedom. On the rare occasions an ATA pilot had to climb up to 6,000 feet in a Spitfire or a Hurricane, there was the most incredible release from the pressures and concerns of life back down on earth. It could be exhilarating. At other times it would simply be terrifying.

The late autumn of 1941 brought with it a thick fog which made flying treacherous. Veronica Innes didn't have much experience of dealing with faster aircraft, let alone in bad weather. She had only just started flying the fast fighter Hurricanes when she had to bring one in to land at Squires Gate near Blackpool one day. The weather clamped down and, to make matters worse, she suddenly saw that a plane was coming in the other way. She very quickly realised that if she didn't do something fast they would almost certainly collide. She pulled the stick and was immediately forced into a spiral dive.

The Hurricane rolled on to its back and Veronica found herself hurtling nose-down, twisting and turning towards the hangars. Her stomach heaved. She gripped the stick tightly and pulled hard to bring it up. *Oh, God*, she thought as the ground got closer. *He was right all along, that horrible beast of an instructor.* As the plane tumbled through the air all she could think of was her ground-school tutor and his malicious premonition. She saw his face with vivid clarity and heard again his sneering that she would be one of the ATA pilots to die. She had a horrible feeling it was about to come true. Somehow at the very last minute she managed to pull herself up and out of the dive and level the plane off. The ground staff below were watching it all with a mix of horror and suspense as the plane put down at the airfield.

'Did you see that?' she asked as she came striding across the aerodrome after landing. Her hands were still shaking and she had gone completely white. 'That plane came from nowhere. Nearly hit me!'

'We saw it all!' said one of the fitters. They all agreed it had not been her fault. In fact, everyone there congratulated her for getting out of it so niftily. The other pilot was duly reprimanded and it turned out that Veronica had been forced so low in her dive that she had brought the telegraph wires around the aerodrome down.

I'm glad I didn't realise quite how low I was, she thought. *Otherwise I might have bottled it altogether.*

Veronica turned out to be a very good navigator with the ATA. She completed her conversion course to the single-engined fighter, and when she returned to Hatfield she discovered that many of her friends and colleagues had been relocated to the new all-woman ferry pool in Hamble. Marion Wilberforce had taken over running Hatfield, which Veronica didn't mind because she had always got on very well with her, but she was sad to see her chums gone and it felt quite quiet at Hatfield all of a sudden.

Pauline Gower had moved from Hatfield too, and was now based at White Waltham. From there she had overall command of the two women's pools, Hatfield and Hamble, as well as overseeing recruitment and training, and monitoring those who were on occasion sent to work at one of the other ferry pools alongside the men. Her new office at HQ was unostentatious. The walls were lined with maps, and a chart in many colours showed the job of each of the female pilots across the ATA.

'It is not a question of sex but of ability,' she once said in her pragmatic style. 'The most useful person does the job.' Pauline had already done a fantastic job for the women pilots. They had now been cleared to fly the fighters and twin-engines. But she had more to do. There were the four-engined bombers to go, still viewed as an all-male preserve, and there was the small matter of equal pay. Women were still paid less than the men for the same job. Pauline continued to quietly and effectively persist with her battles.

'Invasion orders,' said Alison King. 'Surely they won't come sneaking up the river one night here and pounce on us.'

Alison and Margot were in the new operations office at Hamble unpacking and sorting out the various documents, chits, personnel files, aviation books and official papers they needed for setting up their new ferry pool. Among the papers was a large brown envelope containing instructions on what to do if the ultimate emergency happened.

Hitler's plan for invasion, Operation Sea Lion, had been called off, but that didn't stop people worrying that he might take the country in a surprise attack. All pools had been given a large envelope inscribed with the words

'Only to be opened when German invasion imminent'. Although they couldn't open it, they had a rough idea of the drill should the worst occur. Thirty or so women were to go inland, with a skeleton staff of pilots, an adjutant, drivers, the medical sister plus the operations officer, together with a few cadets and the engineers. They would take the Anson and Fairchild taxis and wait at a designated airfield which was actually a former racetrack and now home also to one of the new secret Spitfire factories near Salisbury Plain. It was on a sloping chalky down and well hidden among the surrounding trees.

'I don't suppose we'll be needing the kitchen staff if they do come,' said Alison, tucking the envelope in a secure place.

'A strict diet of tinned spam and bully beef for everyone, no doubt,' said Margot, trying not to believe it could ever become a reality.

'Hello,' said a large, jovial man appearing at the door. 'Armstrong Payn,' he added, holding out his hand. 'Mind if I come in?' He didn't wait for an answer before entering and leaning against the door frame. 'You settling in all right?'

Armstrong had fair hair with a centre parting, and round spectacles. He also had a mischievous grin and looked as if he knew something about you which he might spring at any moment.

'We're feeling our way around,' said Margot, putting a pile of books on the shelf.

Behind Armstrong lurked a shy, awkward-looking man who was the antithesis of the other's exuberance. He followed him in and introduced himself as George Dutton. George and Armstrong had been working with the men's pool which had been based at Hamble before the women had arrived en masse.

'They've left us here to show you the ropes,' said Armstrong. 'Though I'm sure you won't need us.'

Armstrong and George showed them around the single-storey red-brick building. There was the mess and lounge, the locker rooms, maps and signals room and the Met room. Hamble was a lot bigger and more organised than Hatfield had been.

After their tour Alison and Margot left the aerodrome and went to their new accommodation, walking through the town to get there.

'It's like stepping back in time, isn't it?' said Alison.

'Yes, something out of *The Old Curiosity Shop*,' Margot agreed.

The town had rows of quirky, misshapen old cottages and shops with names which did indeed seem to have come straight out of a Dickens novel. There was no shortage of pubs. There was Ye Old White Harte and the Bugle, and also a smart yacht club in the harbour, which would be useful for entertainment. The air was fresh and salty and the whole sleepy place seemed far away from the war. In reality it was quite close, since, as the site of numerous aerodromes, factories and maintenance units, the whole area was a vulnerable target. It would also be the centre of things in due course when preparations began for D-Day. But for the time being it seemed very pleasant and a refreshing change from Hatfield.

Margot and Alison had been allocated digs in the top flat of a house overlooking the river. Out of the window they looked across the river at the tranquil pale horizon and listened to the faint lap of waves and the flapping and squawking of a few gulls diving for fish.

The other pilots were also settling into their own new billets. Most of them were given the name of a house or family to live with which had been arranged by the ATA, although some found their own local accommodation. Philippa Bennett and Lettice Curtis were given a cottage together, and Jackie Sourer, the young South African pilot, was handed a bit of paper with just the name of the residence of a local family written on it. She got hold of a rickety old black bicycle and rode to meet her new hosts.

Creek Cottage. Well, it sounds lovely, she thought as she rode through the town and along the peaceful Hamble riverside, the wind blowing freshly across her face. When she arrived at a row of little bungalows and caught sight of the sign to her house she slammed on the brakes. That was when she discovered the brakes were not working and promptly fell off the bicycle and on to the wet grass. She extracted herself from a tangle of wheels and gear cables and scrambled to her feet as a kindly-looking elderly gentleman appeared from the cottage and helped her up.

'You're not by any chance looking for us, are you?'

Jackie did her best to brush off the leaves. 'Yes, er, sorry about this. I didn't mean to arrive quite so unceremoniously.'

She needn't have worried. The Greenhills, who were both retired, were perfectly charming and more than happy to have her staying with them, whatever state she arrived in. Their home was right on the edge of the river, with weeping willows all around, and they had a small motor boat which they used for summer's day jaunts. Jackie was shown to her new room, which was sweet and cosy, and she made it even more homely by putting up a few family photographs and cut-outs from magazines. Her new surrogate grandparents insisted on making sure she had enough to eat that night and prepared what seemed to her a feast, even though it was concocted from rations.

This paradise didn't last long. Jackie shot out of bed the following morning, not wanting to be late for her first day at Hamble. She was bleary eyed and disoriented after the night in a new house. She gobbled down a quick breakfast, grabbed her bag and hopped on the bicycle. Riding more carefully this time, she made her way to the aerodrome, where the women had gathered in the operations room to collect their chits.

'There's quite a backlog to clear,' said Alison. 'So it's all hands.'

'We'll all have to bear with things as we get used to these new surroundings,' Margot added, before showing everyone to their lockers. 'But I know you'll all take it in your stride.'

Hamble was already a large and fully functioning pool. There was a Met room full of weather charts, where they got their weather reports each morning. There was a room for signals and maps, detailing the signals for landing at the aerodromes, and another room for parachutes, plus the mess where they gathered in the lounge on 'off days' if the weather was bad, and a dining room and kitchen.

From the moment they got their first chits, the deliveries were relentless. There were several aircraft factories nearby, and there were many types of aircraft to be ferried from this strategic South Coast site, including a lot of Spitfires. There were so many planes to ferry in those first few days that Jackie spent five nights on the trot at a range of dreary, soulless hotels between deliveries. She was disappointed that she didn't even make it back to her new home once. Mr Greenhill rang the office asking after her, concerned that she might have gone astray. She was relieved when the busy first few days were over and she was finally able to return to the tranquil cottage and enjoy the comforts of her new room and home-cooked food.

Veronica Innes had to get used to the new drill at Hatfield without many of its most experienced pilots. It consisted of a lot of very long and arduous trips in Tiger Moths and, as the other pilots had done in their first year, she endured many long train journeys back from aerodromes around the country and as far afield as Scotland and Wales. She often found herself sporting a 'most unladylike drip' at the end of her nose due to flying in the cold open cockpit. She and her friend Mary Hunter got the train together if they had been flying in a gaggle and they slept where they could bed down in the corridors or luggage racks after their long trips.

On one occasion when they did manage to get a seat, a woman in their carriage looked over at them with some distaste and they overheard her whispering to her friend, 'If they only knew what a fright they look in those trousers, they'd never wear them.' Mary and Veronica were too exhausted to care and they just looked at each other and burst out laughing. If the women had known of all the trials and tribulations they had been through that past week, they might have been kinder.

There were a lot of Hurricanes on the books at Hatfield

and the work of clearing them now fell to the newer pilots. As Joan Hughes had discovered a few months earlier, many of these fighters had stiff undercarriages which were very difficult to pull up. Quite a few ATA pilots, both men and women, struggled to get them up and down again for landing. Not only that, there were also problems with brake pressure which made ferrying Hurricanes, however attractive they had been at first, an altogether dicey experience at times. As more aircraft appeared on their chits, they began to note them down and tick off the new ones. There was even a bit of jovial competition with one another about who had flown what, and who longed for what next. If a new aircraft rolled off the production line, they were always intrigued to get it on their chits, but some got a reputation for being plain awful.

Lettice Curtis picked up her chit from the wooden table in the operations room at Hamble.

'A Walrus!' she said with a raised eyebrow. She had heard quite a lot about this notorious plane.

'Ah, the waddling duck!' laughed Rosemary Rees. 'That's another one to add to your ever-growing list.'

The Walrus was a bulky plane which could land in water. No one particularly longed for it. But Lettice was prepared to give anything a go and always rather liked a challenge.

The Walrus was interesting at least because it was an

amphibious aircraft. It was a biplane with an enclosed cockpit at the front and a huge engine hanging suspended above on wide struts. It was made by the same company who produced the Spitfire, Supermarine, but it had none of the fighter's sleekness. Despite its shortcomings on land, it was an effective reconnaissance plane which also rescued downed RAF pilots from the sea since it was able to launch from aircraft carriers and battleships.

As she went to collect the Walrus, Lettice asked one of the maintenance staff at the airfield if there was anything she needed to know about it, any snags or quirks.

'Tends to weathercock a bit and it's quite nose-heavy on the runway,' he said. 'Oh, and if you're in a cross wind, make sure you don't hit the ground with the floats. They tend to scrape along and get damaged if you're not careful.'

She climbed into the cabin with some difficulty via the roof and found herself clambering through all manner of equipment, anchors and ropes and other essentials for an aquatic plane. Inside there was quite a roomy area, where an entire crew would normally sit. To Lettice, who was all alone, it felt vast and not like a plane at all. She had been told not to land it on the sea, which was a shame because that might have been rather fun. As she started the taxi she took it carefully along the airstrip and the aircraft did indeed move like a duck on the land.

As she picked up speed, the waddling Walrus moved left and right, and it was still swinging from left to right as she took off.

It's more like flying a ship than a plane, she thought as the plane heaved its way through the sky. She made her first Walrus delivery without any hitches, but she wasn't in a hurry for another one any time soon.

14. Balloons Up

Every pilot had to check in with Maps and Signals before they flew. This was a room with a large map of Britain which clearly laid out the latest information about barrage balloons, anti-aircraft gun emplacements and any prohibited flying areas. They always had to make sure the anti-aircraft gunners knew where they were going, because they could be quite trigger-happy if they did not recognise an aircraft.

One of the biggest challenges at Hamble was the balloon barrage which protected this most vulnerable area. The huge silver balloons had thick cables which made flying near them perilous. When the pilots were coming in to land or taking off, the balloons were brought down to allow them passage and then lifted up again when they were finished.

One afternoon the CO at Hamble, Margot Gore, was bringing a Hudson into Eastleigh after it had been repaired. She had a young ATC cadet called John on board with her, who would help with the lifting and dropping of the undercarriage if needed. There were quite a few teenage cadets from the local Air Training Corps who helped ATA pilots out on board the planes while they learnt about aviation. Margot navigated well through some very poor visibility, and as they approached Eastleigh after what had been a rather difficult journey, she expected the balloon barrage to be hauled away as usual to clear the way for her to land. The balloons would be lowered to create several narrow lanes for planes to pass through. They were codenamed for secrecy things like 'Charlie', 'Harry', 'Alfred', 'Bertie', 'Donald' and such like. This led to quite a few jokes among ATA pilots about whether they were 'familiar' with Donald or Charlie.

Margot wasn't thinking about jokes as she approached this time, but was concentrating hard as the path began to clear. She turned into Charlie and with the help of the cadet put her wheels and flaps down. On either side the cables moved gently in the wind. The balloons flew up to the cloud base, or at about 5,000 feet, so it was really the cables that most ATA pilots risked getting tangled up in, not the balloons themselves unless they were very high. She began to relax when she saw the others in front of her on the ground out of harm's way.

Just as she had started the descent she saw a movement below in her peripheral vision. One of the balloons was rising up again right in her path in front and billowing all around as it filled with hydrogen gas. Margot couldn't quite believe it. She looked again and sure enough it was rising up and had got above the line of the hedge already. All the while she was heading straight for this row which had only just been cleared for her land-ing. Then she saw it wasn't just one balloon rising up again: the whole lane was awakening like a giant pod of whales swimming to the surface. Her only chance was to increase the power enough to climb up over them before they reached her. She put the flaps and undercar-riage back up and throttled forward. Then, whoosh, she was up in a flash. The balloons kept rising and she missed them by what felt like a fraction.

'Lucky we didn't get tangled up in all that,' she said, trying to keep an air of calm for John, the cadet. In real-ity she felt anything but calm, and when she looked over at her young companion he was positively green with fear. By the time they had landed, Margot found herself in a state of high fury. This was a rare occurrence because she was usually very composed, and her anger meant she must have suffered a true injustice of some kind.

'They should have let me in,' she said as she marched into the watch office. They were all apologies in there, aware that they had made a serious error.

It turned out there had been a sudden air-raid warn-ing. Someone had got the instruction 'Balloons Up' and, not realising she was coming in, had hauled the balloons up again. Margot made it very clear in no uncertain terms to HQ that she wasn't at all happy; there was a swift report and the rules were changed to prevent something like it happening to anyone else.

*

Before they flew, pilots were also under strict instruction to check in with the Met, who obtained all the information they could about the weather. With so many prohibited wireless areas and the risk of torpedoes they could not have all the usual weather ships out in the Atlantic, which meant they didn't always get the weather perfectly right. Sometimes they got it very wrong and many an ATA pilot found themselves caught out in bad weather. Nevertheless, there would be consequences if a pilot had not checked in to the Met Office and then an accident occurred due to bad weather.

The pilots were strictly forbidden from flying above cloud, because without any radio on board they had to maintain visual contact with the ground in order to navigate, but it wasn't always possible when the rain came in suddenly. On just such a day, when the Met had not been able to predict a particularly heavy downpour, Veronica Innes found herself stuck above some dastardly-looking black clouds on the way to an airfield at Millom. Unable to see which way she was going, she looked around for any landmarks to reorient herself. There was nothing but heaving black and grey all around. In the murk she caught sight of what she thought was the shape of an RAF Hudson plane some way off.

I'll follow him, she thought, *and see where that leads.* She banked and climbed to follow the Hudson from a safe distance. The last thing she wanted was to crash into an operational plane. She had no idea where it was going and was relieved and slightly amazed when she discovered it was also destined for Millom. This was one of her favourite aerodromes and she didn't mind being grounded due to weather there. Once she had landed she put on her ATA uniform and spent the evening at a local dance, laughing and joking with the pilots and WAAF girls. It was all a great relief from the stress of being a ferry pilot.

When she was back at Hatfield she discovered that a tall, handsome pilot called Terry Volkersz had been posted there for a refresher course. He was a lieutenant in the Netherlands Naval Service and had escaped from Holland during the invasion of the Low Countries. He had been attached to the RAF and was now flying Spitfires. Between the daily deliveries and conversion courses and trying to stay on top of the job, Veronica took rather a fancy to Lieutanant Volkersz.

She had another passion that year, too. It was time for her to fly her first Spitfire. She needed to deliver one in order to get her second stripe and become a first officer. Luckily for her, it wasn't long before she got one, a Mark VB, which she collected from Cowley. As soon as she got into the Spit, her love for the Hurricane faded away. This was an altogether different experience, a lighter and much more manoeuvrable aircraft, with none of those dratted snags with the undercarriage. She was in a state of high excitement when she went in to get her first delivery chit signed after landing. Some RAF boys were on their way in to collect their planes. When they saw what she had just flown they looked at each other in disbelief. 'Women flying Spits – we might as well give up, old chap,' one said to another, shaking his head. Veronica didn't know whether to be amused or offended, but in the end nothing could take away the exhilaration of delivering her first Spit.

When the weather was bad and the pilots couldn't fly at all they spent the day in the lounge room on sofas and chairs or on the floor, knitting or reading or playing bridge. One chilly afternoon at Hamble a group of them sat around passing the time in their different ways. Rosemary Rees was pressed up against the radiator wrapped to the gills in an assortment of scarves and coats, refusing even to remove her furry boots. Next to her, working on some sewing, was Philippa Bennett, who was by comparison to perfectly poised Rose rather more like an excitable puppy.

Armstrong Payn would sometimes hang about and joke with the women on 'wash-out' days, often getting up to no good with a bit of cheeky good humour. On this particular day, he came into the lounge area with a mischievous look on his face. Rosemary looked up from her knitting. 'I want to find out if any of you really *are* women,' he said and looked around furtively.

Rosemary thought nothing of it because he was always joking about. Armstrong skulked around for a bit and then a few moments later pulled something out of his pocket.

'What's that?' asked Rosemary. He opened his hands to reveal a tiny brown mouse. To his utter delight, one of the girls in the mess did actually jump on to a chair.

Having a couple of men about the place at Hamble in the form of Armstrong Payn and George Dutton was quite fun and added to the atmosphere. Lettice Curtis felt it made the pool feel a bit less like a girl's boarding school, and this, coupled with the new planes, was more satisfying and challenging. George and Armstrong fitted in perfectly and were something of a double act, with the delightful combination of Armstrong's rambunctiousness and George's endearing awkward shyness.

There was a man in the maintenance unit whose job it was to get signatures, but he wasn't very good at remembering faces. With it being ostensibly a women's pool, he would sometimes, if surrounded by an eager gaggle of women vying for their chits, ask in exasperation for the ladies to wait, and request 'Miss Dutton's signature first'. George, hanging back out of the crowd, would step forward with some embarrassment to announce his presence and suffer an endless amount of teasing from some of the pilots. 'Miss D,' they would say, 'You really mustn't come on duty without your skirt.'

At the end of a morale-boosting briefing from Margot after a particularly difficult delivery, Armstrong would sometimes stand up and chime in with a flourish, 'And thank *you*, Margot, for being a bloody good CO!' He had a jolly character but he also suffered with chronic stomach pain – but that didn't stop him. On those rainy or low cloud days, he also had a habit of making his way around the large sitting room without touching the floor, clinging to walls and leaping from chair to sofa and radiator to window sill like a restless leopard.

Rosemary would pass the time in odd ways too. Having been a ballerina, she would join Armstrong with her own antics, practising odd positions on one leg, or what she called her 'limbering up'. And the diminutive and agile South African pilot Jackie Sourer had a penchant for standing on her head, saying it helped the blood to get to her brain. All in all, they made for quite an eccentric bunch.

Since the first days back at Hatfield the press had not been quite so fascinated by the women and generally left them to get on with things, but every now and again some twitchy bloke would come and hover about at Hamble trying to get a news or social piece out of the women pilots. Margot would try fending them off as best she could, but also knew that it was important to keep the public on side and at least give them something. She would steer some unsuspecting pilot on their way back from a job towards the more persistent journalists to try and give them something by way of a story to keep them quiet.

The pilots were amused and a little wearied by what the papers liked to pick up on. Often it was the fact that many of the pilots were mothers, or in the case of Lois

Butler, a grandmother. This seemed very intriguing to them. Alison and Margot also laughed at the other picture often portrayed: that they were a bunch of glamour girls constantly shaking their golden locks out of their flying helmets, a perfect combination of Hollywood chic and womanly heroics. None of them recognised this fictitious version of themselves when it came to the daily grind and realities of ferrying. The press and magazine people tended not to mention the desperate hunting for somewhere to go to the lavatory, or the sweaty, stressful searching through the mist for somewhere to land, or the shivering, oil-covered hours waiting at railway stations, instead preferring the perfectly coiffured look for their front covers.

The pilots had got used to not drinking too much tea before flying but now and again they could be caught short and desperate by the time they landed. Some male pilots, they discovered, had access to a 'tube' for disposing of their waste if it was needed. When the women couldn't find any lavatories, they had to resort to desperate measures on occasion. Forthright and fearless Anna Leska amused everyone with her tale that on arriving at an aerodrome with no facilities for females she had resorted to 'going behind a hangar'. When someone asked her, 'But what if a man had seen you?' she replied, 'My dear, if the King of England had walked past I couldn't have stopped.'

15. Crossing the Atlantic

In autumn 1941 demand was such for ferry pilots that there was a radio appeal for more people to join. A young Oxfordshire farmer's daughter, Mary Wilkins, heard the broadcast. She had been bitten by the flying bug as a young girl after seeing Cobham's Air Circus. Her father had agreed to pay for lessons at her local club in Witney, where she had been taught by a young Jackie Sourer before the war. Mary had only managed to clock up a few hours solo before war broke out and the flying clubs were shut down. What she lacked in hours, though, she made up for with enthusiasm in her application. She was asked for a flight test at Hatfield and taken on for training. It was a big change from the 600 hours originally required.

Diana Barnato had had to delay joining the ATA after her horse riding accident, but by the end of 1941 she was also ready to start. She turned up for her second flight test looking striking in her mother's leopard-skin coat without really thinking it was anything strange, and the instructor was obviously flustered and taken aback. He said rather bumblingly that he thought she was far too attractive to be able to fly, which Diana, rather than be offended, decided to take as a good sign that at least her face had healed acceptably.

It was perhaps fortuitous she had delayed joining because it was only by then that they were really ready to take pilots with so little experience and had set up a rigorous training school at White Waltham which taught new pilots everything pretty much from scratch. Diana and the other new pilots had their medical checks. They also had to sign a form to say they wouldn't give away any secrets, and then it was on to the ground school. They learnt about the weather and Met reports and the dangers of flying, including balloon barrages and how to negotiate them, as well as navigation, how to read maps and fly with only a compass, and the landing signals. Then it was on to the real business of flying, with the open-cockpit Magisters, and Hawker Harts, then the Miles Master and the Harvard, the engine of which Diana thought sounded rather like an angry wasp. Technical courses were given by a man called Gribble, who didn't suffer fools and marvelled wearily at how ignorant these people could be about engines and the physics of flying and yet still fly.

They had to do an awful lot of cross-country flying in their training in order to get to grips with the layout and hazards of wartime Britain. The weather, of course, was always a problem, but there were also the barrage balloons to be marked in red pencil on the maps, and they had to practise over and over again finding and landing at the various key aerodromes.

After her initial training, Diana was posted to Hamble for a few weeks on a temporary basis, where she mainly did Fairchild taxi work to get her hours up. The principal work at Hamble was delivering Spitfires from factories in Eastleigh and its environs. They had to move around 300,000 aircraft because it was being urgently cleared out due to the fact it was such a vulnerable target for German bombing. There were more ATC cadets at Hamble, who helped out in the Anson taxi, winding the heavy undercarriage up. They also had a Fairchild three-seater single-engine taxi. Now able to be moved easily between short hops, the pilots would regularly ferry up to three or four aircraft a day between Eastleigh, Brize Norton, Llandau, Cornwall and High Ercall, and numerous other tiny airfields which had sprung up since the war broke out.

Not long after they started at Hamble, some of the more experienced pilots were sent on another conversion course called 'Class 4', also at White Waltham, where they learnt on a Bristol Blenheim to fly medium twin-engined bombers. This meant they could fly many different aircraft in the same class including other twin-engined bombers like the Armstrong Whitworth Whitley and the famous Vickers Wellington which was used as a night bomber in the early days before the heavy four-engines came along, and they could also now take another bomber called the Handley Page Hampden, all rather larger planes than they were used to. After having only been cleared to fly operational craft a few months ago, and now it seemed like they were coming thick and fast.

In early December compulsory military conscription in the United Kingdom was extended to include all men between the ages of eighteen and fifty, and many women were now serving in women's auxiliary forces, fire brigades and the Women's Auxiliary Air Force, or WAAF. Aerodromes had originally been very much male domains, but as the WAAF grew in size, and more women became involved in work for the RAF such as transport, maintenance, radar and engineering work, the ATA's female pilots no longer found themselves quite the novelty they had been in January 1940 when they first started.

This also meant there were more changing and lavatory facilities for them to use, and there was even some accommodation on some of the aerodromes in which, while the WAAF women were working at night on radar stations, ATA pilots could get some sleep between flights. Even with the expansion of the WAAF, though, at some airfields such as Ternhill the CO apparently still refused to allow women in the officers' mess, and female pilots continued to be brought their lunch by a waiter in a white jacket to eat on their own in a dedicated ladies' room.

By December Veronica and Mary Hunter had managed to fly the necessary quota of Spitfires to fully convert to 'Class 3' and they celebrated getting their second stripe.

They flew all throughout Christmas without any let-up, but they didn't mind a jot. They were riding on the success of their promotion, and the weather was bright and sunny. Veronica was also riding high on the first flush of her new-found love for Dutch fighter pilot Terry Volkersz. She thought to herself as she sped along one crisp, clear winter's day, *Who wouldn't want to be flying one of the world's greatest fighter planes?*

By the end of the year both Armstrong Payn and George Dutton had become 'one of the girls', as it were. They didn't want to leave Hamble. The women didn't want them to go either, but four months after the women had arrived they got the orders that they had to move elsewhere. It was a sad day when they left. Margot organised a big party in their honour, and awkward George and cheeky Armstrong hugged and clapped everyone on the back as they sadly bade goodbye to the first chapter of life at Hamble.

Other things were about to change. Churchill had been working hard behind the scenes, and even publicly in radio broadcasts, to persuade America to join the war and boost Allied forces. On 7 December 1941 the American naval base at Pearl Harbor on Hawaii was hit by a surprise Japanese attack. Early on a Sunday morning the sky filled with planes which proceeded to bombard aircraft and battleships in the harbour. Over 2,400 people were killed and around 1,000 injured. With America reeling from the shock of an attack on home territory,

President Roosevelt gave the order and the United States declared war on Hitler's ally Japan.

As the country was being drawn into the increasingly global conflict, one of the most experienced American female pilots, a woman called Jacqueline Cochran, announced she was putting together a group of the best women fliers to join the ATA in Britain. Jackie had met up with Pauline Gower at White Waltham already to discuss the idea. The two women were very different. Jackie was much more glamorous and connected to high society than pragmatic Pauline, but they were both determined in their own ways to prove women would be capable pilots in the war.

In January 1942 Jackie Cochran made the announcement to a glitzy crowd at the glamorous St Regis Hotel in New York that she had put together a group of female pilots to join the ATA. A celebrity publicist, Harry Bruno, was charged with drafting the press release, and they all met at Jackie's newly formed 'Headquarters' at the Rockefeller Plaza. Jackie had sent telegrams to 125 of the best women pilots, and around 25 were selected. Cochran even met up with Eleanor Roosevelt, another vocal advocate of women pilots, to discuss details at the White House.

The selected pilots were sent to Montreal in Canada to be tested and checked before they could depart for Britain. The pay was to be about $300 a month. The minimum number of required flying hours was 300.

They also had to be between twenty-one and thirty-five years old, and at least a high school graduate: they were a young, educated and athletic bunch.

Jackie travelled to London first, and her girls followed on in separate ships in small groups between January and July to avoid the risk of being wiped out in one hit by a torpedo. They were well aware that this had happened to a group of male pilots in the Atlantic the year before when the SS *Nerissa* was sunk in April 1941, with the loss of eleven American pilots destined for the ATA. If ships in a convoy were hit, there was no stopping by the other ships to pick up survivors. The passengers stayed below the water line and there would be little chance of getting out if they were hit on the way.

The women's journeys were all thankfully uneventful in that sense. One of the first to arrive was a ship called *Beaver Hill,* which was a former coal carrier that had been converted into a troop carrier. Some of the journeys were eventful in other ways. One of the pilots who made her way to Britain, Dorothy Furey, got engaged to a Canadian lieutenant called Richard Bragg she met on the ship, to keep the others who approached her 'at bay', she said. They married a month later and Dorothy Furey became Dorothy Bragg. The pilots exchanged imaginings about what might await them in Britain. They had heard varying stories about the level of destruction and hunger which had afflicted the fog-bound island. As they looked out of the portholes of their ship, the other vessels in their convoy at times seemed to disappear. They didn't know whether they had been sunk in the night or just gone off on another mission.

Ready to greet the first five at Liverpool was Pauline Gower, together with the adjutant from White Waltham, who was Margaret Fairweather's sister Kitty. They greeted the new pilots and hoped to reassure the bewildered transatlantic contingent that they were most welcome. Pauline offered to give them all dinner at her hotel, an invitation she assumed they would realise was official and gracefully accept. The pilots misunderstood the context and, as they were all quite exhausted from their journey, rather embarrassingly not one of them turned up. It wasn't a great start to the joining of this aviation sisterhood.

On a confusing train journey to Maidenhead they got their first taste of England, the strange accents and customs of an alien land, and the first five American women reported to HQ at White Waltham. When Dorothy Furey met the head of the ATA, Gerard 'Pops' d'Erlanger, she was not impressed with his little talk to the new Americans. It consisted of a lecture on 'ill-mannered Americans'. She was amused by the fact that his stripes were gold, like an admiral's, and she and her fellow pilots nicknamed him 'the man with the runways on his shoulder'. Pops had nothing, as it happens, against Americans, but had encountered a group of men who had come and got drunk and apparently behaved badly and been sent back home. His little talk did not endear him to Furey, though, or the others who were tired and a bit deflated by what appeared to them to be a very drab-looking Britain.

The male contingent at White Waltham was waiting in eager anticipation for the arrival of the American women and they tried to sneak a look through their curtains as they arrived. No doubt the men were hoping for an injection of some kind of mystical American glamour into the daily ATA routine. The travel-weary pilots were probably too exhausted to notice or care that they were the objects of wide-eyed inspection. What did get their attention was when they heard that the chief medic, Dr Arthur Barbour, who was apparently known to keep a few 16 mm 'adult films' about the place, insisted on people disrobing in front of him for their medical checks. This was usual for men and women, in fact, but the prospect was not much appreciated by the new US contingent. When Jackie Cochran got wind of this peculiar procedure and was faced with the prospect of her girls being examined 'in the buff', she made her views known to the Air Ministry. The Americans managed to escape Doc Barbour's nude ambitions and were allowed to be examined fully clothed.

The new pilots found Britain an alien place, with some strange manners and conventions, and they were relieved to meet up with their male American counterparts who had already arrived.

The weather in Britain at this time was, to say the least, unpleasant. January 1942 was extremely cold. There was snow and ice and it was not at all favourable for flying.

Veronica Innes was taking off in a Hurricane bound for Ratcliffe one morning in typically wintry conditions. With her window freezing with frost, she knew she had to stay as low as possible and keep an eye on the railway line. When the snow came down on top of the ice she could barely make out the edge of Ratcliffe Aerodrome, and her cockpit canopy was covered by a thin sheet of ice. It was never easy to see out of a Hurricane, but now it was impossible. She had no choice but to open up the hood. As soon as she did a great gust of freezing cold snow blew into her face, up her nose and into her mouth. She managed to land the Hurricane, but on the ground, things did not improve. It was windy and gusting and the snow was driving hard and forming in thick layers on the runway. Veronica realised that in all the confusion she had forgotten to put up her flaps for landing. In her haste, she opened up too quickly while taxiing and the Hurricane was caught by the wind and flipped suddenly forward on to its nose. She was not hurt and the Hurricane wasn't too badly damaged, but Veronica was the first to admit she could be a bit careless at times while taxiing. Perhaps she relaxed too soon after the concentration of flying and landing. When she went before the Accidents Committee she thought their finding of 'pilot responsible' was a bit harsh, given the atrocious weather. *Better to be a bit careless on the ground than careless in the air*, she thought.

Another pilot, Honor Salmon (née Pitman), who had got married the previous June, found herself getting into trouble a bit too often in her aircraft.

Once while taxiing a Spitfire into an unmarked 'soft patch' she had an accident with her plane. After that, she had the starboard undercarriage of a Hurricane collapse on landing. These accidents took their toll on Honor's emotional health and she was given a month off to recover. She was sent on a refresher course, but things did not improve. 'Her chief fault is her attitude towards her job,' said one instructor's report. 'If she can be persuaded that flying is, after all, a very ordinary occupation, with common sense the main ingredient, and that an ordinary sensible woman makes a better ferry pilot than a temperamental prima donna, she will do better and inspire greater confidence.' The criticism continued. She was called 'an unstable type', admitting herself that she got into a flap flying with an instructor but claiming that she had no difficulty in navigating solo. 'Apparently' one report stated, she 'tends to rely on Bradshawing [following railway lines].' Another one said she was 'very self-important at times' and another, 'This pilot occasionally flies well – but not as well as she thinks she does. Her progress will need very careful watching.' Poor

Honor Salmon was having problems with flying, but she was very well liked by the other pilots. She was kind and funny, and any time there was a new person at Hamble she helped them as much as she could. It was unfortunate that her sparkling personality didn't help when she had problems in the air.

With more planes to fly, more women were sent on conversion courses, and in April Veronica and Anna Leska were sent to White Waltham to do their light twin conversion Class 3 Plus, on the Oxford. The Oxford, Veronica found, seemed rather dull after the Hurricanes, but the training cleared them for the Anson and a passenger and radio navigation plane called a Dominie. More importantly, it was the next step towards conversion to heavy twin-engined bombers like the Wellington.

Since the Polish RAF had formed their own squadrons in Britain, Polish pilot Anna Leska always looked forward to ending up at one of their aerodromes. She was pleased when she bumped into fighter pilots she knew from her time flying Air Force missions in Poland, and she was especially keen to see her new bomber pilot boyfriend, Mieczysław. When Veronica and Anna ended up at a Polish squadron at Northolt one day and stayed for dinner in the mess, they came close to going on a 'sweep' to France with some of the boys in their

Spitfires. It was probably fortunate they didn't join them, fun though it sounded over the comfort of dinner, because it would have been pretty dangerous, not to mention against every conceivable ATA regulation.

16. A Whirlwind Romance

While the new team at Hamble were settling into their busy schedule, most of the original eight, minus Rosemary, remained at Hatfield. The two Margarets, Fairweather and Cunnison, flew the Anson taxi quite a bit, while Marion Wilberforce and Winnie Crossley were running operations. However, there were to be changes at Hatfield as well. Production of the new 'wooden wonder' Mosquito bomber had intensified, and the ATA had to move out to make way for its expansion. In April 1942 Ferry Pool Number 5 moved to its new location at a mixed pool in Luton. It also incorporated the new training school, the ATA Elementary Flying Training School, where Margaret Cunnison and another of the first eight, young Joan Hughes, took up the role of instructing new ATA pilots.

With all the flying at White Waltham, the grass airfield had taken something of a heavy pounding and that spring it was decided to put a top surface on the landing field. No sooner had the surface gone down than there followed a horrible succession of burst tyres, much to the annoyance of the pilots. It turned out that the material used was somehow mixed with a load of nails and tacks, broken glass and goodness knows what other sharp objects. There were rumours of sabotage, but no one really knew, and it may have just been carelessness.

Diana Barnato had been posted to White Waltham for her cross-country practice, but when the problem with the new surface was discovered flying was stopped immediately, and she and the others based there were ordered on to their hands and knees to pick out the rogue items one by one. It was gruelling work and ultimately fruitless. There was simply too much of the blessed stuff, and no sooner had you cleared one lot than another seemed to appear. In the end heavy magnets were brought in to clear it out. ATA work had to be moved to a nearby airfield and continued there, although it was somewhat hampered by the whole business.

When flying was back on track, Diana was sent on a cross-country on a very windy day. It was so turbulent she feared she might bring up that morning's breakfast, and her plane, a Magister, was dropping and shaking all over the place in the wind. She put down at RAF Debden near Saffron Walden. Over lunch in the officers' mess, she found herself seated next to Fighter Squadron Leader Humphrey Gilbert. She couldn't help noticing how blue his eyes were, though his hair was a bit strange to say the least – in fact it was the worst haircut she had ever seen, all in a big heap on top of his head. They got on very well and chatted all through lunch. He told her he had been shot down in the Battle of Britain and led a squadron over Northern France. Diana was disappointed when the wind dropped and it was time to leave, but she had no excuse. She had to get back to her Magister.

As if by some strange twist of fate, when she tried to start the Magister up it gave her nothing. The engineers said they'd look at it, and while she was waiting for a call from the ground crew she was forced to spend the evening in the mess chatting with Humphrey. She didn't mind a bit. When no call came from the ground engineers she had no choice but to spend the whole night at RAF Debden. The following day the Magister still wouldn't start, so Humphrey showed Diana his Spitfire which had a blue painted nose for camouflage when flying alone. Diana, who had yet to finish her training, longed to fly one. Later that day the Magister still wouldn't start and Diana was delighted at having to stay another night at Debden getting acquainted with charming Humphrey Gilbert. Her CO, on the other hand, wasn't so happy.

Humphrey had rung White Waltham to explain the delay, and although the CO hadn't taken it well, there wasn't much they could do. She couldn't stay there forever, though, and when the Magister finally got going she bade him a sad farewell. They had only known each other for a few days but it felt like ages. They arranged to meet again in London a few times in the following weeks. They danced and talked and shared their stories and she stared into his blue eyes, and even tried to love his hair. Whenever she had her day's leave she met up with Humphrey, including a trip from Heathrow with her friend Bob Sarll, who helped her out. Heathrow was then just a simple grass airfield. Diana made the trip to Debden then back to White Waltham after two days, and whenever she could she was dropped off at Debden by Bob, who became her unofficial taxi, only to be whisked swiftly back by plane the next day for duty at White Waltham.

It was truly a whirlwind romance, but they had also found a true and deep connection in a very short time. He was brave and funny and a great storyteller and handsomely tall and broad-shouldered. Before the month was out they were engaged and busy planning for the big day. They arranged to meet at Diana's London flat one morning when she had a day off. When Humphrey didn't turn up, she assumed he must have had to fly unexpectedly that day and she returned to White Waltham not feeling too concerned. She telephoned Debden to check anyway. He wasn't there. Still not very out of the ordinary. There were always last-minute ops.

The following day Diana was asked to do a cross-country in a Tiger Moth. She was only supposed to stop at Hatfield, but she would fly over Debden. She wondered whether her CO was testing her to check whether she put down there. She didn't dare land, although she was sorely tempted. Everyone by now knew about her romantic attachment to the place. As she flew over she craned her neck to look down for Humphrey's blue Spitfire. It wasn't anywhere. A chill went up the back of her neck and she had a sick feeling in the pit of her stomach. It was like nothing she had ever experienced, even on the diciest of flights.

After she had landed at Hatfield and was on her way back to White Waltham, she tried not to think about what might have happened. She focused intently on the joystick and kept one eye on the ground for navigation. As soon as she landed she ran into the office and telephoned Debden. Her mouth was dry with fear as she was put through to a succession of people. Increasingly exasperated, she eventually reached the Station Commander. There was no easy way for him to tell her that Humphrey Gilbert had been killed the day before. She wasn't told how it happened, and right at that moment it didn't really matter. He was gone and that was that. Her legs seemed to melt away. She burst into tears and leant against the wall of the telephone box. It was only when another pilot knocked on the glass that she found the strength to leave the enclosed space. The same day her curt, unsympathetic CO slapped her wings on to the desk in front of her. Her eyes were still red from crying. So, this was it. She was now a fully-fledged ATA pilot. It didn't feel very ceremonious at that moment. As if to add insult to injury, her CO said, 'Just because you've got your wings, Miss Barnato, it doesn't necessarily mean you can fly.'

Diana went to Humphrey's funeral in a daze of tears — it was a whir of people she didn't know very well dressed in black. She was told nothing about how he had died. In that moment she didn't care. No kind of explanation would bring him back. Although she had been very sad at the passing of dear Bobby Lowenstein the previous year, this was altogether different and the first time she had lost someone she had felt so intimate and close to. It was a pain that dug deep, but there was no real time to mourn openly. The news of death was now a quiet, daily occurrence for so many people. But the fact that it was happening all the time didn't make it any more bearable. She had met Humphrey on 6 April. He had been killed on 2 May. They had known each other for less than a month but their love had been real. The day after the funeral she was given a ferrying job. She had to fly over Debden. As she passed over the airfield she saw the space where Humphrey's Spitfire had been, and she couldn't hold it in any longer. Her grief burst out in a loud, primordial wail. No one was there to hear her and that was as it should be. She saw only the earth far below and the infinite sky ahead.

17. Spitfires for Malta

In early 1942, dramatic events on the island of Malta would lead to one of the ATA's busiest periods yet. Under virtual siege by Axis powers since the summer of 1940, the strategically crucial Mediterranean outpost found itself in a desperate situation. A period of intense bombing by German aircraft based on the island of Crete meant vital supplies were unable to reach the population and the military base there. The Hawker Hurricanes defending the island had been seriously depleted. They were short not only of aircraft, fuel and ammunition, but also food. The RAF Squadron Leader on the island put out an urgent plea for a delivery of Spitfires to deter attacks by German and Italian aircraft. The request was not easy to fulfil. It was dangerous and difficult to transport the planes across the Channel safely. It didn't help that, just when the ATA ferry pilots were required to carry out urgent deliveries, much of the country was blanketed in heavy snow.

Following the bombing of the Supermarine factory near Southampton, large-scale Spitfire production had continued in secret. At a former First World War aerodrome at Chattis Hill in Hampshire, Spitfires were being hastily built to expand the RAF fleet and replace lost aircraft. The airfield was on a sloping chalk field, well hidden by the surrounding trees.

In response to the Malta SOS, a number of Spitfires appeared on the books at Hamble. The deliveries were marked P1W, which stands for *Priority 1 – Wait*. This meant they had to provide their best pilots, and that they must fly to their limits when it came to skill and endurance. In other words, there were few excuses for not getting the planes out as quickly as possible. The women at Hamble got wind that these planes were destined for Malta, and that their delivery was a matter of life and death for the island. It was also a matter of life and death for them. The weather was just about as bad for flying as it could be.

A group of pilots including Ann Douglas, an experienced pilot who had formed the Surrey Gliding Club before the war, Anna Leska, Philippa Bennett and the CO Margot Gore, were taken to Chattis Hill to transport the aircraft urgently. This was the first stage in the Spitfires' journey, taking them to sites in Wiltshire, including Colerne, or to Brize Norton to get their guns calibrated and radios fitted, before going on to Renfrew for further transportation. The pilots made the forty-mile journey by car and were ready to fly at first light. When they arrived, visibility was so poor they couldn't even see the trees at the end of the airstrip.

'There's no way we'll make it out today,' said Margot. 'We'll have to wait here.'

The thick snow was combined with a sticky and cling-ing fog. They trudged into the small hut on the edge of the airfield which was draped only in thin camouflage netting and encamped themselves there in their Sidcot suits and flying boots, ready to fly at any moment as soon as the weather lifted. As the sun came up the snow grad-ually melted and dribbled down the insides of the hut, while the snow outside left its slushy brown entrails across the airfield. With visibility still at almost zero and cloud on the deck, Margot and the others had no choice but to sit huddled in the freezing cold with their thermos flasks and soggy sandwiches, waiting for it to lift. By the time darkness fell, there had been no change and they departed frustrated, tired, cold and feeling rather guilty they had not managed to get the Spitfires out.

The second day they repeated the same procedure, driving again from Hamble to Chattis Hill, where they waited once more in the freezing hut with nothing to look at but fog and snow and each other. Margot kept in sporadic contact with Alison King by telephone from Chattis Hill. The pressure was on from Central Ferry Control, demanding to know what was causing the delay. Alison King was on the front line on the telephones, caught between knowing the pilots couldn't very well be expected to risk their lives, but also aware that this was a most pressing emergency. They tried to maintain a sense of humour, all the while remaining in a state of nervous anxiety about having to fly at any moment. Alison advised Margot that it was just as bad in the surrounding areas.

'It's hopeless here too,' Margot replied. 'This weather just will not shift. It lifts every now and again, so we might get off, if there's a gap. Fingers crossed.'

There was no change and they left again at the end of the day, deflated and cross at their lack of control over circumstances. There were more questions from Ferry Control. There had even been a question in the House of Commons. Why the delay when these Spitfires were needed so urgently?

On day three, the cloud seemed to lift very slightly but there was another thick layer of snow on the ground from an overnight fall. Margot and Ann Douglas were ready in their planes with mechanics on standby, just in case. Ann had a map out and was carefully planning her route. If the opportunity arose to take off, she could possibly make it by going along a railway line. If she could see it.

A snowplough was hurriedly trying to shift the snow that had fallen during the night. Just as they had all but given up hope again, Margot spotted a change in conditions outside. The fog had started to thin out, very slightly. With visibility at about 700 yards, and a cloud base of no more than 300–400 feet, she and Ann leapt into action. This was the best they could hope for, and they were under so much pressure they decided to risk it.

'Maybe we can get a couple through,' said Margot.

The Spitfires had to be held down on the field, due to a short take-off, and could only go one at a time, which made it even slower. There was no time to lose. Ann started her Merlin engine and taxied off, doing her checks on the way. Margot ran hers up and ten minutes later she took off too, hoping to make the most of the slight gap.

Ann disappeared into the distance, but almost as soon as Margot got up in the air and did a circuit the fog and cloud came plummeting back down. She couldn't see a thing. She had to fall straight back into the airfield and it was pot luck as to whether she would actually land on it at all. She did manage to get back down, and as she got out of her aircraft she thought she could hear the sounds of a distant Spitfire in the hazy cloud above. She couldn't see anything up in the whiteness.

It's probably Ann trying to land, poor thing, she thought. *I do hope she makes it.* The remaining pilots sat in the hut and waited for any signs of her plane overhead. The buzz of Ann's engine faded away. There was silence.

Margot's mind was thick with worry. She had seen a glimpse of what it was like up there; she may as well have been flying with her eyes shut. She rang Alison, who tried to reassure her that Ann would surely find her way and contact them as soon as she could. Margot felt the weight of responsibility. Should she have let one of her pilots fly in such treacherous conditions?

As Ann took off she stuck to her plan and followed the railway line in a loop, but the fog soon wrapped around her. She tried to maintain her control and keep as low as she possibly could to keep contact with the ground. She was flying at no more than a few hundred feet. Even having slowed the plane by flying with the flaps down, she was still whizzing at a good 140 mph over the barren white landscape, with nothing to guide her but vague, unidentifiable shapes every now and again through the dim fog. They seemed to shift and change like mirages. Her breathing sped up. She began to sweat. She was literally flying blind. She made out the possible hint of the railway line here and there and tried to follow it, then she traced the line of a road uphill. After about twenty minutes she saw a large white area which might, she dared hope, possibly be an aerodrome. As she landed on it everything around was quiet and white and still. Thank goodness it was Colerne. No sooner had she got her breath back than a collection of anxious maintenance staff appeared out of the mist. As Ann departed to deliver her chit they practically flung themselves at the plane, so desperate, and under such pressure, were they to get it fitted with its equipment.

Ann's legs and whole body were shaking as she made the journey across to the watch office to telephone Hamble. She was in shock and her voice was also shaking as she spoke to Alison King. She felt as though she had encountered something unearthly and experienced a brush with death, so close had she been to losing sight of the ground completely. She was relieved when she saw a sprightly junior ATA pilot called Bridget Hill emerge from a Puss Moth taxi plane which had just managed to land. She had come to collect Ann and had even brought some newspapers for her to read. Ann could sit back and relax on the return journey, while Bridget picked her way back through the murk. It was fortunate that Bridget knew the area well since her parents lived near there, because it was almost impossible to see a thing.

On the fourth day, now being harassed by Central Ferry Control virtually on the hour every hour, two more pilots, Anna Leska and Philippa Bennett, managed to take off in their Spitfires. They both had terrible trouble finding an airfield, as Ann had done, and only just about made it to Lynham in Wiltshire through a combination of nerves, skill and no doubt a fair bit of good luck. When they met on the airfield they were so relieved to see one another they almost cried. Anna expressed her thoughts in characteristic forthright fashion, probably including a few four-letter words. They had made it, they were relieved, but there were many more Spitfires required and at this rate it wasn't going to be enough. On day five, the fog began to lift just enough for the others to finally manage to get away. Eventually, after some similarly hair-raising flights, the jobs were all completed.

The only British aircraft carrier available, the *Argus*, was in the Mediterranean. It was sent back to Britain to load fifteen Spitfires on board. These were the first Spitfires to go overseas and they sailed in convoy on 16 February to Gibraltar, where the RAF fighter pilots picked them up. A British freighter had also managed to sail from the UK with another sixteen crated Spitfires. But not long after that some defects were discovered in the fuel tanks of the first lot and they had to be fixed. More Spitfires were delivered on freighters in March but it was simply not possible to deliver the quantity required using the British fleet. These small deliveries were not going to be enough to defend the island for long. Malta needed more Spitfires and it needed them quickly.

18. Drama at White Waltham

In early March the Fairchild Argus taxi plane took off as usual with four people on board bound for their various deliveries. There were ATA pilots Bridget Hill, who had helped Ann Douglas fly home after the emergency delivery of Spitfires, and a tall, dark-haired friend of Bridget's called Pamela Duncan, as well as a pilot called Betty Sayer. They chatted together about the day ahead above the familiar rumble of the Fairchild's engine. They were being flown by an experienced male pilot, Graham Lever. As the aircraft approached the aerodrome at White Waltham, the plane unexpectedly stalled. After that it came in too low and, unable to regain height, began to descend. It was heading right for a bungalow on the edge of the aerodrome of the ATA Headquarters.

A group of people on the ground watched in horror from below, unable to do anything to help. When the plane crashed through the roof, the stunned crowd ran to the bungalow to try and pull those on board from the mangled wreckage. The petrol tank had exploded after coming into contact with a fire in the kitchen of the bungalow and the plane was covered in fiercely blazing flames. Over two dozen people on the ground were injured in the chaos. Among them were some children who had been playing in the street outside. A man named Croft, who was living in a bungalow next door, was blown through a window into the street. Remarkably, a child who was in the front room of the bungalow was rescued with almost no injuries.

Bridget Hill, Betty Sayer and Graham Lever all died from the injuries they sustained. Pamela Duncan, who had been thrown clear of the house on impact, incredibly survived with only cuts and bruises. Betty Sayer, who had come to England all the way from Shanghai at her own expense in 1940 in order to be an ATA ferry pilot, was buried in Maidenhead cemetery. Bridget Hill was buried at a small church near Salisbury. Her fiancé mourned the loss of the young, brave woman he had hoped to spend the rest of his life with. Surviving pilot Pamela Duncan and other ATA pilots from Hamble, including Honor Salmon, who had been at school with Bridget, mourned their friends. In total six people died in four separate crashes that day. The 15 March 1942 was a very sad day for the ATA.

Irene Arckless, whose fiancé Tom Lockyer was a POW in Germany, had got herself into a bit of a fix. Pauline Gower invited her into her office at White Waltham about something of a 'delicate matter', of, she said 'a very serious nature'. The report says that:

The accusation had been made that at an (unnamed) aerodrome an also unnamed duty pilot was reported to have said to Irene – when she requested the delivery chit to be signed:

'I will, if you give me a kiss first.'

Horror of horrors. After her meeting with Pauline, Irene was distressed enough by the whole debacle to write to her boss about it afterwards:

I wish to emphatically deny these words, as never, on any occasion, has such a familiar attitude been adopted by any duty pilot wherever I have been. Further, I would like to place on record that far from adopting a familiar attitude myself – I get my chits signed as soon as possible, and depart from the duty pilot's office.

Having served six months in HM Forces prior to joining ATA I consider, that as an Officer and I trust, a lady, I know how to conduct myself both in and out of uniform . . .

I would like to add that recently at a number of aerodromes visited, & by a number of people, I have been mistaken for another female member of the ATA, whether there proves to be any connection with the charge made & the above – will no doubt, after investigation, come to light.

I am Madam, Your Obedient Servant,

Irene

Pauline replied, somewhat wearily:

With reference to your letter to me of today's date, I would point out to you that you have not been charged with any offence. Certain matters have been brought to my attention and I took the course of discussing these with you in order to clear them up. Under the circumstances I shall make a further investigation but in the meantime I am fully prepared to take your word concerning the particular instance mentioned in our conversation this morning.

A few weeks later, on 15 March, that same tragic day for the ATA, Irene encountered another drama. She was ferrying an aircraft from Catterick to Prestwick via Carlisle. As she came in to land she was in the unfortunate position of being under the eagle eye of a very experienced pilot, Margaret Fairweather. Margaret had been nicknamed 'Cold Front' on account of her at times somewhat severe demeanour. On this occasion she was not impressed with what she saw. In fact, she was so unimpressed she filed a report against Irene.

The final turn into the slight wind which was blowing was done in a series of jerks, in the nature of flat turns, and the machine was then under-shooting by several hundred yards. The engine was now used to recover, and height was again gained. Thereafter the machine made a perfectly good landing on the grass. I was shocked to discover the pilot was 3rd Officer Arckless, who is known to have some experience.

Margaret decided to confront the younger pilot and proceeded to list her errors in no uncertain terms, citing her turns, and the height she had chosen to circuit the aerodrome. She left nothing out of her cross-examination. Irene went red with a mixture of anger and embarrassment. She felt she was being utterly wronged and proceeded to defend herself. She said there had been a fuel leak, which was why she had taken on so much fuel at Carlisle. Margaret queried this and then requested a 'snag report' for that particular aircraft. If it showed no problems, Margaret concluded, Irene would have a lot to answer for. Irene continued to fight her corner, which made Margaret even more critical. She thoroughly disapproved of over-confident pilots and later wrote: 'Her whole bearing during our conversation convinced me that her extreme confidence in herself as a pilot has no justification.'

Irene was having none of it and parried with her own, 'Personally I feel that there is some personal prejudice existing in the whole of Captain Fairweather's attitude.' She ended her own version of events with a characteristic flourish: 'My one ambition is to be an asset to ATA. and not a menace!'

Irene did manage to argue against all of Margaret's criticisms but she was sent back to school for a check flight with the chief instructor as a precaution. She felt very pleased with herself when she was pretty well vindicated:

Miss Arckless . . . has given us such a good report that we have no alternative but to return her to full flying duties. Her explanations on your various points seem fairly satisfactory, but we shall, of course, keep this Officer under observation.

In spite of this Pauline Gower herself weighed in:

Miss Arckless suffers from over-confidence and I am not at all satisfied with her ability as a Class I pilot. I should be grateful therefore if you would keep a careful check on her flying and general airmanship.

It's not inconceivable that the class differences between Irene and her bosses may have played a part in these encounters. Irene was from a relatively humble background compared to many of her ATA counterparts. It may well just have been clashes of personality, and Pauline and Margaret had a duty to be watchful and strict with all their pilots when necessary. In any case, it seemed that no matter how Irene tried, she could not convince those in charge that she was up to the job.

Diana Barnato was grieving the loss of her fiancé, Humphrey, in a Spitfire accident. Although she didn't know at the time, she eventually found out from one of his pilot friends that Humphrey had been killed taking a passenger up with him in his Spitfire. The planes were only meant to carry one pilot in the small cockpit and there had already been a few accidents when pilots had decided to take someone with them to parties or just for jaunts. The news that his bravery had tipped over into recklessness was saddening but their squadron had been under immense pressure at the time, and his spontaneity had for Diana been part of his charm. She also found out from the friend that when she had been grounded at Debden Airfield in her Magister, been forced to stay and fallen in love with Humphrey, the whole thing had been planned. He and a few friends had taken the plugs out of the plane.

She smiled when she found out, remembering the good times. It had been a devastating loss but she had plenty to occupy her now that she was a fully-fledged ferry pilot. Diana was posted at White Waltham, and flew her first Spitfire in October 1941. She had flown seventeen different types of aircraft in the lead-up to her first Spit, including the Hurricane, Swordfish, Lysander and something called a 'Wicko Warferry' – a high-winged monoplane which was designed by an Australian, Geoffrey Wickner, and used as a taxi plane.

Diana's thirteenth Spitfire was an interesting experience. She was taking it from Llandow in Wales to RAF Hornchurch, a fighter station in Essex. As she flew over London the sun was setting into a murky mist and visibility was very poor. A sea fog had rolled off the estuary so that all she could see were the tips of radio masts, and she couldn't possibly land at Hornchurch. She made her way west up the River Lee and tried to find an airfield she knew was at the small town of Broxbourne. In the mist she made out the shape of a plane on the ground and thought she must be in luck and have stumbled upon it. Little did she know it was absolutely tiny – really just a small field – and she might not have room to land before ploughing into a hedge. She went around again.

By this time it was almost dark. She flew very low to get a better look – too low for comfort as she sped over some large glasshouses which housed vegetables being grown for market. She came in as slowly as she possibly could without falling out of the sky and made it in to land, stopping just short of the hedge. When she got into the small aerodrome she realised she had only just missed hitting a tractor which had been on the edge of the field and had crept up behind her plane as she taxied in. The driver was hard of hearing and didn't realise how close he came to having a Spitfire plough into him.

As Diana took the train back to London she was still shaken and worried about how to get the Spitfire out of that tiny airfield the following day. She soothed her jangled nerves at her favourite night club in Leicester Square with some of her RAF chums and took the advice of her more experienced friends about how the devil she was going to get the aircraft out.

One trick of the trade was to use the wind for uplift, but when she got back to Broxbourne she found to her dismay that it was dead calm. The only way to do it would be to pull the aircraft right up against the hedge and have four, instead of the usual two, ground crew lie on the tail to hold it down as the engine was started. That way she could fire it up as much as she dared, and at the crucial moment she released the brakes and nodded her head, and they rolled off as she sped up the field. It all went well and she prayed there would be enough space as she rocketed forward with a roar. She happily lifted off, missing the telephone wires, and the Spitfire disappeared into the distance towards London. The four ground crew brushed themselves down from their fall and stood up to watch the successful lift-off. It had been the first Spitfire in their airfield and all in all had been quite an adventure.

19. Fire-watching

The island of Malta was once again in dire straits. In April of 1942 Hamble got an urgent request for another delivery of Spitfires. The island needed extra supplies or it would almost certainly fall to the Axis powers. An urgent appeal had been made to President Roosevelt for American assistance with an aircraft carrier. There simply wasn't sufficient space in the British fleet to provide the number of planes required. The President agreed to loan the US aircraft carrier *Wasp*, which would depart from Glasgow with several dozen of the planes on board. But first they had to get the planes from the various secret factories around the country to the maintenance unit and then north for departure.

After more P1W deliveries, ATA pilots around the country were waiting with their planes, sometimes all night, for the weather to clear while Central Ferry Control asked again why they couldn't get them out more quickly. There were numerous calls to the Met Office asking if the weather was going to improve any time soon. The ATA pilots weren't allowed to fly at night because the RAF preferred the skies empty in case of

German attacks, and all anyone could do was sit and hope and wait for the clouds to lift.

When the weather cleared and the planes got out, the *Wasp* was eventually loaded up with Spitfires from various sites around the country. She sailed out of Glasgow on 12 April under escort and headed towards the Mediterranean. All but one of the Spitfires reached Gibraltar, where they left for Malta with their pilots and landed safely. Unfortunately for them, the Germans had spotted them approaching on the radar and they mounted a massive attack with around 300 bombers as soon as they arrived. Forty-eight hours later there were only a handful of useable Spitfires on the island.

An anonymous RAF sergeant wrote afterwards:

The Spitfires came waggling their wings as if to say 'OK, boys, we're here.' But that very same evening the 'gen' went round that a big plot was building up over Sicily and within half an hour or so we were to see that Jerry really meant business. Standing at a vantage point in the village of Zurrieq, I saw the first waves of 88s coming all the way over the island. They dived down on Takali where the whole batch of Spits had landed. We tried to count them as they came in, but it was an utter impossibility. Straight down they went . . .

SOS. Send more Spitfires.

*

Almost the entire delivery of Spitfires had been destroyed as soon as they had arrived on the island of Malta. On the brink of being taken by the Axis powers, there was no option but to mount another operation straight away to send more fighter planes. The aircraft carrier *Wasp* had already reached Scapa Flow on its return journey to America, but near the end of April she returned to the Clyde for reloading. There was another P1W, Priority 1 – Wait scramble by the ATA to get the planes up to Scotland. The Spits were delivered to Renfrew to be fitted, and also Brize Norton and Prestwick. Eventually fifty Spitfires were found and squeezed on board and the *Wasp* departed, and a smaller Royal Navy vessel took some too. A few of the planes crashed before they arrived but about sixty Spitfires were already in the air and ready within about half an hour of their arrival on Malta. This time the operation was a success and the air power of the Axis powers was substantially reduced.

By the spring of 1942 the RAF bombing on German cities had begun to have a noticeable impact on morale in Germany. Shocked by the intensity of the retaliation, Hitler turned his attention back towards Britain. He ordered that the 'air war against England' become much more aggressive, with preference being given to targets 'where attacks are likely to have the greatest possible effect on civilian life'. The resulting retaliatory raids on ports and industrial sites were also to be carried out on places outside London. Baron Gustav Braun von Stumm, who was with the German Foreign Office, is reported to have said in response: 'We shall go out and bomb every building in Britain marked with three stars in the Baedeker guide.'

This led to the nickname 'the Baedeker raids' for the extended bombing campaign on English towns which followed. Between April and June, the Luftwaffe began targeting the country's most appealing historic towns. They included Exeter, Bath, Norwich, York and Cowes on the Isle of Wight, Hull, Canterbury and Deal, and some of their historic landmarks were destroyed in the raids. In June 1942 the Luftwaffe targeted Southampton, and the pilots at Hamble were on edge knowing they were vulnerable. They all lost a lot of sleep during air raids as they lay awake listening to the buzzing aircraft and anti-aircraft fire overhead.

At one point the local civil defence requested that ATA pilots sit up at night and do fire-watching in case of incendiary attacks. If they were lucky, the pilots who did this managed to catch some sleep beforehand between 6 and 7 p.m. Eventually CO Margot Gore had to mount a mighty battle of her own with the civil defence to put a stop to it.

'How can you expect pilots to sit up all night and then fly the next day?' she asked them.

'But we all have to do our bit. Everyone is making sacrifices. None of us *wants* to do it,' they replied.

When Margot reminded them that they were flying valuable RAF planes and if one crashed as a result of pilot fatigue, possibly on civilians, there would be questions, chiefly: why were the pilots so tired in the first place? They finally somewhat reluctantly relented and the women at Hamble were henceforth exempt from night-time fire-watching duties if they were working.

Lettice Curtis had moved out of the house she was sharing with Philippa Bennett in Hamble and into new accommodation at a hotel in Southampton with two other pilots. Living in the middle of this port city, they found themselves in the thick of the nightly air raids as soon as they arrived at the hotel. There were 'red' air-raid warnings, which meant there were aircraft directly overhead. For five consecutive nights Lettice listened to the roar of the aircraft overhead and the anti-aircraft guns firing back at them.

Although the sounds were frightening, she couldn't resist going for a look, strictly against regulations, from the roof of her hotel. She watched as the beams of the searchlights flashed across the skyline of the city. The planes and the tracer bullets were lit up every now and then before the raiders shot off into the blackout darkness again. The planes tended to congregate on the other side of the big expanse of estuary, Southampton Water, because it was away from the barrage balloons. Lettice couldn't help marvelling at the spectacle in spite of its deadly cargo.

20. The Blue Bible

'How do you fly so many different planes without having training on all of them?' was a question often asked of the pilots. Unlike the RAF pilots, who were rigorously trained on a few, very specialised aircraft, the ATA pilots had to be able to fly just about anything at a moment's notice. Now that the pilots were being cleared for the different classes of aircraft, the women too had to become acquainted with the categories which had been worked out to enable them to carry out the job of a ferry pilot efficiently.

With more jobs on the books, more pilots were needed and they also had to be confident to fly any aircraft presented to them, often planes they had never even seen before, let alone flown. To help achieve this, A. R. O. MacMillan, the ATA's chief instructor, had worked out a careful system for classifying the aeroplanes, which meant in theory a pilot could fly any plane in a particular class if they had passed the conversion course.

Class 1 was the first that they were able to fly as they became ferry pilots. These included Tiger Moths and Puss Moths, Magisters and the Fairchild Taxi. Class 2 saw them able to fly single-engine fighters, the Hurricanes and Spitfires, and the Fairey Barracuda, which was an RAF dive bomber developed in 1941. There was a Class 2 Plus, which meant they could add an American plane called an Airacobra, as well as the Typhoon and Tempest, which began to appear later and were even faster, and the American Tomahawk. Class 3 was the twin-engines, the Airspeed Oxford and de Havilland Rapide. Class 4 was the twin-engined-bombers: the Blenheim, Wellington, Dakota and Hampden. Then there was a Class 4 Plus, which they could do if the CO thought they were fit for it, which included bombers like Mosquitos, Hudsons and the Baltimore. This also meant that they would be able to fly the loaded Anson taxi.

By summer 1942 no women were yet cleared for Class 5, which was the four-engine bombers like the Flying Fortress, Lancaster, Halifax and the Liberator, since there was still an idea that they weren't physically capable of managing the bigger planes. After all, the wheels alone were bigger than the pilots! This misconception was about to change.

In order to familiarise themselves with all the new planes, and the others of their class, the pilots were also given what they referred to as the blue bible. This was a ring-bound, or sometimes shoelace-bound, blue leather book entitled *Ferry Pilots Notes*. It contained a page or more of concise notes for every plane they might encounter. There were about 130 of them in total and they all had their own quirks and differences. The pilots also had to study detailed handling notes on each aircraft. They were supposed to read and absorb these in advance, and they had to sign that they had read the handling notes for each aircraft and couldn't take a chit until they had done so. But the blue bible was really what they focused on most and was a godsend for the pilots, who kept it with them at all times. The *Ferry Pilots Notes* gave them everything they needed to know about a plane in easily readable form – landing and take-off speeds, engine type, details about flaps, gills and tanks, stalling and gliding speeds, and ATA-specific cruising speeds which were different to the RAF, who flew a lot higher and faster.

There were also pages of notes about what to do in case of an emergency or forced landing. For example, they had to get someone to guard the plane while the pilot telephoned the Watch Office or ATA operations room. They also had to check that if the aircraft was armed, any guns on board were not loaded before they left, and take details of any damage to the aircraft. The book also contained all the useful checklists for take-off, including one of the most common, HTTMPPFGG. Some of the pilots had their own little sayings for remembering this one, including such gems as Hot MP Fancies Girl. The book also contained other useful information about rpm, gills, climbing boost, ATA cruise and revs, slow flying, stalling speeds, effect of flaps being put down, landing checklists and checklists for after landing, such as unlocking the tail wheel, opening the gills, putting the flaps up, and so on.

When it came to the individual aircraft, there were precise notes about things to look out for. For example, that the Spitfire had a heavy nose on the ground. You had to prime a Stirling's starter engines before landing. You had to pull the Tempest's emergency exit handle 'really hard'. There was advice on everything, from starting, brakes, tanks and propellers to fire extinguishers. On the Dakota, there was a useful note: 'Warning: tail wheel lock is under throttle NOT (as marked) next to oil controls.'

As well as the blue bible, pilots found other ways to remember all the details and quirks of all the different aircraft they were given. Jackie Sourer wrote notes about how to fly on all kinds of scraps of paper, including her 'To do' list, alongside such domestic concerns as 'mend stockings' and 'buy tea'. Sometimes the pilots gave airmen a lift back in bad weather, and on one such occasion when one was hitching a ride with Jackie, he told an officer afterwards that the journey had been all right, but he had been concerned the pilot had been, as he thought, reading a novel through all that bad weather. 'Oh! That wasn't a novel,' chimed in Jackie cheerily, 'that was my *Pilots Notes*. I've never flown that plane before!' upon which the airmen looked even more horrified.

This was the only way the pilots were able to handle the ever-increasing number of different aircraft they might encounter as the war went on.

One of these new planes was the de Havilland bomber, the Mosquito, which started rolling off the production

17. Margot Gore (*left*) in a Tiger Moth just after the war.

18. Lady Mary Bailey and the light tourist plane in which she did an 18,000-mile trip around Africa in 1929. She joined the ATA only briefly.

19. Hawker Hurricane – the first operational fighter the women pilots flew.

20. Avro Lancaster B-1 on a test-flight.

21. Supermarine Spitfire and Hawker Hurricane.

22. The Spitfire became a favourite among the ATA pilots.

23. Spitfire factory.

24. Lettice Curtis, Jennie Broad, Audrey Sale-Barker, Gabrielle Patterson and Pauline Gower with an Airspeed Oxford.

25. Eleanor Roosevelt visits the ATA Headquarters at White Waltham, with Pauline Gower, Gerard D'Erlanger and pilots Opal Anderson, Jane Plant and Virginia Farr.

26. Engine aircraft and theory class: Helen Richey, Irene Arckless, Faith Bennett, Honor Pitman, Jennie Broad and Louise Schuurman.

27. Jackie Sorour climbing into a Spitfire.

28. Irene Arckless in her ATA uniform.

29. Pauline Gower (*left*), Commander of the ATA, and Jacqueline Cochran, Flight Captain in charge of the American women pilots welfare.

30. Diana Barnato Walker after the war.

31. Pilots picking up their chits at White Waltham: Benedetta Willis, Elizabeth May, Zita Irwin, Roy Mary Sharpe, Irene Arckless, Faith Bennett and Lucy Falkiner.

line in 1942. Most of the women were delighted to fly them when they started appearing on the books because they were quite lovely in the air. But they had a few vices, too. If a pilot went too slowly, they literally fell out of the sky. And they had to be careful not to let them overheat.

'Watch your step. They're inclined to bite,' was the word of warning. The *Ferry Pilots Notes* warned them to avoid swing in a Mosquito on take-off, and not to open throttles beyond +2 boost until the first third of a run had been completed, and on landing to guard against undershooting.

With their *Ferry Pilots Notes* safely tucked in their pockets, the pilots also usually got a test pilot or an engineer to show them around a new plane and cockpit. On one occasion, a pilot was intrigued to discover a long rubber tube in the plane. When she enquired what it was, she was told in a knowing whisper that it was for 'gentlemen pilots'.

The other item the pilots always carried was their log book, where they meticulously recorded their pilot hours, number of passengers, type of aeroplane, where and when it was collected, and destination and length of journey.

They sometimes found themselves flying some real old crocks nearing or past the end of their working life, and this could be quite risky. There were some planes most people didn't like. One of these was the Airacobra, which had a 'tricycle undercarriage'. It was an American aircraft which arrived in crates and had to be reassembled, tested and flown to Cosford in the Midlands, where it was taken to pieces and then sent to Russia. It was unpopular because it had a tendency, when the pilot was switching from one wing tank to another, for the engine to cut out. Two pilots had to make a forced land them, which was a frightening moment for them, because the engine was at the rear, and if the plane crashed the engine would most likely come right through the pilot's back. The propeller would probably also end up through your legs. Moreover, it was difficult for the pilots to see out of the Airacobra's thick armour-plated windscreen, which essentially meant navigating backwards. The women at Hamble tried their best to get rid of them as quickly as possible.

Another plane which wasn't everyone's favourite was the Tomahawk. Margot hated it, as she found her legs were too short. It had toe brakes and a stick which dug hard into the stomach. She could keep the plane straight only if she could lock the tail wheel, but she found it very hard to reach. Whatever their quirks and difficulties, though, they couldn't refuse a plane.

By 1942 Hamble had grown considerably in scope and scale. They had their own WAAF officer and assistant, and a teleprinter linked to weather centre forecasts, which gave them detailed printouts every morning as to the likely weather. There was an old man in the office overnight whose arduous job it was to write down the details of all the aircraft in a book. Margot and Alison King would then make out a programme of who was to fly what and where and whether it was safe the following morning.

Margot's main job as CO was to know all her pilots very well, then to decide when a pilot was fit to move on to something more complicated and go on a conversion course. She also had an adjutant, two operations officers and a Met officer called Jackie (who was called Jackie Met to distinguish her from South African Jackie Sourer). Everyone liked her. There was also a sergeant, transport section staff, a flight captain, first officer and several flight engineers, as well as canteen staff and a medical nurse. All in all it was a large and efficient organisation with many people involved in maintaining its smooth operation.

Alison would, with the help of Margot, or Rosemary the Deputy CO, co-ordinate the daily running of the pool. This involved everything down to making sure all the pilots had a meal, had their Met forecasts, the right vehicles, and liaising with operations officers at HQ and Central Ferry Control to piece together this complex jigsaw. Alongside her, Margot was a well-respected and capable leader. Behind her natural confidence, however, she felt the weight of responsibility. Her job became ever harder as they took on less experienced pilots. Each pilot, whether new or old, also had their own foibles, quirks and characteristics which Margot had to keep an eye on. Some didn't like bad weather, others didn't mind handling trickier aircraft, some were a bit nervous of some planes, others were over-confident. The strain of making crucial decisions for so many other people, especially the less experienced and more vulnerable, took its toll.

21. A Bit of Luxury

Nancy Miller arrived at Liverpool dock exhausted and relieved. She had survived the perilous journey from North America across the Atlantic. Despite several alarms along the way, there had been no actual attacks by German submarines aimed at her ship.

Nancy was one of the final group of women to arrive from Jackie Cochran's group of American pilots. Before she left home, she had heard that the Brits were starving and had packed accordingly. An old-fashioned travelling trunk and three suitcases were crammed to the gills with canned food, peaches, apricots, pears, baked beans, spaghetti, lima beans (known to the Brits as butter beans) and peas, and even a bottle of special salad dressing. She also had an ample supply of winter clothing just in case, although it was mid-summer when she arrived.

The barrage balloons and bleak, bombed-out streets were a shock to Nancy, who had not long before been in sunny, carefree California. She stayed at a local hotel where Jackie Cochran had arranged to meet her new charges. While she lay in an unfamiliar, dingy room, Nancy was woken up suddenly that night by an awful sound. She wondered for a moment whether it was coming from under her own bed. Thank goodness, in the basement where the other guests were sheltering the bar was open. They explained it was an air-raid warning and the 'Wailing Willie' or 'Moaning Minnie', as they called it, was a regular occurrence people had come to expect at any moment.

Everything was new to Nancy. Not just the war, but all things English. Cars and moustachioed taxi drivers careering about on the wrong side of the road. Strange linguistic expressions she had never heard before. Even the money was peculiar and made no sense. Railway stations were confusing and there were no clean soda fountains on the streets or shining drugstores on the corner. Most distressing of all, there was a distinct lack of proper ice cream. At every turn Nancy was reminded she was in a foreign land and far away from home. She didn't have time to dwell on it for long, though. There followed a swift procedure of security checks, alien registration cards, photographs, medical checks (fully clothed, thank goodness) and then on to a billet in Luton where she was staying with a local family. It was here she started elementary training and ground school.

The course was rigorous and unrelenting. There were RAF maps to get her head around, and the different instruments on all the British aircraft to learn. Morse code and cross-country navigational theory were taught in the classroom, before she took to the air.

She started to familiarise herself on the map with the

bendy medieval roads, a stark contrast to long, straight American highways. There were numerous strange landmarks which made up the British landscape. There were new words and phrases in general use in English, such as pavements for sidewalks and trousers for pants. Someone offered her orange squash. She said 'yes, please' expecting a large vegetable and was confused to be handed a glass of sickly orange drink. But there were also things which were differently named when it came to aircraft, petrol and gasoline being the most obvious. It was very amusing for Nancy when she found out that what she knew simply as 'take-offs and landings' the British called much more descriptively 'circuits and bumps'.

After ground school, it was time to get to the real flying. Nancy was shocked when she found herself climbing into ropey old Harts, 1930s fighters which were well beyond their best. She prayed every time she landed in one of those that the wheels wouldn't buckle under her.

The weather was something of a shock, too, compared to Nancy's home town where skies were often clear and it was certainly a lot more predictable. Aerobatics were off limits to ATA pilots. But some of the more playful instructors couldn't help throwing them in for a bit of fun, to test the pilots' reactions.

Nancy was being instructed by a tall, straight-backed, well-spoken chap called Pennington-Leigh. He had a voluminous handlebar moustache, which some pilots joked they used (or really did use) as an artificial horizon if they were behind him. As he and Nancy took off one morning, Pennington-Leigh suddenly did a few slow rolls. Nancy's stomach heaved but she wasn't sick. Then he made a sudden dive towards the airfield. She gasped. The air speed indicator was soon 'off the clock' at around 300 mph. They pulled up and then the aircraft went over again. Then it went right side up, but this time it was heading straight towards the endless blue of the sky and beyond. Before Nancy knew what was happening, Pennington-Leigh abruptly 'cut the gun'. The engine stopped.

'Over to you,' he said nonchalantly.

When they got back on solid ground, Nancy was shaken but happy to have made it. Pennington-Leigh was not looking so happy. During the aerobatic rolls, 30 bob had fallen from his pocket. It had been an expensive ride.

As rationing had tightened, food was in short supply, but people had got quite used to eking things out and felt quite healthy. The ATA pilots devoured their ration of chocolate if they were hungry, or if they didn't need it, they saved it for their younger nieces, nephews and children, who were eternally grateful for any sweet stuff in these lean times.

As the Americans had set up squadrons across Britain there were some surprise moments of luxury. The Americans had access to their own plentiful food supply since they were not subject to rationing and were able to import their favourite things from the US.

Sometimes the British ATA pilots got a taste of how the other half lived. One day, Margot Gore took an aircraft to an American squadron in Christchurch, and the Commanding Officer asked if she would like to stay for lunch in the officers' mess. Not one to turn down a meal, she stayed. She was in utter disbelief at what she saw when they brought out the food.

'I haven't seen steak for years,' she said. The said piece of meat was so huge and juicy it resembled a doormat in comparison with the thin slivers she had grown used to. Margot began to tuck in, but she very quickly found after about four mouthfuls that she was unable to eat any more. Clearly her stomach had shrunk and her appetite had decreased from the rationing.

Must be about half a pound, she thought, and then there was a huge pile of vegetables on the side, too.

The American pilots beside her were laughing as she put down her knife and fork. They simply couldn't believe she hadn't eaten steak for so long. She cut off a little two-ounce strip.

'See that there,' she said. 'That's all the meat I've had per week for four years.'

Their faces fell. She realised at that point that the Americans had had no idea about the scale of British rationing.

'But how do you look so well, with so little food?' one of them asked her.

'You don't need all that meat, really,' she replied, and

at that moment, the thought of putting away that whole lump of cow simply made her stomach turn.

'It was lovely, though,' she said, trying to force one more, tiny mouthful down and not wanting to seem ungrateful at their largesse. When the meal was over the CO of the squadron came out with a small packet in his hand. By this time, Margot had acquired a little pet dachshund.

'This is for your pooch,' he said jovially.

The pooch won't be having that, she thought as she pocketed the meat.

Later that week she regaled her fellow pilots with the story, some of whom had experienced something similar on their own visits to American squadrons. She had made a whole meal for Alison and their housemate Helen from the remaining steak which had been meant for one person. The pooch, not wanting to be left out, had to make do with the back end.

Apart from the odd moment of luxury at an American base, most meals were quite bland in Britain at the time, unless you bought on the black market. There was a lot of gloopy macaroni cheese, baked beans, cauliflower cheese, and very little meat. It all seemed to be the same colour. When the Dig for Victory campaign kicked off there were more vegetables, but formerly available luxuries like oranges, sugar and butter became quite scarce. There was no particular shortage of the *amount* of food, it was just that what they did have was often very dull.

22. Heavy Twins

After her recent trouble with Margaret Fairweather and Pauline Gower, Irene Arckless was finally promoted to second officer. She desperately hoped her fiancé Tom might be released, or even mount an escape from the prisoner of war camp in Germany.

She sent him a birthday card with two dogs on the front. It found its way eventually by air mail to Prisoner Number 470, Stalag Luft 1. The card was printed with the words:

To Greet you Heartily
this Birthday Morning
and to Wish you
a Host of Happy Days
from

Then in Irene's own swirling hand it said simply:

Renee
With all my love darling

Throughout the summer of 1942 there were still a lot of Mk I Hurricanes on the books. Irene Arckless had her fair share of them. With these aircraft, the undercarriage often had problems with retraction on take-off. One day, Irene was faced with the situation where, although the starboard leg had gone up, the port leg had not. As she said in a report afterwards, she 'flew around for about half an hour as I tried either to get the port leg up, or the starboard leg down'.

She used the emergency methods they had been taught, but it was no good. She couldn't shift either of them. Irene did a circuit of the aerodrome, wiggled her wings and did all kinds of other 'amazing actions'. She elaborated in her report that she

> [. . .]*trimmed aircraft to fly hands off as well as was possible under the circumstances, took both hands off and feet off everything and tried brute force to move the selector lever . . . during this period the aircraft certainly appeared to perform some remarkable antics! I then did a further circuit and went in to land. Port wheel fortunately retracted and I made a normal crash landing.*

Having survived this rather terrifying incident, Irene was sent on a conversion course to fly more aircraft. The report on her performance was, once again, positive.

> *from A. G. Head, Temp. O.C. Training Pool*
>   *a keen and safe pilot who has shown considerable initiative and resourcefulness. A likeable personality who is inclined to be*

*rather high spirited but whose work is of a high standard. An
extremely good navigator who will make a most useful ferry
pilot. She had to cope with a difficult problem in a Hurricane
with undercarriage selector trouble recently, and belly landed it
with less damage than the Engineer Officer of the Station had
ever seen before with similar circumstances. She was exonerated
by the Accidents Committee, thus proving her School reports to
carry considerable weight. All her work in Training Pool has
been very satisfactory.*

Another vindication for Irene Arckless.

Veronica Innes was also sent on another conversion
course. This time on heavy twins, Class 4, which meant
training on a heavier Wellington bomber. Although
some people hankered after the larger planes, Veronica
didn't like them much.

'It's like flying around in a pair of railway carriages,'
she said to her friend Mary Hunter. 'No finesse required
whatsoever. In fact,' she huffed, 'the more ham-fisted
you are with it the better.'

In the end she found the only way she could fly the
Wellington effectively was propped up with four cush-
ions, lying practically flat on her back. On her first solo
flight she came up at such a flat angle she nearly hit the
watch office. After that, and fourteen hours on the Blenheim, it was back to Luton converted to Class 4. Despite
her promotion, she still preferred the nifty single-engine

fighters to these big double-engine brutes. But a ferry pilot couldn't afford to be picky.

Veronica's skills on two-engines would soon be tested. As usual, she went in to check the Met report before a collection, and it was clear, although with storms across the rest of the country. She decided to risk it and get away quickly, rather than be grounded for ages. While she was warming up the engine, a thick black dog of a storm was just hitting the edge of the airfield. She decided that she could just get away before it hit. As she took off, thick plops of rain were beginning to come down on the cockpit window. Then there was a terrific crack. Dust whirled about the cockpit and into her face. She looked up and saw the dark sky above. The hatch had blown open just after take-off. With a deafening noise, and the rain and wind whirling about the cabin, and the hatch flapping, she had to put her goggles on. She braced herself. There was no choice but to carry on to the next airfield. On arrival after a literally hair-raising journey to Ternhill, it was discovered that one of the engines had caught fire. When the Accidents Committee tried to blame Veronica for not carrying out proper engine checks, this really took the biscuit. Eventually she talked them round, and they put it down to 'cause unknown'. It didn't do anything to improve Veronica's love of the Wellington.

There was a flurry of concern when one of the original eight pilots, Mona Friedlander, collapsed suddenly. She had developed a splitting headache and was swiftly sent home to bed. She stayed there for a week but was still unable to focus and felt generally awful. No one knew what was wrong with her, and she was very alarmed when she came out in boils and all kinds of pain and discomfort. When she collapsed again, a doctor eventually came to the conclusion that Mona must have suffered from carbon monoxide poisoning. There was one likely culprit.

A new single-engine aircraft had been developed with a view to improving on the Hurricane and Spitfire. It had become increasingly urgent to compete with the Luftwaffe's prize fighter, the notorious Focke-Wulf FW 190, so the powerful Hawker Typhoon had rolled off the production line. It transpired that Mona had flown one of the new fighters before she collapsed, and that there had been several accidents with these planes, even pilot deaths, especially when it was on the ground taxiing. The news finally broke when a male pilot parachuted out after being poisoned and lived to tell the tale. The Typhoon had a short exhaust pipe coming up through the cockpit floor, which meant the deadly and odourless gas had been able to seep into the cabin. Fortunately for Mona, her journey had only been a short one, but she was seriously weakened by the effects of the carbon monoxide. ATA pilots were issued with oxygen masks after that, but it was too late for Mona. She never really recovered properly and was invalided out in October 1942. She had flown over thirty types of aircraft.

23. Licensed Bandits

The autumn of 1942 saw a thick fog and heavy clouds come down, making flying quite treacherous for the ATA. This was no problem for Margie Fairweather's husband, Douglas. The rather rotund, energetic and loveable character got on with all the pilots, who had nicknamed him 'Poppa' Fairweather, and also 'Captain Foulweather', on account of the fact that he was definitely not a fair-weather flier, as his name might suggest. Everybody agreed that he had the keenest eyes: he seemed to be able to see in almost zero visibility. Rosemary teased him jokingly that he was too big to fly anything but the Anson, but in truth he was the best navigator anyone knew, and he loved flying the Faithful Annie in all weathers.

Poppa was often there with the Anson taxi plane to rescue a stranded pilot who found themselves stuck at an airfield, hundreds of miles from home. Diana Barnato found herself in just such a situation after flying to Prestwick in Scotland in a Miles Master. She was bracing herself for a freezing, crowded journey home on the overnight train when Poppa appeared in the mess and offered her a lift back to White Waltham. He had to first get permission from the CO of the training pool where she was based, and in no time he had sweet-talked them round, saying he could get her there much more quickly than if she took the train, even via Belfast where he was headed. So they headed out over the Irish Sea to Belfast. They couldn't find two hotel rooms, so Diana contacted some friends who were stationed there, and Douglas took a room. In the morning they climbed aboard the Anson again and took off in a thick fog.

Diana was amazed when Poppa took out a tiny, crumpled map, propped it up in front of him and set off in virtually zero visibility in roughly the direction of England. He proceeded to smoke one cigarette after another the whole way and the cabin filled with thick smoke. After some time in the haze of both the cabin and the murky cloud and mist outside, Douglas stubbed his latest cigarette out and hid it. He then started to descend. Diana could not believe it when they emerged from the clouds and were right above Maidenhead. Poppa really did have a navigator's sixth sense. Douglas brushed away the piles of ash which had collected all over his rather large belly and grinned as he pulled back the joystick. Diana gawped in amazement as they taxied into White Waltham. She had no idea how he had worked out the way, without wearing a wristwatch. He told her it was simple. He had calculated the length of the journey by the number of cigarettes he had smoked. 'A total of twenty-three, with seven minutes per cigarette,' he said.

'But promise not to tell them I've been smoking.' The powers that be thoroughly disapproved of his smoking mid-air, but they never could stop him. As they came to a stop he opened the window and it became impossible to tell what was cigarette smoke, and what was fog.

While great strides had been made when it came to female equality in the ATA, women had still not flown the four-engined aircraft. As more of these were required it wasn't long before the argument for training the female pilots to fly them gathered momentum. The Advanced Training School at the ATA was extended to train more pilots, and Lettice Curtis, who was in an all-male ferry pool at the time, found herself put forward. She was glad that the ATA's chief instructor, MacMillan, was not anti-women and had no qualms about letting her join the course. The plane she practised on was a Mk II Halifax, and her instructor was a Polish pilot, Klemes 'Dluga' Dlugaszewski, who had been one of Poland's first commercial pilots and escaped Poland before joining the ATA. They would take the aircraft for circuits together around the various RAF airfields. The pressure was on both of them: Dluga was expected to bring his 'girl pilot' up to speed, while Lettice felt she couldn't fail, because if she didn't do it right, then she would muck it up for all the others and it would be declared that women simply couldn't fly the heavy planes.

While Lettice was in the middle of her training,

Hamble got some shocking news. Jovial, funny Armstrong Payn had died of complications with his stomach condition. It felt wrong, somehow, to everyone who knew him at the ATA that he had died of something so prosaic as a stomach ailment, given the risks they all took every day. But it didn't much matter to Armstrong now. His funeral was scheduled for 26 September.

It was also a perfect day for flying a Halifax. Lettice Curtis was reaching a crucial moment in her training when she got the horrible news of Armstrong's death. Somewhat sick at heart, on the advice of her CO, she took her lesson in the Halifax and missed his funeral. She briefly took the controls of the plane and made some circuits. She was the first woman to take the controls of a four-engined bomber.

Not long afterwards there was a buzz about White Waltham. The DRO (Daily Routine Orders) said all pilots must wear 'full dress' in a few days' time. *Must be a parade or something*, thought Nancy Miller, one of the American contingent, as she passed the notices. Skirts would be the order of the day. Positively no slacks. And hair strictly above the shoulders.

As the big day approached, everyone was rushing about making sure that nothing was out of place, and rumours circulated that some bigwig must be coming.

'Could be the King and Queen, or the Prime Minister,' were among the speculations. It transpired that not one but three dignitaries were heading their way.

Eleanor Roosevelt was on what the press called a 'hustle tour', studying what women were up to in wartime Britain. She was joined by Churchill's wife, Clementine, and a visiting Colonel (Mrs) Hobby of the US Women's Army Corps. The ATA arranged a greeting party, with groups of the new American women pilots selected to stand in front of various aircraft on the tarmac. The air of ceremony was somewhat dampened, literally, by the pouring rain which arrived without apology just in time to greet the VIPs. The First Lady was draped in a huge fox fur complete with tail and wearing a jaunty hat. She was accompanied by Gerard d'Erlanger and Pauline Gower, who took her on a tour round the airfield where she exchanged words with some of the American pilots.

Nancy Miller was fortunate enough to find herself standing under the protective overhanging wing of a Fairchild Argus, until she had to step forward to receive Mrs Roosevelt, who was being followed along dutifully by a fireman in a flat cap who was holding a vast black umbrella. Some of the other girls got a thorough soaking as they waited for their turn to meet the President's wife. Pauline Gower got drenched as she couldn't very well shuffle under the First Lady's umbrella with her. Mrs Roosevelt posed for the press in front of a Lockhead Hudson plane which was draped in the American flag.

The Americans found the visit exciting and were happy to get a chance to gorge themselves on the home-style feast laid on in the guests' honour. The excitement continued even after the VIPs had left. An air-raid warning sounded and the sirens wailed around the aerodrome. The rain may have prevented an accurate hit, because the bombs missed White Waltham and landed in a nearby airfield. There was gossip in the shelter about whether, and if so how, the word had got out about Mrs Roosevelt's visit. Whether or not it was a fluke or inside information, ATA HQ had been spared.

Another pilot sheltering from the rain that day was Lettice Curtis, who had been brought in from her Class 4 conversion course to stand under the wing of a Halifax in honour of her achievements. On hearing that a woman was training on a big bomber, the press revelled in announcing the momentous news the following day: 'Girl Flies Halifax'.

Two days later, now feeling the weight of immense pressure having had her training announced publicly at a critical moment, Lettice braced herself for her first solo flight on the four-engined plane. Her instructor smiled and got out of the Halifax, leaving her and the flight engineer completely alone. She didn't find it too hard to handle, only noticing that it took a bit of welly to shift the ailerons. Other than that, it didn't seem much heavier than a Wellington. When she came in to land, her instructor, Dlugaszewski, greeted his student at the edge of the runway with a proud salute.

*

Margot Duhalde returned from White Waltham, where she had been sent to learn some mechanics, and some more English. Once she had arrived at Hamble, she got into a sticky feud with Anna Leska. No one could work out exactly what had sparked it off, but they were both forceful characters and were very soon at each other's throats, at times almost literally. It may have been something to do with Margot's connection to the Free French and Anna's experience in Paris, but whatever the cause, it became something of a dangerous situation, which resulted in their cutting each other up on the runway and even fighting in the air in mock dog fights on the odd occasion.

Margot Chile, as they called her, had a boyfriend, Leader Gordon Scotter, who made her tell Margot Gore, the CO, what was going on. He was really quite worried it could end up with one or both of them killing themselves. In the end Chile had to apologise in front of Margot Gore. Afterwards, though, she threatened to knock Anna's teeth out.

In October 1942 Veronica Innes got the news that she was to be posted to Hamble with her friends Mary Hunter and Honor Salmon. The same month she was involved in making a film with the Crown Film Unit at Pinewood studios. They recorded some low flying at Aston Down, as well as formation flying, and Veronica was filmed with her parachute over her shoulder, and then in a mock-up of a Hurricane with a Spitfire canopy.

They had set it up with a machine puffing smoke all around the place in the studio.

The main story of the film involved the delivery of a Hurricane being complicated by the pilot being unable to get the undercarriage down and having to do a belly landing. Veronica had to step out and say one line: 'All right, boys, I don't think she'll burn.'

At first it was quite amusing, then they kept shooting the scene over and over again and eventually she found the whole thing rather ridiculous. She was quite relieved when she saw the film later in a cinema and discovered that they had cut her line.

The lounge in the mess at Hamble was a comfortable room with easy chairs and tables where the women played cards, knitted or read on poor weather days while they waited for it to clear. Anna Leska and a few of the other pilots were keen bridge players and it sometimes got quite heated when they were playing a tight game. The lounge had heavy blackout curtains, which gave the room something of a dull atmosphere. On a very dreary day it wasn't much fun sitting around in a darkened room, and Jean Bird, a pilot who was something of an artist, decided to give the curtains a bit of life. She coloured them in bright yellow, and everyone signed their names on them. After that, any distinguished visitors were instructed to add their names to the curtains, and it became something of a Hamble tradition. Among the signatures were 'Pops' d'Erlanger and Sir Stafford Cripps, a fighter pilot who was now Minister of Aircraft Production.

Christmas 1942 was sad for many. There were more husbands, sons and brothers killed or missing. Irene Arckless's fiancé, Tom, was still imprisoned. She went home to her parents on 28 December to celebrate her twenty-seventh birthday. She was a bit shaken by an accident she'd had a week earlier, when an Airspeed Oxford she was flying developed low oil pressure in its starboard engine and she'd had to make a forced landing. The incident was investigated and she was found 'not to blame' but it had been a shock.

She returned to work for the ATA in the new year, more determined than ever to do well for her Tom. On 3 January she was taking another Oxford from an airfield near Cambridge. It was late in the day and her engine cut out during night take-off. As the machine stalled she tried to stay clear of a nearby house and the tip of the wing scraped the ground. Those on the ground saw that the plane was unusually low and saw it skim and shake a hut near some anti-aircraft gunners. Another anti-aircraft gunner said the engines were spluttering as if in trouble. Irene turned to the right and kept losing height. Momentarily she gained some height again, but not enough.

The plane crashed into the kitchen and bedroom above

it of the house she'd tried to avoid. There was a baby in a pram who was not hurt. Irene was pulled from the plane and rushed in an ambulance to Addenbrooke's Hospital, where Dr Ruth Bell, a casualty officer, said that she was suffering from severe shock when she was admitted. Irene had a large laceration of the scalp and a compound fracture of the femur as well as evidence of a fracture at the base of her skull. She did not survie the injuries.

Irene's parents did not identify their daughter's body. Instead, her brother-in-law, LAC Oswald, came and confirmed it was Renee. The plane was officially found to be satisfactory and it remains a mystery why she crashed. There was speculation that the aircraft must have touched a tree as she swerved to avoid the house. The verdict was accidental death.

Irene's funeral service was held at St Aidan's Church, Carlisle, and she was buried at Stanwix Cemetery, her coffin covered in a Union Jack. A firing party from the RAF stood present on the way to the church, preceded by a detachment of ATA pilots. The music included 'Be Thou Faithful unto Death' and Beethoven's 'Funeral March'. Irene had been the first female member from the Border Flying Club, and the first woman in the North-West to qualify as a pilot. 'She went into it with all her zest,' said her father. 'Always, I think, she thought of her sweetheart.'

*

That freezing early winter Diana Barnato was still based at White Waltham. She was on a series of runs around Cardiff and the Bristol Channel delivering various aircraft and had discovered that the area was quite tricky for a number of reasons. Firstly, the ack-ack boys, or anti-aircraft gunners, around Bristol seemed to be a bit trigger-happy. Diana noticed a few times while she was ferrying Hurricanes that she was surrounded by puffs of smoke from their guns. Fortunately she wasn't ever hit.

'I do find it rather incredible,' she said to a friend, 'that they really can't spot the difference between a Hurricane and a Messerschmitt or a Focke-Wulf, but there you have it.' This happened to quite a few people, it turned out, when an enquiry was instigated and pilots came forward.

There were also a lot of seabirds in the area which when flocking together could cause quite a nuisance on and off the runway. Pilots also had to fly in over a dyke past the Bristol Channel, which meant they couldn't come in too low, and there was the inevitable balloon barrage over Cardiff to make things as difficult as possible for take-offs and landings. On one occasion that winter Diana was a passenger in the Anson taxi when it hit a series of gulls on take-off. One smashed the windscreen and was catapulted right down the cabin to the back passenger seats, where it was impaled on an axe which was hanging up. Another was caught in the wing. There was a mess of white feathers, and the cabin was freezing cold, but the Anson managed to put down again without too much trouble.

The next day she had to put down in a Hurricane due to bad weather and was picked up by the Anson again, with another load of ATA pilots. The plane was heavily loaded with twelve people, but they were quite trim due to wartime rationing and it was probably not too overloaded. Quite a few planes had put down, but the pilot, Jim Mollison, Amy Johnson's former husband, was confident he could get through and that it was clearing up. They traced their way up towards Reading, when suddenly, out of the clouds, they saw another plane. Diana thought it was a Mosquito at first but it wasn't long before they saw tracer bullets zipping through the sky towards them. Then, painted on the tail, they saw the swastika. It was a German Messerchmitt Me 110.

'It's a bloody Jerry!' said Jim. He yanked the stick and pulled the Anson up into the clouds. The plane was still firing as it whizzed past them.

When they finally landed at White Waltham there was an air raid in full swing. They all felt quite smug as they stepped out of the Anson while everyone was dashing to the shelters because the plane had flown overhead, when they had actually been shot at by it. The Anson had been fired at, but not hit, by what turned out to be a lone hit-and-run raider. It also turned out to have already discharged its deadly load at Reading railway yards.

As a result of this and a few other encounters with the

enemy, for a while the ATA recruited rear gunners to sit in the gun turret of the Anson taxis. When one of the gunners was asked by an official at the Labour Exchange what exactly his role was as an air gunner if he wasn't in the RAF, the gunner replied that he was in the ATA, which was of course a civilian organisation. The official sighed and said, 'Well, what the heck do I put you down as, then? Licensed Bandit?' Although these licensed bandits fired on occasion, they were not known to have actually shot anything down.

24. Heavy Losses

In the spring of 1942 Tom Lockyer was warned to prepare to move to Sagan, in Silesia, to a big new RAF prison camp. After 'much flap, and under very heavy guard', they eventually arrived. The camp was very new and about two miles from the town in a stretch of young pine forest which had been cleared by cutting down the trees just above ground level. They had no flushing toilets, and seepage pits in lieu of drains, and with the exception of the cook house, only four cold water taps in the whole of the compound, serving over 1,000 men. There were still plans afoot to mount an escape, but the Germans decided to move some of the more troublesome of the inmates to Oflag XXIB, at Schubin, between Posen and Bromberg, in Poland, and Tom was moved again. He wrote in his diary:

> We eventually arrived there, after a rather hectic journey, with a couple of train breaks and much yelling and chatter gun fire, and found that we were under the German Army, a scruffy mob of morons, compared with the Luftwaffe, who looked down their august noses at this green uniformed shower. Security arrangements

by the Army were just laughable, and the Luftwaffe were horrified.
All attempts to reason with the Army proved fruitless (how like our
own bunch of opinionated daffodils), and having got a receipt for so
many bodies, the Luftwaffe departed, muttering darkly that the
bastards could bloody well learn the hard way, blast them.

And they did. Life was tough in the camp and the prisoners talked of little other than how they could plan their escape. One monotonous day Tom was chatting with a bloke who had not been a POW very long, less than a year, and he mentioned that he had just received a letter from his girlfriend who was in the ATA. 'She mentioned that she knew a girl in that mob,' said the man, 'who was engaged to a bloke called Lockyer in your camp. Do you know him?'

Panic stations, I wrote home and to Renee right away. Many
months later got a reply from Renee, saying not to worry, she was
being very careful, and she had wanted to help towards getting me
home, so, being a licensed pilot (A licence), ATA came back into
her mind. Remembering my previous objections, however, she had
made a special journey down to my home to ask my parents'
advice. They thought it a very good thing and advised her to go
ahead. When reminded about my objections, they advised her not
to tell me, then I could not do anything about it, or worry.

Had I known at the time (this happened within a month of
my being reported a prisoner, and letters were only taking about a

month), I could have (a) prevented her from joining, or (b) pulled quiet strings to get her out, if necessary on phoney grounds, as I still knew quite a few people who would have done this for me.

Prior to receiving her letter, however, I was summoned to the SBD's office late in January 1943, and was informed by W/Cdr Hyde that she had been killed in an accident on January 3rd. My people, when they did answer my letters, were full of pompous patriotism. My father, an ex-regular soldier, was full of flag-waving and drum-beating, with all the usual blah of a damned pompous prig who knows he is too old to risk his neck and is determined that everyone else should risk theirs. I did not write home any more.

In June 1943 Diana Barnato was posted again to Hamble, permanently this time. It was always hard for new pilots coming in to such a tight bunch of experienced pilots, but they were all friendly and took her under their wings. In particular Honor Salmon, who had been in some trouble over her flying but was well loved by everyone as a character and had a warm, friendly smile, made Diana feel very welcome and took every opportunity to show her the ropes. Honor lived with her parents near Marlborough, which may account for why she flew nearby in bad weather. Not long after she had joined Hamble, Diana heard the awful news that Honor had flown into a hill near her parents' house in an Oxford. Rosemary Rees was Deputy CO at the time and she took the news and had to go and view the crash site.

The RAF got her body out and set a guard on the wreckage while Rosemary gave instructions. They had salvaged an overnight bag, a watch and, most tragically, Honor's wedding ring. Half an engine was left with a large bit of it intact. The ATA inspector of accidents looked perturbed when he viewed the wreckage and commented that the medics hadn't done a very good job. There was a helmet there, and he told Rosemary not to touch it.

She didn't want to look. She drew a map of the location and had the difficult job of writing to the relations. The only thing she had to comfort her in any way was that more often than not the death of an ATA pilot was instantaneous.

It turned out that Honor had hit a solid wall of cloud and rain. Another pilot, Mary, had waited out the cold front, which had cleared in a couple of hours to clear blue, but Honor did not arrive. Alison King spoke to Mary afterwards and she simply could not believe it.

Six ATA pilots went to her funeral, where they stood to attention and saluted. Her mother had said that she wanted it to be a 'jolly funeral'. Pauline Gower said of this popular pilot, 'Honor will be very much missed, not only as an excellent pilot but as a friend. She was a charming and gallant person.'

When they got the news, Margot had called over the tannoy at Hamble and gathered all the pilots together to tell them. Although she wasn't the first, and wouldn't be the last ATA death, it hit everyone hard as she had been very popular. Diana was shocked and deeply cut up by the news. Honor had been so kind to her. Margot asked if they would like to keep any of her possessions from the locker as a memento and Diana found herself being handed one of Honor's shirts. With clothing rationed, she reluctantly accepted it. She tried it on once and cried so much she could never wear it again.

25. Little Lady Bulldogs

Most pilots could not fix their own engines and they had separate ground engineers for the mechanical side of things, but one pilot who could was Molly Daphne Rose. Molly was the daughter of David Marshall, who founded the Marshall Aviation company in Cambridge. After spending a year at a finishing school in Paris, Molly joined the family business as an apprentice engineer. She learnt to fly in her brother's old Tiger Moth out the back of their place in a field and got her pilot's licence aged seventeen. In 1939, when she was only nineteen, she married the love of her life, Bernard Rose, who became a captain in the 4th County of London Yeomanry, Sharpshooters.

Molly joined the ATA in September 1942 and ended up at Hamble. She progressed to the twin-engine bombers, and fast fighters like the Typhoons and Tempests, and the Mosquito. Her scariest incident was in a Swordfish, an open-cockpit biplane bomber, which was something of a relic from the 1930s. It was unwieldy to handle and nicknamed the 'string bag' by some pilots because of its similarity in shape to a shopping bag. It was an effective and crucial aircraft, though, particularly good at hitting submarine torpedoes. As Molly was flying it the engine cut out suddenly.

Molly knew this had happened to other people. She never expected it to happen to her. There was no time to panic. She was completely alone in the cockpit with no radio, and reliant solely on a map, compass and good old-fashioned eyesight. Scanning the landscape for somewhere suitable to land, she spotted a small field. She levelled up as best she could without an engine, hoping she had room to do a forced landing. The plane was silent but for the whistling wind around her face. It partly glided, partly dropped and veered from side to side in the air currents. Facing into the wind to try and slow down the approach, she gripped the control column and did her best to control the cumbersome 'string bag'.

It came in to land just on target but she soon realised to her horror that it wasn't rolling to a stop, but was hurtling towards a large hedge. Molly hadn't been able to see that the field was sloping downhill from the air, and the plane ran straight through it. On the other side a young lad was ploughing a field, oblivious to the drama unfolding a few feet away. As the aircraft came crashing through the hedge Molly saw him at the last minute, swerving hard left to avoid a collision. The Swordfish shuddered and shook and eventually turned over. After some creaks and groans from the aircraft, there followed an eerie silence.

The lad put down his plough and walked over, unsure

what had just happened. Could it be a German spy coming in under cover? After a few minutes Molly wriggled herself free from the cockpit and climbed out from the upturned aircraft. The young man hadn't expected anyone to land in his field, let alone a woman pilot. 'Will you mount guard while I go and get someone? I can't just abandon it,' said Molly, brushing herself down. She was shaken and dazed but, remarkably, uninjured.

'Oh heavens, look at the state of it,' she said, surveying the upturned and battered plane. 'We can't let anyone get their hands on it.' Before she had left Molly had been warned that it had been fitted with some highly confidential military equipment, something on the undercarriage, she was told, for locating ships. Nobody, but nobody, should be allowed to get hold of it, even if it meant destroying the Swordfish altogether. So the bewildered farm labourer mounted guard for the night, while Molly went off to the nearest aerodrome to alert the RAF that she had crash-landed their plane, and its top-secret equipment.

That night she thought about what she'd say to the powers that be. Could she have avoided the crash? The engine had cut out. It wasn't her fault the field was on a slope. But there would no doubt be questions. Planes were expensive, urgent commodities. All accidents were thoroughly investigated. Molly Rose had no idea what the outcome would be. The RAF came from Cosford. It was a Saturday and all the RAF boys were going to a dance. Molly wasn't very popular when two of them had to miss it to watch her Swordfish all night. The Accidents Committee investigated and Molly was relieved when she was found 'not responsible'.

It's hard to imagine the sheer complexity involved in organising the ferry pools across the country. All the deliveries to be made on any given day meant each of the COs and operations officers had to think on their feet and deal with any sudden changes, mishaps or stranded pilots, and work around mechanical failures. A typical day at Hamble might involve one pilot taking a Spitfire to Brize Norton, followed by a trip in a Fairchild or Anson to Yeovil for another pick-up, taking a Seafire to Lee-on-the-Solent, followed by a Walrus to Cowes, and so on. It was the same story across all the pools, and for Central Ferry Control too, it was like a very complex jigsaw allocating each job to a particular pool.

At White Waltham HQ, the senior commanders issued instructions, and the aircraft were all monitored at Central Ferry Control in Andover, which was the hub for all ATA movement. The operations officers produced a chit with the name of the pilot, type and number of the aircraft, where it was and where it was going. When the pilot delivered the aircraft she tore a bit off the chit and handed it to whoever was in charge at the aerodrome, who then signed to say it had been accepted. Then she either took off again in another plane or was picked up in the taxi, or took the train back. The pilots were routed safely into aerodromes with no radios by flying control, then the operations officers would ring to ask, 'Has Spitfire number x taken off?' Those in charge at the aerodrome would reply, 'Yes', and give the time and the ETA at the destination. The pilots didn't carry much except their ID, flight authorisation card, ferry-pilot notes and their overnight bag, and, of course, their parachutes.

At Hamble Alison King and Margot Gore were always trying to arrange the schedule so as to save as much time and petrol as possible, which meant a constant shifting and checking to see what had been delivered, who was where, who needed picking up in a taxi and who could bring back what from which aerodrome.

When the weather was very bad, Margot had to make a judgement call as to whether it might be a 'washout' and not lift at all. If that was the case, she would let the pilots go home or into Southampton, which had several cinemas where they could catch a film. Southampton was quite bleak by then, bearing the open wounds of recent devastating bombing on many of its streets. Sometimes they went instead to the pretty little cathedral city of Winchester for shopping or tea. It had not been hit so badly and retained much of its olde-worlde charm.

More often than not, if they were ferrying, they were so tired by the end of the day they just had a meal and fell into bed. But when they had days off they found things to amuse themselves and take their minds off the hard work. Some of the younger ones went out to late-night parties and clubs in London if they got the chance. There were lots of men in uniform about, naval officers and other service people, and there was a party-hard mentality for those who wanted it. Some were simply too tired, like Margot, whose job was very demanding, and Rosemary and some of the slightly older pilots, who preferred to avoid the very late and raucous parties if possible. They did enjoy a whisky at the Yacht Club in Hamble, or something to stiffen the nerves in the Bugle, where they could chat and relax after a tough day's flying.

Some of the more active among the pilots found time for some sports and leisure activities in and around Hamble. Margot played squash on the court there. She even had a small sailing boat moored on the River Hamble and a fishing permit. She and some of the others went off for sailing trips in the Solent on their days off, or they hired horses in the New Forest and went riding. Others were good at athletics, or played an instrument, rowed or did gymnastics, all of which helped them with flying, maintaining their co-ordination and quick thinking.

They were by now used to flying aircraft they had never seen, so it was no surprise one morning when an Albemarle, a twin-engined transport aircraft, appeared on Jackie Sourer's chit. She looked at her blue book and got herself ready for take-off, waiting for the green light from the 'caravan' at White Waltham. Then suddenly it changed to red. Someone came running over. The Air Marshal wanted an urgent lift. He did not notice until he was fully on board and Jackie was turning for take-off that he was being flown by a female pilot who didn't, he thought, look much older than sixteen. He made a dash for the door and demanded to be let out. He was not at all happy about being flown by a schoolgirl. It was too late. They were off. Jackie, who had a darkly humorous streak, did nothing to reassure him and said airily, 'You know, I've never flown one of these before.'

'Don't let's talk of heroines of the air,' Pauline once said. 'Flying is a job and like any other it is done by the people qualified to do it. Women are treated exactly like the men. That is one of the things for which I have fought.' Although she had gained something close to equality in terms of work, there was one issue Pauline Gower still felt very strongly about: equal pay for equal work. The female pilots were paid in line with Treasury rules about women flying during wartime, which deemed women's work worth some 20 per cent less than men's, but Pauline was adamant that they should be paid the same.

In 1943 she met up with Sir Stafford Cripps, Minister of Aircraft Production, to discuss the issue of equal pay. At first he said there was nothing he could do, but Pauline had an ace up her sleeve. Most likely she herself had arranged for an MP, Mary Ward, to raise a question in the Commons about it. Pauline told Sir Stafford that this was going to happen, which could potentially be embarrassing for the Treasury. When he left White Waltham, she could only wait for the outcome of the question in the House.

In April it was announced in the House of Commons that women ferry pilots would be getting equal pay from the following month. Mary Ward asked the question of Sir Stafford Cripps and he replied in the affirmative. Tellingly, though, he added that this in no way indicated that equal pay was to be a general rule going forward. It was, it seems, more a momentary wartime 'aberration' thanks to Pauline's tenacity rather than any kind of real progress in terms of equality (as subsequent and current battles being fought on this issue testify). For the women of the ATA, though, it was a momentous achievement. They finally felt they were valued as much as the men and it was a great boost to morale.

On 25 February Lettice Curtis finally completed her Class 5 conversion to four-engined bombers. She had to prove herself worthy more than her male counterparts: instead of the usual seven perfect solo landings she had to pull off no fewer than ten of them. She also had to learn radio procedures for the first time, because the pilots had to radio in for landing. She did all this anyway and passed, the first woman to do so.

On one of her solos, her new instructor Flight Captain

R. H. Henderson was watching as she came in. When her plane didn't bounce or even swing on landing as they had expected in a heavy cross-wind, Henderson was amused by the observing station master's remarks that, contrary to what his boys had told him, those Halifaxes 'must be easy if a little girl can fly them like that'. Lettice was no little girl, and Henderson reminded the SM that her flying record was no fewer than 2,000 hours. Although she had passed, Lettice was very worried for some time afterwards about any small mishaps, or large mishaps, that might happen which would create a sensational news story and jeopardise the chances for everyone else.

In early 1943 Alison and Margot were informed there would soon be a lot of four-engined bombers near Hamble. Some American Fortresses were to be fitted out nearby, and there was a contract for Halifaxes at a local factory. Although Lettice Curtis had converted to the heavies, there was still reluctance in some quarters about letting the women get carried away with themselves and having too many flying them about the place. Pauline was adamant that it made no sense whatsoever to keep her women from flying the planes, particularly since there would be so many near Hamble. She won, again, and Margot was the next to convert to Class 5. She was also sent for the extra training it took to fly the heavy Flying Fortress. Rosemary Rees and Philippa Bennett followed suit, and Joan Hughes not long after.

They all went to Marston Moor in Yorkshire for the

Halifax Conversion Unit and stayed with WAAFs there, who had their own ATA hut. Rosemary and Philippa overlapped on their courses and spent a very amusing evening watching entertainment put on by a Major Gilbey. He brought a concert party which featured sketches and songs performed by a group of young soldiers, who had been taught the routines by Gilbey himself. It was riotously funny and included an all-singing, all-dancing finale of 'Boys of the Bulldog Breed', after which Gilbey ran on stage dressed as a WAAF. He was hoisted on to the shoulders of the soldiers and he sang 'And the Little Lady Bulldog Too'. Rosemary and Philippa were henceforth nicknamed 'the little lady bulldogs'.

While Rosemary was on her conversion course, one day she had four terrified flight engineers on board 'hanging over my shoulder', she said, 'horrified by the idea of a woman flying it with them'. When she started ferrying the four-engined planes, Rosemary was coming in to land when the Air Vice-Marshal was in the office. Hearing a woman's voice on the radio, he asked who it was and waited to meet her afterwards. 'By God, I've seen everything now,' he said when she came in with her chit.

Rosemary absolutely loved the four-engines, and when she got her hands on an Avro Lancaster bomber, she rated it more highly than the Halifax or the Flying Fortress. 'They handle like a car,' she said to her Hamble colleagues, 'more like an eager horse wanting to gallop off than those lumbering Fortresses.' These American planes were a lot more complicated, with lots of electrical switches, although they were very effective and deadly in operations. The pilots always had a flight engineer with them in the four-engined planes because they couldn't change petrol tanks or alter cooling, since they would have to leave their seat and walk to the back. The engineers were trained at Hamble and they knew their duties, which included watching engine temperatures and inspecting the plane overnight to make sure it was ready the next day after a stop-over.

In total eleven women converted to Class 5 across the pools. With its new contingent, Hamble began the job of clearing out the Halifaxes from the nearby factory. There was some bewilderment when these 'little lady bulldogs' suddenly started appearing from the bowels of those ginormous planes. The wheels alone on these heavy bombers were taller than the pilots. One day Joan Hughes and her non-pilot flight engineer were making their way inside after landing a Halifax at an RAF aerodrome.

'Hello,' said Joan cheerily. She produced her delivery chit and put it on the desk in the duty pilot's office.

The duty pilot barely looked up. She stood there for a while, then cleared her throat. He lifted his head. 'The pilot's got to sign in,' he said. Then he looked back down at what he was doing.

'I've just brought this one in,' said Joan. Another silence.

Eventually he looked up at her properly and seemed

really quite cross. 'I said the pilot. Passengers can't report,' he said very slowly, as if speaking to a stupid person.

'I am the pilot,' said Joan, also slowly but trying not to seem too exasperated.

The reality finally dawned on him when he saw her uniform. Unless the Halifax had spirited itself there by some form of black magic, which perhaps seemed to him the more viable explanation, there was simply no alternative other than that she was indeed the pilot. He muttered, 'Then maybe I'm the Air Marshal,' and eventually found it in himself to sign the delivery chit. Even presented with the object in human form herself, resplendent in blue uniform and gold wings, it was sometimes hard for people to believe a mere woman could actually do this job.

Because Rosemary Rees enjoyed flying the bigger planes she also quite often ended up piloting the Anson taxi. She always felt the cold, though, and as the Anson was not very well insulated, being just bare metal, during the winter she would huddle up in as many furs and coats and blankets as she could manage to squeeze on board. Sometimes, if it was very cold, she didn't leave the Anson at all at the various aerodromes and had one of the passengers on board do the necessary reporting in with the air controllers. At one aerodrome at Winchester they were quite perplexed that this mysterious pilot never appeared in person and asked who was 'this fellow Rees who never comes in. Ask him to show himself.'

Rosemary reluctantly extracted herself from her cocoon of blankets and presented herself to the controller as not a fellow at all.

Ferrying a large group of pilots who were also great friends could have its tormenting moments for the Anson pilot. They were often chatting and talking to one another in the back seats and could get quite carried away with their stories. Every now and again, invariably when Rosemary was negotiating a tricky balloon barrage or landing in fog, there would be a great shriek from somewhere at the back. She would sit up and think there was an emergency. 'Everything all right back there?' she would call out anxiously, thinking someone had seen something horrific. The reply would come back, 'Oh, you must hear this. Jackie has just told a most hilarious story.' Rosemary would sigh and request that all amusing anecdotes be confined to the ground in future.

In 1942 Margaret Fairweather was promoted to the position of Flight Captain, which meant there were now two captains in the family. She was given control of the women's flights out of Prestwick Ferry Pool. Known to be a 'reliable and steady' pilot, she also became one of the women cleared to fly the four-engined bombers. She did have a small 'incident' once with a Halifax but was deemed not at fault when it was discovered that 'the bolts securing an engine cowling broke away and fouled a propeller'. In May 1943, however, someone wrote to

Pauline about her in relation to an altogether more serious matter:

> *It is observed that F/Capt Mrs Fairweather is not complying*
> *with Standing Orders re. her hair. Also, this pilot still persists*
> *in wearing grey coloured stockings, whereas black is the order.*
> *Will you please be good enough to point out to this pilot that the*
> *Commanding Officer's Instructions in regard to 'Dress Regula-*
> *tions' must be complied with.*

Margie's husband, Douglas, had been too heavy for ferrying originally, at a portly 16 stone, but he was cleared to fly the Anson and became a regular taxi pilot and ran the group of Anson regulars. By 1943 Douglas was the head of a new communications flight unit, which he had set up himself at White Waltham, called Air Movements Flight. His job included flying service agents, commandos and equipment to the locations of secret sabotage missions, as well as bringing sick and injured servicemen from around the country to various military hospitals.

He preferred to fly without a map, instead using his remarkable sixth sense for navigating. When some people complained about this he appeased them by fixing up a map in his aircraft. On closer inspection it was revealed to be a map of Roman Britain. Douglas often had a cigar or cigarette in his mouth and ash all down his tunic. His methods and his character were unconventional to say the least. He was described by one colleague as a most likeable personality, but 'complex and not uncoloured by guile'. The guile could be very useful when he was negotiating the tricky world of wartime aviation, including getting the aircraft he needed for his demanding job in Air Movements Flight. He could be very funny, too. Once when he was taking a group of pilots in the Anson over Scotland, he suddenly shouted at them all to get to their feet in his broad Scottish accent. They all stood to attention in hurried confusion, then sat back down again. When they asked him a little while later why they'd had to stand, he replied, 'When we're passing over Bannockburn, laddie, every bloody Englishman has to stand up!' Douglas was certainly a character, and Margie loved him deeply. In September 1943 there came the following note:

> *Flight Captain Mrs Fairweather is pregnant and I recommend that her contract is terminated with three months' pay in lieu of notice.*

Margaret was nearly forty-two and her husband was fifty-three. She and Douglas had found out they were to have a baby.

26. Invasion Orders

The pilots had to have a medical check every year, and they took health matters quite seriously. If you had a cold, you were grounded and weren't allowed to fly, so they started giving injections against colds, mainly because it was not good to fly at altitude with a blocked head. If a pilot was pregnant, she had to stop flying too, but they weren't always discovered as quickly as Margaret was. Mary Hunter went off to have a baby when she got pregnant. Later Jackie Sourer, who in January 1945 became Jackie Moggeridge after marrying a soldier called Reg, turned out to be seven months pregnant and still flying. Eventually she went off to have her baby and moved to Taunton.

In early 1943, before she went off to have her baby, Jackie Sourer was crying in the locker room. Veronica stumbled upon her red-eyed and sitting looking as though the world had ended.

'What's wrong?' she asked and put an arm around her, thinking something awful must have happened to Reg.

'I'm on the list,' she said, gasping through the tears.

'What list?' asked Veronica.

It turned out that Marion Wilberforce was going off

to become CO of another all-women's pool in the Midlands at RAF Cosford. It had already got something of a reputation: they had heard that the 'tough babies' were going there, while the 'glamour girls' were staying at Hamble. In the end neither Veronica nor Jackie went to Cosford. Like Hamble, it was located next to key factories and maintenance units which needed to be swiftly cleared out, and Marion Wilberforce ran a tight ship there. Women were also posted to some of the male pools, at Prestwick, Kirkbride, Ratcliffe and White Waltham among others, but this was usually on an ad hoc basis, and the ferry pools were never fully integrated in any real sense.

By all accounts, all of the women who spent their time at Hamble were happy to be there. For those who lived with local families, they had the benefit of going back to a home. Jackie was with the Greenhills, who were retired. Veronica and her friend Mary Hunter ended up in Burseldon with a Mrs Sheila Norris and her ten- and eleven-year-old sons Peter and Michael. Honor Salmon had lived there with them before she died, and a woman called Lorna Parker also lived there with her mother, so all in all it was quite a crowded household. The whole place was warm and homely, though, with its big roaring fire and large living room where they all sat round the radiogram together after work and talked about their different days, and they all loved living there. The food, which was cooked by Mrs Parker, was also spectacular, in spite of the rationing, particularly the puddings. The house, High Firs, was actually a small-holding with a pig and a cow in the garden and Mrs Norris spent much of her time dealing with this, which also accounts for why they had a bit more food than other households.

Nancy Miller from America also found herself billeted with a local family, the Whitcombes, who had two sons, Mervin and Peter. Nancy was also in the fortunate position of having a great cook in Mrs Whitcombe. She was in fact quite spoiled, having a hot water bottle every night and her washing done, and even real eggs. She even had her own little sitting room next to her small bedroom. The two boys found it amusing to take turns calling up to her each morning for breakfast, and then their regular 'Good morning, Miss Miller' was always a delight to hear from those chirpy little boys. Although Mrs Whitcombe did her best to feed Nancy as well as possible, there were some things she missed. Certain vegetables which had been plentiful at home were barely obtainable, and meat and sweets were very reduced, of course.

She looked forward to the chance to drop in at an American squadron and taste the delights of the unrationed, such as steak, peach pie, peanut butter, jam or fruit juice, as well as American-style hospitality. Not long after she joined Hamble, Nancy converted to Class 3, and she soon got a taste of an American plane she had seen before, the Mustang. These were designed for very low-level attacks and she delighted when she got one in going as low as possible, hopping over telegraph wires and trees at a whopping 275 mph. It was quite a thrill to see the ground whizzing underneath at such a momentous speed.

For the American pilots, receiving mail from home was the greatest morale booster. Each pilot had a pigeonhole for mail which they checked religiously even if there was no hope of anything. But when something did come, including packages of food, make-up, clothes and much sought after American magazines, it would keep them going for weeks until the next time.

Nancy was asked that summer if she wanted to take part in a radio broadcast to the States from the American Red Cross Club on Piccadilly in London. The place was abuzz with American servicemen and Nancy was interviewed by a lieutenant before an interlude from a swing orchestra. It was all quite amusing and the interviewer even joked that she should marry him and be the main breadwinner while he did the washing-up! Best of all, it was broadcast to her parents in the States on her twenty-fourth birthday. What a birthday present to know her parents could hear her voice all the way across the Atlantic!

When they weren't working, the Americans found ways to amuse themselves, either going to the cinema or the swimming pool in Southampton, or arranging their own games at Hamble. They didn't have the luxury of going home to London or wherever, like the British pilots did. One day they organised an impromptu base-ball match. They cobbled together a bit of wood to use as a bat and found a red tennis ball. They used bricks for the bases. It was hilarious and the British contingent were all thoroughly amused by this sport they had never played themselves.

Throughout 1943 the pilots at Hamble continued to convert to the different classes. Veronica did her Class 4 Plus, which meant she could fly the Mosquito bomber and the trickier American Hudson. She didn't find it too hard 'if you treat it with a bit of respect', as she said. It was inclined to swing a bit on take-off. Landing was trickier and it was hard to do a proper three-point land-ing, though Veronica managed to pull it off. She actually found the Hudson easier than the Wellington, which she wasn't very keen on. At Aldermaston, where they did the training, she met some American soldiers who were based there and she got hold of some American luxuries, including a face flannel and a hot water bottle from the Post Exchange. There were also some very British luxu-ries, including plenty of strawberries for sale by the side of the runway, which Veronica also enjoyed gobbling down at any opportunity. The soldiers watched as the pilots took off and landed and some had their own secret hankerings to fly. One day when a Hudson was struggling to take off it turned out a cheeky lot of GIs were sitting on the tail trying to get a joyride.

Once she converted, Veronica got her longed-for Mosquitos. She was also cleared to fly the Typhoon, or Tiffy, which was a fast new fighter. Some found it very tricky to handle, but Veronica loved it. It cruised at a whopping 300 mph, which was very fast for the ATA, and you had to handle it very carefully, particularly in bad weather. Veronica, who seemed to enjoy the challenge, ferried one hundred or so without any accidents. She had married her Dutch pilot, Terry, and by January 1944 she was Veronica Volkersz. Her friend Mary Hunter went off to have a baby, and in March Veronica was promoted to flight captain. It was hard to believe she had only joined the ATA three years earlier as a nervous sprog. So much had happened, and she was now flying some of the world's fastest fighters.

By the end of the year tensions on the Continent were rising. Something momentous was brewing. There were more aircraft than ever and numerous 'secret' airfields springing up around Hamble. Some were no more than tiny fields hidden by trees.

The need for pilots was such that, whereas the first woman had needed 600 hours, by 1944 they were taking women to train *ab initio*, who had never set foot in a plane before. When it was announced that a group of WAAFs could join, over a thousand applied. Only a few lucky – or smart – ones got through. They weren't all well connected, though some were; others must just have impressed. They were taught from scratch, and some of them got to fly the fast fighters before the war wound down.

On 3 April 1944 a call came through to White Waltham's Air Movements Flight from the Royal Canadian Hospital at Taplow. There was a Canadian soldier who required special medical assistance. Could they fly to Prestwick and pick him up and bring him back to White Waltham for medical treatment? Douglas Fairweather volunteered to go to Prestwick in a converted Anson air ambulance himself, as he knew the weather was bad. There was a military hospital near White Waltham. Douglas was notoriously capable of navigating in poor visibility and he decided to do this job himself rather than give it to any of the other pilots. When he left, the weather was indeed appalling in the South but it was worse in the Midlands. Douglas took the Anson rather than the Rapide, which had a radio, because he was more comfortable in the Anson in bad weather. On the way he picked up a second officer, Nurse Sister E. Kershaw, who had offered to help, and they loaded on the necessary medical equipment before heading north. Douglas no doubt sat with his cigarettes timing the journey puff by puff and cracking his usual jokes along the way. The plane was last seen entering low cloud near the Chilterns. It never arrived at Prestwick.

Nobody knows what happened that day, except that the rain had dropped so low the cloud base was only about 100 feet above the Irish Sea. They must have drifted over the sea, because Douglas washed up on the Ayrshire coast nineteen days later. Nurse Kershaw's body was never found. Margie's daughter, Elizabeth, was born a few weeks after he disappeared. Margie had to battle with the competing emotions of joy at the birth of her daughter and grief at the death of her dear Douglas.

The pilots at Hamble were devastated at the loss of such a character and they all refused to believe it could have been the weather that got 'Poppa' Fairweather in the end, so legendary were his navigation skills. 'It must have been something else,' Diana Barnato insisted. 'Or maybe he just ran out of cigarettes.'

At Tangmere Airfield one day, Diana met a man with sparkling blue eyes, a mischievous grin and curly short brown hair. Wing Commander Derek Walker was twenty-eight. He had a lean figure and a high-spirited nervous energy. He was constantly scanning the skies for planes he could identify. Diana had flown a replacement Typhoon into the RAF squadron and she got chatting afterwards with Derek, who joked that although she had delivered it in one piece 'they get broken later on anyway'. He had many entertaining stories about his time with the RAF. He had been in Greece and had even helped evacuate the Greek royal family. Later he was in Desert Air Force in Egypt, where he was hit in the shoulder. He was hit again and sent home to recover but still managed to be jolly about it all. He was sent back out on Typhoons and that was when they met.

Diana found him brave and jolly and able to cajole even the most melancholic or downcast person into high spirits. He was what she needed after her many recent tragedies. They had a whirlwind but deep romance. One day not that long after they had met they were sitting together in a big green armchair and Derek announced to Diana that he simply couldn't live without her and that was that. He said, 'Shall I ask?' She said, 'We'd better,' and without much ceremony they were engaged to be married. When they set the date of 6 May 1944 she didn't realise until afterwards that it would be two years to the day since the heart-breaking funeral of her last love, Humphrey. She decided not to change the date. This jolly wedding and Derek would be her new beginning.

On the appointed day, Diana waited nervously in her white dress at the altar of St Jude's Church in Englefield. She looked elegant with her hair curled and her eyes shining with a mix of anticipation and nerves. The cere-mony was sweet and moving and they felt very in love, hardly noticing there was an audience. Derek had his hat tucked under his arm as they left the church arm in arm. Diana had a delicate bouquet and a floral headdress. The wedding cake, in addition to the usual happy couple model, was also topped off by a model of a Typhoon, in honour of how they had met. Derek sported his cheeky smile and Diana looked beautiful as ever as they posed for photos cutting the cake together. The party was raucous – some of Derek's chums fell into a fish pond, while some of Diana's fell into the swimming pool. A few of them lay prone on the floor while photographs were taken.

The honeymoon was short and jolly, just a few days in Totnes in Devon with a couple of friends who had been married the day before them, and for whom Derek had been the best man. The festivities were short-lived and it wasn't long before they were both back to flying.

Despite the joyous mood in the Barnato-Walker household after the wedding, the general mood in Britain had become tense. It wasn't long before Derek also became unusually jumpy. Diana didn't yet know the full reason why, although it soon became apparent to everyone that something momentous was about to happen.

When Molly Rose's husband, Bernard, came back from Italy and Sicily, where he had been based, he began to re-equip for another big operation which was very hush-hush. Margot was generous and flexible and gave Molly adequate leave to see him. She made the most of it. They knew that Bernard would be off again before long, and who knew when they would see each other again.

At White Waltham and Aston Down, some male

ATA pilots had started to ferry planes across to the Continent. They had not been asked to do this at Hamble and it was still felt women should not be making a nuisance of themselves and getting in the way. Some were quite peeved and longed for a bit of excitement across the Channel. Veronica was quite excited when one day they were all inoculated. 'This means we're to be going to France, of course,' she said. 'I knew we would eventually.'

Her suspicions seemed valid when they were all bundled on to a bus and taken to the Southampton swimming baths to practise a dinghy drill. They stood along the edge of the pool fully togged up in flying gear, Mae Wests (life vests) and parachutes and were told to jump from a 15-foot diving board with their dinghies into the water. Veronica's initial excitement turned to alarm when she got to the edge and looked over. Margot took the lead and jumped first. The idea was they were to shed the parachute before landing by giving it a sharp tug. Veronica forgot this crucial bit and duly sank to the bottom of the pool. Then they had to inflate the dinghy and get in it. Once they were inside they discovered to their delight all kinds of amusing things: some chocolate, a Verey pistol flare gun, some yellow dye to stain the sea. Somehow Veronica managed to lose her dinghy and had to scrabble around the pool getting it back. 'I'd rather drown, I think,' she said with her mouth full of swimming pool water and thoroughly exhausted when it was all over. By the end of it she had rather gone off the whole idea of going to France after all.

By the end of May things were moving fast in Hamble. Alison King and Margot Gore watched, intrigued, as some Americans arrived and built a jetty just outside the yacht club. The streets in Southampton and its surrounds were also gradually filling up with armoured trucks, tanks and amphibious vehicles.

'Something they're planning to land here, do you think?' said Alison as they watched the workmen assemble the jetty with both precision and speed.

'There are a lot more ships in the Solent, too. Jammed with them,' said Margot.

Their sleepy town was being transformed into a military zone and fast becoming the heart of the action. Then things happened quickly. They got new 'Invasion Orders' marked in big red letters 'Top Secret'. This time it wasn't that they were expecting the Germans to descend. The invasion of Nazi-occupied Europe by the Allied forces was imminent.

In London, Derek and Diana watched from the window as storm-force winds kept them up through the night. Derek was pacing anxiously and kept looking out of the window. Heavy aircraft were heading south. Some were towing gliders. Derek knew what was about to happen.

As D-Day approached, things got increasingly busy

at the airfield and military locations around Hamble. Soldiers 'appeared in the woods' as Rosemary Rees loved to say in her wry tone, 'draped in camouflage'. Many women in the ATA knew men who were out there and ready to leave. Molly Rose discovered that her husband, Bernard, was leaving for D-Day. They wondered how many would return. There were thousands of them billeted in the woods around Southampton. There were hundreds of tanks, jeeps, trucks and Bren-gun carriers filling up the surrounding roads. There were even bridge sections being towed on to boats, and a whole floating harbour was ready to be towed across for the landing in Normandy.

Aerodromes sprang up along the South Coast with wire netting laid on the ground. Hedges were cut down and the aerodromes were camouflaged with dark paint to hide the Typhoons and Tempests. A factory at Marwell, which was a target as it was making Halifaxes, was also camouflaged with paint to blend in with the surrounding woodland and was very well hidden. The pilots had to do a lot of ferrying to Group Support Units at Lasham and Biggin Hill, where aircraft were armed and their radios fitted. They flew numerous Spitfires, Tempests, Mosquitos and Typhoons over the next few days.

The Solent began to fill up with vessels, packed nose to tail and side to side. The Winchester bypass became a great car park and was all of a sudden lined with tanks and trucks. Nobody could come in or go out that way, and it meant they were short of fresh food. The troops were ready to leave, awaiting Eisenhower's signal.

On 5 June, pilots returned to report that a huge collection of aircraft had gathered at Hullavington Airfield, painted with black-and-white stripes for easy identification. That night they took off. On their way home along the riverside, Alison and Margot marvelled at large numbers of landing craft setting off one after the other. The sky was filled with RAF and US fighters and fighter-bombers to protect the vessels going across. Alison looked at Margot. After all the excitement and build-up, it was finally happening. But it was tinged with sadness. This wasn't going to be an easy fight. Then they heard it: the noise of engines. All these vessels and military equipment were now making their way up the Hamble en masse. From her cottage in Hamble Rosemary heard the constant drone going overhead and the engines of the boats on the river.

Then, as if they had never been there, Hamble was suddenly empty and quiet again. The Solent was just a rippled expanse of water and a scattering of local boats. The invasion was on. There was no flying at Hamble that day: the aerodrome was shut in case any damaged fighters needed to land. Several of the pilots sat round together and listened to the wireless as Chester Wilmot, an Australian war reporter, described the landings in vivid detail on the BBC. Chester had flown in a glider with the 6th Airborne Division into Normandy on 6 June and reported from the heart of the action for most of the ensuing liberation of Europe. When the German high command eventually surrendered, Wilmot reported on that too.

Codenamed Operation Overlord and nicknamed D-Day, the Normandy landings were the largest combined naval, air force and land operation in history, the aim of which was to liberate Europe from Nazi occupation. They began on the beaches of Normandy, at Utah, Omaha, Gold, Juno and Sword, and by the end of the first day began to make their way inland to confront some of the fiercest and most dangerous fighting of the war, with heavy losses on both sides over the following several months. The troops were not only British, American and Canadian but also included Australian, Belgian, Czech, French, Polish and other forces.

Alison and Margot spent the evening quietly sitting outside and thinking about what might be happening across the Channel. They watched the sun setting but couldn't much enjoy its early summer hazy glow. 'I wonder what's happening now?' said Margot. Then a while later Alison would chip in with 'You don't suppose they . . .' and so it went. All questions they simply couldn't answer. As the sun finally disappeared they moved inside and had a fretful night. In the morning the BBC announced that Allied forces had landed between the Cherbourg Peninsula and Caen. The same day the first

Spitfire was already back at Hamble, where it was to be repaired. The battle was so near and yet felt a world away. The Spit came in with its black-and-white stripes and caused quite a stir at the aerodrome. They felt closer than ever to the real stuff of the war.

27. D-Day

On the night of the D-Day landings, Molly Rose had taken a radio to bed and heard at 6 a.m. that the invasion had started, knowing her husband, Bernard, was in it. Not long after, she got a communication from the War Office. Her husband had been reported missing, presumed dead after his tank had been hit. A Mrs C, who worked in the canteen, had also received the same perfunctory message about her own husband. They consoled one another and kept a brave face on things, but it seemed very likely both men had been killed.

A colleague of Bernard's wrote to Molly and told her that he'd seen her husband's tank burning. It was not an image she wanted to picture. He told her that he thought there was no way anyone could have got out. He had seen it shot up and then burst into flames. Margot was sympathetic and gave Molly three days leave to pull herself together. Then it was back to work.

With the invasion underway, ferrying continued with new aircraft on the books: more Walruses, much to everyone's despair, but also more Mosquitos, Spitfires, Typhoons and Tempests. There was an added difficulty on the home front with the arrival of the buzz bombs. These were now being launched regularly from France, targeting London, but also the South Coast where all the preparations and repairs were going on, and Hamble was a prime target. Diana thought one had exploded already some months earlier across from Hamble, but with security a prime concern her father's friends in the know were tight-lipped.

When the explosions became more regular the word got out that it was the VI rocket. They were long missiles, with tail fins, which were launched by jet-propulsion and made their way unaided across the Channel. When they reached their destination, a timer kicked in and the engines cut. The sound of the bombs was terrifying enough but the eerie silence which followed was more so. It meant they were about to fall nearby. A few ATA pilots saw them flying towards Britain from France, and one actually landed in the mudflats in Hamble. Eventually, quite a few ATA pilots flew above them, and from 4,000 feet you could look down and see them quite clearly.

It was dreadful hearing the awful noise, but even worse was when the engine cut and there was a wait for it to drop. It was a horrible moment knowing that it would fall and hit and possibly kill people, and there was nothing they could do. On occasion fighter pilots were known to chase them and tip them over with their wing tips, and they regularly chased them in fast fighters like

Tempests and shot them down over the Channel or over farmland so they landed outside populated areas. Fighter pilots were also attacking the V1 rocket launching sites and other targets in France and there was a constant flow of aircraft returning for repairs, keeping the ATA busy. Hamble became a 'prang-patch', which was a designated airfield where RAF pilots could stop in an emergency, to be patched up or get maintenance done.

With all this going on, Diana thought about her husband, Derek, who was over in France in his Spitfire. She got a surprise when one day he turned up and produced a large Camembert cheese, the first she had seen in four years. He told her he had liberated it, especially for her. She hugged and kissed him and, in that moment, she loved him more than ever. Then she set to devouring the cheese.

Amidst all the excitement of D-Day, Margaret Fairweather was still mourning the loss of her husband, Douglas. Although she had given birth to baby Elizabeth, she had returned to work for the ATA that June. On 4 August 1944 she was on a communications flight in a Percival Proctor III LZ801 with her sister Kitty and a passenger called Lewis Kendrick, who was an RAF VIP, when the engine 'faded out'. She force-landed perfectly in a field near Wrexham but she didn't see that there was a large ditch at one end. The Proctor went nose first into the hole.

She and Kitty, who had severe fractures to her leg, were rushed to Chester Royal Infirmary. Margie had serious head injuries; Lewis had minor abrasions. Margie never regained consciousness and she died later that night. The technical investigation showed that the vent of one of the fuel tanks was completely blocked by a film of waterproof sealant called 'dope', which was applied to protect fabric-covered aircraft. It had blocked the pipe and caused the tank to collapse: 'In these circumstances the petrol gauge is likely to have indicated that the tank still contained fuel, when in fact it was dry.'

There was a horrible game of blame-shifting after the tragedy between the Chief Engineer and the Engineer in Charge at White Waltham, each trying to blame the other for letting the plane fly and failing to ensure that it had been serviced properly. Also involved were the Officer-in-Charge Air Movements Bay and the Engineering Inspector, who were blamed for not checking that the fitters were competent, and then there were the two fitters themselves, who had failed to notice the vent was blocked.

No amount of buck-passing would bring Margaret back, but there was a report to recommend that from then on Proctors be modified to make sure it didn't happen to anyone else. The cause of death was in the end said to be 'extensive skull fracture', although some believed it was actually due to glass from Margie's glasses penetrating her brain. She was buried, together with Douglas, in Dunure Cemetery, South Ayrshire.

*

On 25 August Paris was liberated from Nazi occupation. The commander of the German garrison and the military governor of Paris surrendered to the French, and Charles de Gaulle arrived to take control of the city. In early September 1944 it was Brussels' turn to be liberated. Diana Barnato-Walker's husband, Derek, had been in the country working as an assistant to an air commander. He now had a problem. He needed a Photographic Reconnaissance Spitfire to document pockets of German resistance, but they had no pilot to take one over. Diana's eyes lit up. Might there be a possibility that she could fly the Spitfire there herself?

Women had not been allowed to fly across the Channel and many of them were very disgruntled about it, because the thought of a continental trip seemed to offer the prospect of a bit of excitement after all their hard work in Britain. They were now being denied it by those who thought women might be captured or not able to cope with the lack of female lavatories. Derek had a brainwave. Diana had a few days' leave from the ATA. 'If it's an RAF job, then the ATA can't do a thing about it, can they?'

Diana couldn't believe that she might fly to Belgium under the auspices of the RAF, but amazingly Derek managed to swing it. He got official written permission for 'First Officer D. B-Walker' to 'travel to Brussels and to remain there for a period of four/seven days . . . she is proceeding by air and will be in uniform'. They didn't need to know she would be the pilot.

When she saw the Spit with its invasion stripes, the excitement became real. But so did the nerves. Derek had a radio, but she would not, and, in any case, she didn't know how to use one. She would have to follow his wing tips and trust that he knew what he was doing. Diana had no idea how to navigate across the Continent. Derek warned her before they left not to land anywhere if something went wrong but to get herself straight back to England.

As she flew up in her Spitfire and left the White Cliffs behind her, and with Derek beside her heading for Belgium, she thought they must look quite a sight, husband and wife flying in formation in their Spits. All the way Diana kept a careful eye not to bash into Derek's wings and tip his aircraft over. They made it without a hitch and once the aircraft was delivered they spent a very jolly few days in newly liberated Brussels, where there was a jubilant party atmosphere. Already there seemed to be an abundance of things they had not seen in Britain for years, such as leather and, of course, delicious continental food.

The celebrations, and what effectively became Derek and Diana's second honeymoon, couldn't last forever, though. There was still work to be done and she had to get back to the ATA. But when they were about to leave and Diana was supposed to fly the Spitfire back after its mission, a thick fog came in. She managed to extend her leave, but after six days there they eventually thought they had taken Diana's leave to the limit. She had to get back. The weather still looked really iffy, but Derek said it would be all right, so they made plans to take off and head for RAF Northolt, again flying in formation together. As an RAF pilot Derek flew faster than Diana was used to doing, particularly as she also had to map-read at the same time. In the end she couldn't see a thing as the land only occasionally peeped through the fog. Then, horror of horrors, somewhere over Belgium, she lost him. She was flying over a foreign country, blind, with no radio, in thick fog, with just short of an hour's worth of petrol.

She couldn't land there as she didn't know what she might encounter. She had to try and head back to England. She calculated what she thought was due west and hoped to hit land in a short while. As she crossed the Channel she hit sea fog, and all she could see were glimpses of the sea, which was quite disorienting. The sea seemed to go on for too long and she wondered whether maybe she had miscalculated the direction. She might very well end up over the North Sea. If that was the case she'd never make it to land on the petrol supply in the Spit. She flew to 3,000 feet and didn't dare look down until finally she saw the faint shape of a coastline. It was Britain, somewhere near Bognor.

In the yellow fog and fading light she found her way round to Tangmere, concentrating with every muscle on getting everything right. Eventually she saw the landing lights and Verey lights. She thought they must be for other aircraft coming in. It was nearly dark. She had to land. When she came in her legs were shaking, but she felt a rush of relief when she saw Derek's Spitfire. He had made it too. It turned out that Tangmere was the only airfield open in the whole South of England and those lights had been for her after all. She and Derek embraced. He was almost angry, but only because he had been sick with worry. Diana was in shock for several weeks after her ordeal. Derek marvelled at how she had got there with no radio or instruments. But she had. A month later their little trip caused a flurry in the press:

> the beautiful daughter of the millionaire racing motorist, and her husband, Wing Commander Derek Walker DFC, have flown on a honeymoon trip to Brussels and back, each piloting their own Spitfire.

Not everyone was happy about this. Some members of Parliament had wanted to go to Brussels and been refused. They kicked up a fuss, and the Air Chief Marshal was angry. As a result, Derek had some of his pay docked for arranging the escapade. Neither Diana or Derek regretted it a jot.

*

Although Molly Rose had been informed that her husband had probably been killed when his tank had been hit, she always had a feeling somehow that he was not really lost. Finally her hunch was proven right. In November he was found as a prisoner of war. It turned out that Bernard had been getting someone else out of a burning tank so he wasn't in his own when it had exploded. He had been captured and it wasn't until six weeks later that Molly finally got a card from him from his prison camp. When she discovered where he was, she sent him relief parcels of food and cigarettes, none of which unfortunately ever arrived. Mrs C, who worked in the canteen, had also found out that her husband was not dead but in fact a POW. They may not exactly have celebrated their husbands' imprisonments, but there was a huge amount of relief. The possibility they might all be reunited seemed real once again.

That autumn, continental ferrying by the ATA began in earnest. There wasn't much telephone connection with France at that time, and flying without radios over unfamiliar land with potential pockets of German resistance was a new challenge. This flying was more dangerous than ever, but all the ATA women were keen to take on the continental trips since Diana had paved the way. Before long it had become official that they were allowed to do so, and by January 1945 there were many more women ferrying operation craft to France, Belgium and Holland.

Rosemary Rees flew to Prague and found it very bleak and depressing with 'grey-clad Russian soldiers' and food sparse and inedible. Once battle moved inland there was a Group Support Unit in Brussels, and others went further into Germany. It was a shock to see the extent of the Allied bombing campaign, which had been brutal. Rosemary, who had flown the four-engined bombers, had seen at first hand in the squadrons the contrast between the excited bomber boys before they left and the drained and weary ones who returned the following day. The gaps at the table in the mess were achingly empty signs of those who had not returned. But seeing Germany and the other side, she witnessed what they had been doing. Many cities were razed, with only a few church spires and factory chimneys dotted here and there. When she returned to the East End she found it hardly looked damaged in comparison. The retaliation had been severe.

The war wasn't quite over yet. In December and January, the Nazis launched a massive counter-attack. But it was fruitless. In April Hitler committed suicide in his bunker. The following day Joseph Göbbels did the same and by early May German forces were overwhelmed and began to surrender.

Irene Arckless's fiancé, POW Tom Lockyer, had been sent to a naval camp at Tarmstadt, near Bremen. He wrote that 'Hitler had ordered all RAF prisoners to be shot', because he blamed the RAF for the destruction and the disintegration of Germany. But this order, Tom wrote, 'was too much even for the SS and the Gestapo'.

Having been spared Hitler's order, the POWs were evacuated and walked through Zeven to the Elbe where they crossed the river by boat downstream from Hamburg. On 2 May 1945 at about 12 noon there was a hell of a lot of yelling among the guards. The 11th Armoured Division had arrived to liberate the camp. The guards surrendered and a day or so later 'about 20 motorbikes with pillion passengers arrived from a Commando Unit and escorted our SS troops away.' Tom and the other pilots were taken to an army transit camp, exhausted from their ordeal but relieved the end was in sight. They were deloused and given a medical check before being taken to a large barracks in Luneberg, where they were once again quizzed and medically inspected. Being outside the confines of the camp was actually quite traumatic at first. The traffic in the streets terrified the newly released prisoners and those, like Tom, who had been behind wire for over four years were too afraid at first to cross the road. They had to be more or less escorted across until they gradually got their nerve back. The men were shovelled once more into lorries and driven to an airfield where they were eventually picked up by USAF Dakotas and flown to Brussels. It was 8 May, VE day. The next day they were flown back to England in batches, sitting on the floor of Lancaster bombers, and landed at Westcott, near Aylesbury. Back on home soil they were relieved to have hot showers, not so relieved to have yet another medical inspection, and very relieved indeed to have a hot meal. In the morning they were again checked for any medical problems and 'interrogated by the Security people, kitted out, and sent home, on a month's leave, pending further medical boards'.

Tom was glad of course to have been released after so long behind barbed wire. But the blank truth of the matter was that he was now alone.

'I had nothing to come back to. She had been dead for over two years.'

28. Winding Down

When news broke out on 8 May that the war in Europe was over, celebrations erupted throughout Britain on VE Day. Mona Friedlander, who had been invalided out of the ATA, was now working for the Ministry of Information censoring photos. She saw the VE day passing out opposite the Cenotaph. It was a very hot day and the crowds were packed in like sardines, jubilant and cheering. She was carried feet first by a crowd she didn't know into a doorway.

The troop ship *Queen Mary* came into Southampton and let off a resounding blast of its horns which could be heard right across the city. It was so loud the ground shook and it really did give the impression the war was finally over. That night people lit bonfires and it was wonderful to see all that light and warmth as a sign of approaching peace after so many years of blackout and Blitz. All over the country, people organised street parties and celebrated like there was no tomorrow. Diana Barnato, who had friends who were still POWs in Japan, didn't feel that the war was truly over just yet and she had a quiet night. But there was plenty of partying at Hamble and more than a few drinks downed in celebration.

Not long after, some husbands began to come back from prison camps. One of these was Bernard Rose, Molly's husband. He was given two months' leave. When she told Margot he was back, the ATA released her so she could be with Bernard and take care of him after the shock and trauma of his experience.

In January 1945 Jackie Sorour married an army captain called Reginald Moggridge. During their courtship Jackie would fly over his base and, as the aviation terminology goes 'beat it up' or fly very low. During their courtship they sent each other letters and chocolate bars, and Jackie sometimes attached a love letter to one of her chocolate rations and dropped it from a plane over his base with a note saying, 'whoever finds this please eat the chocolate and give the note to Captain Reg Moggridge'. He always seemed to get it. When it was announced that the war was officially over, Jackie was in the air and hadn't got the news. She flew over Reg's barracks and beat it up as usual, but this time he didn't go out. He thought she knew, and that if she saw him she might do something silly and kill herself. She didn't of course. On their wedding day her dress was made from parachute silk.

In June 1945 Pauline Gower married her fiancé, Wing Commander William Fahie, and many of her ATA girls went to her wedding. They celebrated with their leader on her happy day and no doubt were grateful for all she had achieved for them. She had also made history by being appointed to the board of BOAC, which was a remarkable achievement for a woman in a man's world.

By August 1945 the heady Hamble days were over. The pool was split up and the pilots were posted to other pools around the country. Veronica was posted to one of the designated 'invasion pools' at White Waltham. The new jet fighters had begun to be flown the previous summer and some were being taken across the Channel. Veronica became the first woman to fly an operational jet fighter (a German female test pilot, Hannah Reitsch, had flown one at a German research centre). Amazingly, there had been no special conversion course, or even any instruction, for the new jet planes rolling off the production lines; there was just another page to add to her *Ferry Pilots Notes*.

Veronica flew a Meteor III from Moreton Vallance Airfield to Molesworth and underlined it in red in her log book. She found that it wasn't much different to a fast fighter except for the rush when it reached 16,500 rpm, instead of the usual 2,700. Ironically, perhaps, for a more sophisticated engine, the planes were in some ways easier to fly. They had no complicated procedures like 'variable pitch propellers' – the engines were simply open and shut. Although they represented the future, flying them was more akin to using the primitive old Tiger Moths – though they were much faster and ate up a lot more fuel. You only got half an hour out of them, but you could go a long way in that time.

'It's a bit like a dose of salts,' said Veronica after flying her Meteor, 'and you get an almighty kick in the pants when you open to full throttle.' Amazingly, she found it easier than landing a Mosquito. She was a bit disappointed she didn't get a chance to show off to the boys at the squadron at Molesworth about having been the first woman to fly an operational jet. She was unceremoniously piled into the Anson instead and whisked off back to White Waltham. Her historic flight was given no fanfare, but that was very often the lot of the ferry pilot.

The two jets, the Gloster Meteor and the Vampire, which entered operational duty just after the war, were much sought after, especially by the women, who were aware they might not get the chance to fly the new jet-propelled engines again. It would become a lot harder for women to become commercial pilots than it would for men after the ATA disbanded. Rosemary flew both the Meteor and the Vampire and caused much envy among some of the ATA boys, who were all hankering after them.

On 15 August VJ Day was something of an anti-climax compared to the country-wide celebrations of the victory in Europe. For many people it was just another day at work. Its horrific consequences in the Far East, of course, showed war at its most ugly and destructive.

Some ATA staff stayed on for a while after the war to wind things down, but eventually all the men and women who had done this job returned to their peacetime lives.

Some continued flying. Others went on to do completely different work, but they would never forget their time with the ATA, the friends they had made, and the friends and loved ones they had lost.

There was so much tragedy during those years for all the nations involved in this global conflict. No amount of victory talk would erase the realities for those who had lost loved ones and friends and witnessed unimaginable horror. But for the women of the ATA, they had been granted a strange kind of opportunity amidst all this destruction: to fly some of the world's fastest fighters and largest bombers, and to experience a level of flying no woman would ever do again to this day. Some flew over 100 types of plane in those few short years. Many had only started flying a couple of years before the war. Some trained completely from scratch on the job. Amidst all the death and destruction and loss, there was also a necessary humour and camaraderie which helped people get through those dark days. And there was always a song or two.

> Sung to the theme of 'My Bonnie Lies over the Ocean':
> My Spitfire lies spread on the runway
> My Walrus collapsed in the sea
> I know there was never a pilot
> Who broke up more aircraft than me.

Sung to the theme of 'Popeye, the Sailor Man':
I am in the ATA
I break up whatever I may
I am what I am
And I prang what I can
Whatever they give me each day, poop-poop.

Epilogue

Veronica Volkersz wrote: 'I could not contemplate any other job. Flying has become such an integral part of my life that it is almost impossible to imagine existence without it. I should hate to think that I should never again emerge into the bright sunshine of the world above the clouds, leaving behind the pettiness of everyday life.'

By the end of 1945 it almost seemed as if the war had been a strange, hazy dream, as the women of the ATA prepared for a new and very different world. Although they had been given a remarkable opportunity to fly during the war, most of the female pilots were not able to continue flying commercially during peacetime. Old prejudices returned and opportunities were few and far between. However, a few remarkable pilots did succeed in breaking new ground in aviation.

Jackie Moggridge (née Sourer) moved to Taunton with her husband, Reg, and their new baby. She was awarded a medal for valuable services in the air in 1946 and continued flying with the RAF Volunteer Reserve. In 1948 Jackie was commended by King George for Valuable Services in the Air. In the early 1950s Jackie was one of only five women at the time to be awarded full RAF wings, an under-acknowledged achievement well before the RAF generally accepted women pilots into their ranks. With a great deal of persistence and hard work in the face of prejudice Jackie also got her commercial flying licence and, among other missions, flew Spitfires over the Middle East to India and Burma and co-piloted a sales trip of refrigerators to South Africa. Jackie eventually became the first female air captain on a scheduled passenger flight, flying for Channel Airways between Portsmouth, the Isle of Wight and the Channel Islands.

Rosemary Rees was appointed MBE in 1945 for her wartime service. She also joined the RAF Volunteer Reserve and eventually got her commercial flying licence. She operated her own air-taxi charter firm, Ski Taxi, for five years until deteriorating eyesight eventually put a stop to her flying career. Rosemary died in 1994, aged ninety-two.

Another of the original eight, Joan Hughes, became chief flying instructor at White Waltham after the war and was appointed MBE in 1945 for her wartime service in the ATA. Joan Hughes was also among the first five women to be awarded full RAF wings. In the 1960s, at the British Airways Flying Club, she gained a reputation for being able to fly almost anything and eventually became a film stunt pilot. Joan flew sequences for the 1965 film *Those Magnificent Men in Their Flying Machines* and was a stand-in pilot for Lady Penelope in the 1968 film version of *Thunderbirds*. She retired after fifty years of flying with 11,800 hours in her log book.

By the end of the war Lettice Curtis had ferried nearly 1,500 aircraft. She went on to become a flight test observer at Boscombe Down and worked in Flight Development at Fairey Aviation at White Waltham. By 1962 she was working at the newly formed Air Traffic Control Experimental Unit at Heathrow Airport. At the remarkable age of seventy-seven, Lettice got her helicopter's licence.

Four months after the end of the war, Diana Barnato's husband, Derek, was tragically killed flying a Mustang. Diana had suffered her fair share of tragedy, but she continued flying as a pilot with the Women's Junior Air Corps, inspiring other young women to fly. In 1963 she became the first British woman to break the sound barrier in the RAF's new Lightning jet. Diana was appointed MBE in 1965 and died in 2008 at the age of ninety.

Margot 'Chile' Duhalde also continued flying and became France's first female combat pilot and a transport pilot in Morocco. She returned to Chile and became a private pilot, before opening her own flying school. She also became Chile's first air traffic controller and kept working until she was eighty-one. She died in February 2018, aged ninety-seven.

Alison King, the first female operations officer, joined BOAC after the war, and in 1953 became the Director of the Women's Junior Air Corps. In 1956 she was appointed chair of the newly formed British Woman Pilot's Association.

Not everyone continued flying, but some pursued other childhood dreams. Hamble CO Margot Gore was appointed MBE in 1945. When the war ended she became chief flying instructor at the West London Flying Club at White Waltham, but she had always wanted to work in medicine and eventually became an osteopath, serving as chair of the board of governing directors of the British School of Osteopathy.

Commander Pauline Gower was disappointed to have to tell the pilots who had got their hopes up so high that in peacetime most of them would not be able to fly as a career. 'My answer is a brutally frank one,' she said to those who enquired: 'you can't.' Pauline was being honest and realistic, but some women could and did continue to fly.

In April 1944 Jackie Moggridge had flown Spitfire ML407, the first Spit to register a hit on D-Day. Fifty years later she flew the plane again, thanks to pilot Carolyn Grace, whose husband had restored it, and they re-enacted the flight from the factory to the fighter squadron. When Jackie died in 2004, she went up into the sky one more time, and her daughter Candy scattered her mother's ashes from the Spitfire she loved.

Pauline Gower's own life was cut tragically short in March 1947 when, after giving birth to twin boys, she died of a heart attack. She was honoured with a posthumous MBE in 1956, but for all she achieved, you might say she is long overdue a higher honour.

Acknowledgements

Many of the ATA's female pilots have told their own stories and I have drawn on a few of them for the anecdotes, characters and details of this book. Some of the dialogue is imagined, but the details are drawn largely from the following: Diana Barnato Walker: *Spreading My Wings* (Grub Street, 2003), Veronica Volkersz: *The Sky and I* (W. H. Allen, 1956); Ann Welch: *Happy to Fly* (John Murray, 1983); Lettice Curtis's autobiography (Red Kite Books, 2004); Jackie Moggridge: *Spitfire Girl* (Head of Zeus, 2014); Nancy Miller Livingston Stratford: *Contact! Britain!* (California, 2010), which quotes the two ATA songs; Mary Ellis: *Spitfire Girl* (Frontline Books, 2016); Rosemary du Cros: *ATA Girl: Memoirs of a Wartime Ferry Pilot* (Frederick Muller, 1983); and Alison King's account of her time as operations officer, *Golden Wings* (White Lion, 1975). Jackie Hyams has also collected a number of stories in her book *The Female Few* (The History Press, 2016).

The Imperial War Museum Sound Archive holds a collection of extensive recorded interviews with several of the pilots, including Rosemary du Cros (née Rees), Mona Friedlander, Margot Gore, Alison King, Jackie Moggridge, Molly Rose and Joan Hughes.

For first-rate historical detail about the ATA, direct accounts from pilots including Margot Duhalde, and information about Pauline Gower, Anna Leska and Jacqueline Cochran among others, Giles Whittel's history, *Spitfire Women of World War II* (Harper Perennial, 2008) has been extremely valuable. For information about the life and death of Amy Johnson, Midge Gillies' meticulous biography, *Queen of the Air* (Weidenfeld & Nicholson, 2003), is fantastic. Details of the Siege of Malta, and the quote from an anonymous RAF sergeant, can be found in Martin Waligorski's article on spitfiresite.com. *The Story of the Air Transport Auxiliary* by E. C. Cheesman (1946, reprinted by Maidenhead Heritage Trust, 2008) gives a very detailed overview of the ATA as a whole. *The Air Transport Auxiliary Ferry Pilots Notes* (1941, republished by the Yorkshire Air Museum, 1996) and flying books *Teach Yourself to Fly* (1938, republished by John Murray Learning, 2017) by Nigel Tangye and *The Civil Air Guard Book* (Nicholson and Watson, 1939) by Malcolm Logan are valuable contemporary technical sources.

I am indebted to Terry Mace, who has meticulously collected, collated and written about many of the ATA staff personnel files and biographies on the website A Fleeting Peace, http://afleetingpeace.org. Thank you, Terry, for your help with sourcing letters, reports and photos (Crown Copyright) about the pilots.

For further details about the story of Irene Arckless, thanks also to Jim Corbett, who has been very helpful and put me in contact, via David Layne, with Tom's nephew Chris Lockyer, who kindly sent me his war diary.

I am very grateful to Dr John Hathaway, formerly Flight Lieutenant Hathaway, who took the time to talk to me about his experiences as an RAF pilot during the war.

The RAF Museum has been very helpful with archives, and Richard Poad MBE and the staff and volunteers at the Maidenhead Heritage Centre have been very generous with advice and access to their collection of ATA documents, log books, diaries, photos and newspaper cuttings.

Enormous thanks to Candy Adkins (née Moggridge) for her enthusiasm and help with her mother's story.

Thanks to Daniel, Zennor, Sarah, Amy, Olivia, Nick and all the team at Michael Joseph. And finally, thank you, Gary, for endless amounts of moral support, tea and chocolate.

Picture Permissions

He just wanted a decent book to read ...

Not too much to ask, is it? It was in 1935 when Allen Lane, Managing Director of Bodley Head Publishers, stood on a platform at Exeter railway station looking for something good to read on his journey back to London. His choice was limited to popular magazines and poor-quality paperbacks – the same choice faced every day by the vast majority of readers, few of whom could afford hardbacks. Lane's disappointment and subsequent anger at the range of books generally available led him to found a company – and change the world.

'We believed in the existence in this country of a vast reading public for intelligent books at a low price, and staked everything on it'
Sir Allen Lane, 1902–1970, founder of Penguin Books

The quality paperback had arrived – and not just in bookshops. Lane was adamant that his Penguins should appear in chain stores and tobacconists, and should cost no more than a packet of cigarettes.

Reading habits (and cigarette prices) have changed since 1935, but Penguin still believes in publishing the best books for everybody to enjoy. We still believe that good design costs no more than bad design, and we still believe that quality books published passionately and responsibly make the world a better place.

So wherever you see the little bird – whether it's on a piece of prize-winning literary fiction or a celebrity autobiography, political tour de force or historical masterpiece, a serial-killer thriller, reference book, world classic or a piece of pure escapism – you can bet that it represents the very best that the genre has to offer.

Whatever you like to read – trust Penguin.